To Norma

C000225193

Michael
Lockwood - Edwards.

Best Wishes,

Nick Edwards

Memories of Sheffield, Yorkshire...

'...many people have said they used to come down to the market on a Saturday morning to see us in particular, to watch us juggle and throw the pots about. It was a bit of entertainment, a bit of a laugh, there was a bit of joking and taking the micky.'

THE POTTY EDWARDS

WHAT A WAY TO GET A LIVING

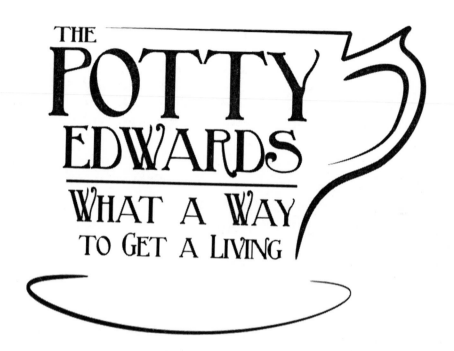

MICHELE LOCKWOOD-EDWARDS

The Derwent Press
Derbyshire, England

www.derwentpress.com

The Potty Edwards: What a Way to Get a Living
by
Michele Lockwood-Edwards

ISBN 13: 978-1-84667-040-4

Book interior and cover designed by:
Pamela Marin-Kingsley, www.far-angel.com

Potty Edwards logo designed by Christopher Dowson of Das Grafik Ltd

The moral right of the author has been asserted.

Published in 2010
by
The Derwent Press
Derbyshire, England
www.derwentpress.com

For Mum and Dad

CONTENTS

FOREWORD

If you have lived in Sheffield for some years, it is quite possible you have some china in your china cabinet purchased from a member of my family. This is the story of my parents, brothers and sisters and how we cobbled together a living for many years by selling pots in the market. We were known affectionately as the *Potty Edwards,* and I'm proud to belong to this family of market traders. I have woven together my memories, reminiscences; fragments and anecdotes passed down through the generations, and told to my daughter. She has been collecting notes for many years and thought it was time to tell our story — of a world that seems long past, and all but forgotten. I'm Mick Edwards, now over seventy years old. My story begins with my early childhood. I hope you enjoy it.

This book is dedicated to my parents: Arthur and Agnes Edwards, and to my brothers and sisters: Joe, Arthur, Bill, Bib and Agnes with love and affection.

Mick Edwards
(as told to Michele Lockwood-Edwards)
October 2009

–1–
THE RAG AND TAG

There was a time when people had to make their own entertainment. Few people had a television. There were very few celebrities and if there were, well the public knew very little about them. Members of our family were a bit like small-time celebrities. Edwards' Pottery, Glass and China stall was known in the market, but admittedly that name was a bit of a mouthful; people simply referred to us as the 'Potty Edwards'. We were known for working Sheaf Market in Sheffield in particular, or the Rag and Tag, as locals had christened the market.

There were quite a few of us in the Potty Edwards clan. There was my father, Arthur Edwards, who owned the business. He introduced us to pitching. Eventually in the 1960s his stall in the Rag and Tag passed to me, Mick, along with my older brother, Bill, who was my business partner for a few years. My other older brothers, Joe and Arthur, were also involved in working the markets roundabout. My brother, Arthur, had a stall right next to ours in the Sheaf Market. We took it in turns to pitch[1]. We were grafters, actively shouting and bawling to sell goods, not quiet standers[2]. Joe worked Barnsley, Rotherham and Doncaster markets mainly. I don't think the public knew our names individually, or could pick us out from one another, which was admittedly difficult with our similar faces, alike in shape, with our large eyes and big, aquiline noses; but Sheffield people felt as if they knew us all; perhaps as if they owned a little piece of us, and we rather liked that.

I don't mean to swank[3], but many people have said they used to come down to the market on a Saturday morning to see us in

---

1 pitch (v)-active selling, gathering an audience to an auction
2 quiet standers-selling passively, waiting for customers to approach
3 swank (v)-to show off (local dialect)

particular, to watch us juggle and throw the pots about. It was a bit of entertainment, a bit of a laugh, there was a bit of joking and taking the micky. We called it 'having a nobble'[4] with the punters[5]. The public came down Dixon Lane and Broad Street in droves in those days to the market. Fridays and Saturdays were snided[6] with folk. They streamed down into the market eschewing the posher shops at the top of town, on the hunt for good value. Women tussled with their brown paper carriers full of fresh fruit and their shopping baskets, thronging around the market, jostling and pushing to get through to the bargains. People came to see the spectacle of auctions, the shouting and balling, and the mavericks and eccentrics as much as to shop. We looked on from behind our stall at the multi-coloured tapestry of flat caps and headscarves, and we enjoyed every moment.

In those days the outdoor market was on a small piece of land in front of the Norfolk Arms pub on Dixon Lane, between Broad Street and Commercial Street. It was quite an informal affair: a small patch of ground bordered by ramshackle wooden boards and tin sheeting, which were forever being re-patched and mended, tacked together with rusty nails, and covered with a patchwork of posters that had seen better days, and dilapidated, shuttered, high shop fronts that were lined with wares. The central roof structure, or canopy such as it was, was made from wooden struts and sheets of corrugated iron, and there were gaping holes where the wind and rain could blow through. The stalls were nothing flash, just basic steel-framed structures with a sales surface, which was just a rough table top, fashioned from dirty boards.

The market came to life when the lights were on; shades hung on chains from the rafters bathing everything with gaudy, harsh electric light, offering a little warmth too from the big electric light bulbs, especially welcome in the wind and rain, for we worked in all weathers. The middle of the market was quite congested, lined with stalls, and narrow thoroughfares. The outside of the market area had a broader path around the perimeter, and various more permanent shop structures and wooden booths facing in towards the crowds, the herbalist, Sadler's Watches, Debson's, and Granelli's cafe. Our stall, Edwards' pot stall, faced Granelli's café. Next to Granelli's was Tom Marsh's

4 to have a nobble-to have a joke or laugh with someone (market slang)
5 punters (n)–customers (market slang)
6 snided with-packed with, full of (local dialect)

grocery stall, and on the other side of it was Tony Smith's Grocers, then came Dibbles' Fruit, Katz's Fruit and Veg, and Holt's fruit stall.

Our stall was a double-width stall, facing out to the thorough-fares both in front of us and behind us, which provided access for the public on both sides. In the next row along, to the rear of us, were the fruiterers, C. Marshall, J. Sargeant, and Frank Rushforth, or Rushy as we nicknamed him. Our distant relations, Gerty Heppell and Betty, had a stall further down our row. Harry Stanton and Dick Ramsay used to pitch for them.

Wilf's TF & S stall was a little further up, in the same row as us. I once asked Wilf what the TF & S stood for, which he'd got beauti-fully sign-written on his barrow, thinking it must be something highly esoteric or technical. He looked at me blankly and said dryly, as if I were a complete idiot, 'Tuesday, Friday and Saturday.' Next to Wilf's was my brother, Arthur, with his pot stall. Then came Benson's, where you could buy nighties and long-johns.

Also down from us in the same row was my relative's stall, Elizabeth Edwards' Pottery Glass and China. Finally, at the end was Syd Wilson's swag joint, selling cheap household items. He sold blankets and bedding and his joint was stacked with dress lengths, sheets, towel bales, pillows and bolsters. We called him 'Over my dead body Syd' as that was his favourite saying. If you made him a cheeky offer for a bit of discount, he fired that phrase at you.

He once got a bloke wanting to have a pop at him at the stall, get-ting aggressive and wanting to start a fight. 'Over her dead body!' Syd yelled, pointing to his wife, who sat innocently beside him.

My experience of life in the market started early on, when I was about eight years old. In all weathers I'd accompany my father there on Saturdays, offering what little help I could, but mostly looking on and taking all in. In cold weather I was swaddled in layers of clothing: liberty vest, shirt, jumper, long trousers, gabardine overcoat, with a balaclava on my head. In summer, I'd run around in my shorts and shirt.

I remember Syd well. He liked to have a joke with my father, and if an attractive woman walked down the market, Syd would shout to him, 'Arthur, pipe[7] the Harris[8]!' My father would laugh. One day I

7 pipe (v)-look at, see, (market slang)
8 harris (n)-backside, bottom, posterior, arse, derived from rhyming slang Aristotle, bottle, which means backside, arse

asked my father what it meant. He gave me a little clip, clouting me for being cheeky, saying, 'Never you mind, lad. I'll tell you when you are older.' Syd used to pull big pitches and sell loads of goods. People used to say Syd must be a millionaire, which made my father laugh, saying, 'He would be, if he put the bats[9] up!'

Sam Turton's Genuine Antiques and Collectables stall was further down. Sam's wife used to sit behind the joint in all weathers. She wore a mink fur stole around her shoulders.

My father warned me, 'Give her a wide berth, that bleedin' dead thing round her neck is chatty[10].' I asked him what a 'chat' was. He told me sagely, 'It's like an insect only bigger, with more legs, and if it cops[11] for thee, the bloody thing'll scran[12] thee!'

The market was always busy. Barrow boys trundled their barrows around laden with boxes of fruit, clanking along, whistling and swerving through the crowds, only stopping to chat up the prettiest girls. People were out hunting for bargains, or on their way to 'the cowsheds', which is what local people called the pub at the bottom of the market, so called because the seating was primarily tight booths with benches. We hardly ever went in there. We might take the lads in at Christmas for a drink, but for most of the time we were too busy trying to earn a living.

The 'Potty Edwards' were well known. In the days when there were few celebrities, the sight of handsome chaps in shirts and ties, with rolled up shirtsleeves, wearing smart trousers was a draw; the public came to see us because we had the gift of the gab, and a bit of front[13]. They stood mesmerised as they watched us auction our wares — while juggling, and throwing pots around to one another — this was our trademark.

There wasn't much to do on a Saturday either, and a walk around the market passed the time. People had to push, to get through the crowds, it was so busy. They used it as a meeting place; somewhere where they could bump into old friends and neighbours, and stop for a chinwag. Most often they ended up in front of our stall, stopping to be entertained, before they went on their way.

---

9 bats (n)-prices (market slang)
10 chatty (adj)-infested with bugs (slang)
11 cops for (v)-gets hold of, grabs (slang)
12 scran (v)-to eat (also noun- food)
13 front (n)-cheek and confidence (colloquial)

Our juggling and throwing techniques took practice and skill. The brand new pots were stored in large oval two-handled baskets full of straw. We'd arrange them neatly, the cups coiled, snaking around in the baskets nestling into one another, cushioned on the straw. The main one of us pitching would get one of the helpers, known as *schleppers*[14], to throw the pots to us one by one, in order; dinner plates, side plates, tea plates. We'd then throw them up, and catch them in order, splaying them broadly in an ornate fan shape, in an arrangement of side plates or dinner plates, holding them up high with one hand, to make them glisten and sparkle under the electric lights to show them off. We might be holding as many as a dozen, or even eighteen plates aloft. They were heavy. We'd then gather the plates up, sliding them under one another like a pack of cards, and hurl them confidently to a schlepper waiting in the wings to catch the clutch of plates from us. The pots were slippery, and our trick to help create a bit more friction was to drop a little powdered cigarette ash onto the surface and dust it on with a handful of straw. We were convinced it helped us manage them in flight and it was part of the ritual we went through to get ready before punters arrived. Though if you couldn't throw pots, of course this couldn't help you.

Sometimes people winced as the pile of plates separated in the air, but when they landed in a pile in a schlepper's hands there was a sense of relief from the audience and tittles of nervous laughter. Sometimes when we had a fanned arrangement of china up for all to see, we'd then throw the whole spread of pots across to a colleague, and he'd catch the display, pots clanking through the air and resettling back in his hands, organised in pretty much the same formation as when the pots left our fingers. He'd then hold the display up high. Sometimes a little ripple of applause would roll round the audience in appreciation, especially when kids were present.

We might vary our tricks; following a fan display we might whizz plates across to a fellow schlepper at the opposite end of the stall, chucking them one by one at great speed. He'd catch them one by one between his thumb and forefinger, then throw each plate into his other hand the second it arrived, stacking them up in order. Then

---

14 schlepper (n,)-helper, subordinate worker (from German verb, *schleppen*, to drag, used in context of undertaking boring work).

with a jolt and deft flick of the wrist, he'd again display the pots in a fan shape to perfection, thrusting them skyward so that people could see the patterns on them. The punters loved it! We liked to think they appreciated a bit of crash, bang, wallop...

We seldom had any accidents. We got new schleppers to practise with old pots in the warehouse. It took some time before we trusted anyone to go live with the skill in public. This was designed to get attention, to create interest, to get the punters talking and warming up to us. We called it giving the punters a 'flash'. Giving them a flash with an eye-catching display led to sales. There were rarely any breakages, but if there were any accidents, or failure of nerve, the public loved it; they savoured our mock reprimanding of the feckless schlepper with threats to dock his wages...

We had various techniques, which were part of the 'dem' or demonstration. We wanted punters to realise that they were buying quality products, bone china and pottery from Stoke-on-Trent, the best in the world. (In my view, nobody should dare drink tea out of anything other than an English bone china cup.) We'd hold a bone china teacup under the hot electric light, near to the bulb to show off its sheer delicate translucence and the lovely thinness of the china. The light shone through it, turning it a lovely creamy ivory colour. We would also demonstrate its strength and capacity for everyday use. This needed practice to conduct. We could knock a nail into a piece of wood by using the foot rim of a china cup, without causing the cup any damage. We'd raise our arms high, banging the rim down on the wood, continuing with our patter all the while, emphasising each phrase, timing our main words of the spiel to coincide with bringing our arm down heavily to place more pressure on the rim as we banged it down. This always brought oohs and aahs from the audience. People in the front row would cringe away, expecting splinters of china in their hair and on their coats. It never happened. (Don't try it at home; the angle of the blow is all-important. If you need to knock a nail in any time, please use a hammer.)

We'd also guarantee the soundness of each piece by 'ringing' a cup. This was done by jingling it upside down briefly on the saucer — to hear it ring like a bell. My family christened me 'Jingle Johnny' as a kid. From the age of six I couldn't resist walking past any pot without ringing it or tapping it gently with my finger-nail to hear that mellow, delightful sound. It was probably irritating to the others working with us. Dad would often growl at me to stop it, saying, 'Nitto[15]! Nitto! Turn it up!' A round, sonorous note signals a perfect piece; a flat, dull sound indicates damage, perhaps a tiny hairline crack, hardly visible, that could break the pot at any time, particularly when boiling water was poured in. This ringing technique is the best method I know to check if a cup is sound; I still can't resist doing it to this day. If an item was unsound, with a hairline crack, or in any way damaged, we'd say it was cackled[16], paggered[17], macka[18] or a demick[19]. We liked to be able to talk to one another without the punters understanding fully. We had a private language that we understood, with a particular vocabulary, which was suitable for any conversation we might need throughout the day.

We always sold perfect pieces (unless we advertised them as seconds, which was not usual) and we prided ourselves on selling best china at reasonable prices. We could beat Cockaynes or Walsh's any time on price for the same goods. I even loved the sound of the company names and brands, so old-fashioned, so British, redolent of a bygone time of prosperity and the days of the British Empire: Crown Staffordshire, Cauldon, Caverswall, Copeland, Tuscan, Balfour, Royal Grafton, Foley, Gladstone, Shelley, S. Bridgwoods & Son, Royal Albert, J. and G. Meakin, Royal Doulton, Roslyn, Ridgway, Radnor, British Anchor, Imperial China, Aynsley, Beswick, Minton, Hammersley, Adderley, John Tams, Wedgwood, Midwinter, Paragon, Radford and Royal Standard. My particular favourite was Tuscan china; I rated the quality of decoration and its egg-shell thin delicacy. I always called Tuscan and Shelley china 'egg-shell china'.

You could not fail to be drawn into working the markets in my family. It took you over, dominating every activity and conversation. I was probably fourteen when I left school. As schooling was never my particular forte, I was very happy to feel the pull of the family business, and I started work at an early age out of choice. Even at eight or

---

15 Nitto- stop it, don't do that (market slang exclamation) possible corruption of *nicht* (German)

16 cackled (adj)-broken, damaged, cracked (market slang)

17 paggered (adj)-faulty, broken, damaged, cracked (market slang)

18 macka, macca (adj)-faulty, broken, damaged, of poor quality (market slang)

19 demick (n)-a seconds piece, faulty item, demonstration piece not for sale (market slang)

nine years old, I used to work with my Dad and brothers in the market on Saturdays. I loved it. The pocket money I earned was a boon, but I'd have gone for nothing. I loved being part of the hustle and bustle. I relished the sounds: market traders shouting to one another with cheeky taunts and accusations, the clank of barrows, the thud and thump of boxes landing on the pavement as people unloaded and set up their stalls, the jingle of cups and the clank of the tea urn. These sounds were part of a familiar landscape, punctuating my everyday activity. Granelli's rumbling tea urn called to me when I was parched, and I'd stop off from my work to go and buy a big jug of tea for the grafters, dodging its hissing jets of water and great wafts of spitting steam. On my way out of the door, I'd pause to chat to any grafters assembled who had stopped for a quick cuppa, cheekily urging the part-timers to 'get back to graft'.

I also savoured the smells. At the end of a busy day's trading the market had an unmistakable smell: a peculiar spent odour of cooked fish and chips in newspaper, the greasy stink of wafting chip papers, rotting cabbage and decaying fruit, and the spicy opulence of boiled sweets, comfits, torpedoes, lozenges, dragees and coltsfoot rock, the air tinged with the faint herbal aromas of camphor, menthol, cinnamon, wintergreen, aniseed, liquorice and cloves from the herbalist's shop. Our stall had its distinctive smells too: the musty woody smell of damp tea chests; the wheaten, grassy smell of dry straw, and the tobacco aromas of Park Drive, Players and Woodbines, which the workers puffed on, as they occasionally halted their routine for a crafty smoke.

It never really occurred to me to do anything else but work in the market. It seemed a perfectly fine and appropriate occupation. I used to mither[20] my father to let me have a go at pitching when I was just eight or nine years old. Pitching was when you took the main lead in actively selling wares, (as opposed to selling them passively) and we'd use a gavel, and bang a wooden block next to the reams of tissue paper, and shout and bawl to get attention, taking pleasure when we pulled the punters in and got them interested in buying our wares. We always called the crowd to order by banging the gavel, rapping it boldly a couple of times on a wooden block, announcing: 'Ladies and gentlemen, if we could have your attention. We're about to start to-

20 mither (v)-to harass, persuade, repeatedly ask for things (local dialect)

day's sale!' My Dad used to tell me that the gavel had been in the family for years. It was fashioned from hickory wood, which is strong and shock-resistant, able to withstand constant walloping.

Usually people would close in and gather near to the front. You could then start the sale with little items to get their interest. In the 1960s, we'd start perhaps with half a dozen Wade animal figures for half a crown, or some fancy glass, perhaps some tumblers, a glass fruit set, a sugar bowl and cream jug, a sauce boat or china gravy boat and tray, or a little vase. These small items were what we called 'pitch pullers'. Gradually we'd build up to auctioning the combination sets or 'combos' as we called them, then finally the bone china dinner sets, bone china fruit sets for Sunday best, and coffee sets. A good punter might buy both a dinner set and a tea set or coffee set, perhaps for a wedding present or special anniversary. After each sale we dropped the change into a wooden bowl, called the damper. We then put the notes in our back pocket, always rolling them up tightly, held together by a rubber band. In my family having a wad of banded notes was a badge of machismo. After our pitch, members of the public would hang around, waiting for the next bit of theatre, chatting to us, talking about what pots they had at home. Those were the days; nowadays the customers are too busy to stop and rabbit[21].

---

21 rabbit (v)-to chat, talk, gossip (slang)

–2–
WAR TIME

When I was a child, people in the family still spoke about the war. We still had recent knowledge of loss and privation, and the stories told of overcoming adversity served to bolster us and cheer us, in the hope for better times. At family gatherings, people told stories of living on their wits, and we always relished the possibility of anyone getting one up on officialdom.

I was three when the Second World War broke out. My first memory of the war is a recollection of heading into an air raid shelter on Penistone Road. I was probably four or five years old. We were on our way visiting when the wailing sirens went off, so Mam ushered me into the nearest air raid shelter. I was wearing my gabardine mackintosh and my knitted balaclava, and clutching my pop gun to me, which was my favourite toy at the time, which I carried with me everywhere. We waited nervously listening for the plummeting whistling sounds as the bombs came down. The adults counted silently in their heads, nervously trying to gauge the likely proximity of any hit. I was in the shelter doorway, peering out excitedly and shooting my pop gun. My Mam tried to haul me back in, but I kept pressing through the crowd back to the doorway through the tightly crammed sentinels, to look out, hovering on the threshold, and to pop my gun at the Gerries. A bomber had been spied overhead, and the threatening drone hovered over the area as it buzzed through the high cloud. All of a sudden there was a terrific bang, and a whistling sound nearby, as a shell burst. I whooped with delight, thinking my shot had been successful, and that I had hit the plane.

'Got 'im!' I yelled.

The bombing passed and we came out into the sunlight again, rubbing our eyes and smelling the smoke in the air. We were lucky that day. We had heard of near misses. My school chum, Mick Berry, was being carried down into an air raid shelter one day by his Grandma when a shell burst and it blew them both off their feet, but they were alright, just a little bruised.

My brother, Bill, didn't like to talk of his army exploits, even though I pumped him for information about guns and bullets. I remember him mentioning a 303 bullet which he used in his gun. I liked to boast to my friends about his army record. I asked Bill why he had to go to fight the Germans. He always said simply, 'Because they killed our Grandad.' This rather frightened me; it sounded as if they had come looking for him specifically.

I liked it when Bill was around when I was a child. He talked to me and indulged me and would answer all my questions. Admittedly he also made use of me. He liked a lie-in and a cup of tea first thing in the morning, and he always managed to persuade me to go and make it.

'Now then, Mick, go and make us a cup of Rosy Lee[22],' he said.

'I'm busy.'

'Go on. Tell thee what; if tha makes it, that can wear t' tea cosy on thi nut for a bit,' urged Bill, as if he was awarding me a great honour. I fell for it every time and would come back upstairs with a cup of tea for him, the tea cosy balancing on my head like an exotic fez.

Of course we had noticed a difference in our livelihood and in our living standards during the war. My visits to the shops with Mam were now a sombre affair, whereas before I might have had the pick of the shop and could ask for anything on the laden shelves. Now we had to use ration coupons when we went to buy our groceries. We had a precious book with printed pages, and had to hand it over to the lady behind the counter. I used to hope she'd forget to doctor it when we'd made our final purchases, but she'd always come with the scissors and cut some coupons out. She had to account for what she'd given out.

We were lucky during the war. For many years selling pots and bone china on the market gave us a good living. We could afford to buy food, and occasionally we could buy supplies on the black market. Occasionally we would deliver a tea set or dinner set to a farm and we'd barter part payment and obtain a chicken or a generous meat ration or half a dozen eggs.

22 rosy lee (n)-tea (rhyming slang)

My father told me this story about a relative of his who was out at black of night hunting for black market pork — rarely to be had and very precious. This happened to my father's relative, Charlie Lavell and his wife, Lilly, during the war. They lived at Parson Cross and we used to visit them when I was a kid. Aunt Lilly was a lovely woman; she'd kiss my cheek when I went in. Before the war, when food was plentiful, she'd cut me great doorstops of spiced loaf slathered with butter saying, 'Pass some of that spiced loaf to our Mick, I'm feeding him up.'

During the war food was scarce in the Lavell household, and Charlie had heard of someone who had raised a piglet for sale, feeding it from neighbours' scraps, and he meant to have it. Such activity normally had to be registered with the authorities, but this unauthorised rearing of livestock went on in many places. People sheltered the animals in outhouses and fed them from what scraps and vegetation they could find, sometimes sharing the slaughtered beast amongst neighbours who had scrimped any food waste from their rations to feed it up. Charlie missed his meat and he was looking forward to paying any price for the taste of a crozzled[23] bacon sandwich and a nice roast joint with apple sauce. He'd heard of this chap in the Wicker[24] and had made arrangements to call at dead of night to pick up his black-market porker. He helped his wife into the van with him as lookout, and they set off in search of their illicit repast. Finally they found the house they were looking for, off a lane down by the Wicker. The man fetched the piglet from the outhouse and he shovelled it into the back of the van, pocketing payment without making conversation. He closed the gate and waved them a quick goodbye and went back into his house.

With the pig locked in the back, they set off again on the journey homeward. The piglet was loose in the van, but it kept scrabbling towards Lilly, trying to get over into the front seat area. She felt its wet nose near her hand as it tried to make contact with her, brushing her arm to get attention.

'I'll be glad when he's in the chuffin' pot,' she said, wiping her palm on her shawl and pushing the piglet back into the back of the van. 'Get down, you soft ha'peth.'

---

23 crozzled (adj)-of food, cooked, well done, crispy (local dialect)
24 Wicker—the name of a city centre road in Sheffield

Charlie and Lilly were undoubtedly drawing attention to themselves, out late at night in a vehicle. There were few cars out on the roads anyway, and to see a big Austin van out at night was indeed unusual. Anyone out on an escapade had to be making an important journey, for they had to be using precious petrol, which was on ration. Aunt Lilly huddled in the passenger seat with her shawl around her shoulders, lurching to and fro as Charlie drove back along the Wicker. It was a cold night. Her breath rose in a steamy cloud in front of her. Charlie squinted at the road ahead. He was struggling to drive, as he dare not turn his headlights on because of the blackout. Suddenly Lilly started and shivered to see the dancing light of a torch up ahead.

'What's that up there?' she asked of Charlie, who shrugged his shoulders and trundled a little more slowly towards the light ahead.

With jangling nerves Charlie drew to a halt; the torchlight was blinding him. As he drew nearer he saw the outline of a dark figure cloaked in a cape, a shiny badge glistened in the half-light, and he recognised the outline of a tall policeman, shining his torch towards the van.

Charlie gulped and felt his heart race. It would be quite a coup for this copper to catch him with a black market pig. The policeman raised his hand urging them to stop.

Charlie had to think quickly before they got too close and the copper could see what they were up to. He kept advancing slowly, steering with just one hand on the wheel, with the other hand he grabbed the squawking piglet and pulled a blanket from the footwell and draped it around it, swaddling it tight like a baby, almost throwing the swathed bundle into Lilly's arms.

'Cover it with your shawl an' all and hold tight on that,' he said to her, stuffing the piglet's sniffing snout back down under the cover. The policeman moved towards the van and strained to look towards them.

'Bleedin' 'ell, now we're for it!' whispered Charlie to his wife, winding the window down.

The policeman came closer and peered into the van, looking around.

'Good evening. A dark night to be out. What'll you be up to, I wonder?' he said.

Charlie was conscious of Lilly sitting frozen beside him. She was holding onto the bundle, clutching it tightly, rigid with fear and unable to speak. Luckily the piglet seemed to have calmed down.

The policeman leaned over and cautiously prodded the coverlet saying to Lilly, 'Cold night to be out with a little babby, love.'

Lilly dare not reply, she smiled inanely and left Charlie to handle the situation. Charlie could not bear the tension and thought they were about to be discovered. He was terrified at the copper's interest in the baby and imagined him undoing the cover to reveal the pig at any moment. Then they'd be bundled into a police van, never to be seen again. He could do time for profiteering. The images running through Charlie's head were terrifying. He could see himself fettered in a dank cell, thin and gaunt.

Mindful of the terrible consequences of his lust for bacon, he could not help his urge to confess all and he gasped and blurted out loudly, 'We've been out to fetch a pig, Officer!' The officer eyed him uneasily, now thinking he had a nutter to deal with, which was always a lot of paperwork, and mused over his next action. The copper found Charlie's declaration ridiculous: he had scant experience of seeing pigs in any circumstances at this time, dead or alive. Lilly continued to clutch the bundled pig tightly.

The copper eyed Charlie, then started to laugh at him. He guffawed at the wild assertion that he'd been to fetch a pig. He gradually got a grip on himself, wiping his eyes, which were watering, and then found he was mildly irritated at this bloke taking the micky out of him.

'Oh. So tha's been to fetch a pig, has tha?' he sneered.

'Aye.'

'Oh aye. A big un, was it?' questioned the copper indulgently.

'No, just a little un.'

'A little un. Oh really?' he guffawed, and then pulled himself together, becoming altogether more serious and professional in tone. 'Go, on, get on your way, you cheeky bleeder!' said the policeman, pretending to scutch Charlie across the head. 'You've been to fetch a pig, have you, you cheeky chuff! Do I look like I'm just off the boat? Get off home with ya! And don't let me see you round here again!'

Charlie couldn't believe his luck. He slammed the van into gear, released the hand-brake and drove off quickly, not wishing to wait to be challenged further. Charlie and Lilly could hardly believe their good fortune. That bacon sandwich was a little bit nearer.

'I'm not hanging round holding onto this bleeder. It's for the chop in the morning,' said Charlie.

My older sister, Bib, courted a chap called Joe Bennett, (known as J.B). When J.B. was in the RAF during the war, Bib did his insurance round for him. Joe was a fitter mechanic and was repairing aeroplanes and was not in any great danger. Before the war, Joe had also had a balm[25] round. He used to buy yeast in great sacks and he'd cut it up into weighed amounts and bag it up, taking it round to the small bakeries, selling it on to them. Some large bakeries might buy half a sack from him at any one time. He used to deliver to a bake house on Portland Street and another on Cross Bedford Street.

All kinds of enterprises sprang up during the war, as people learned to live off their wits, and necessity bred creative invention. Joe Bennett told me this story of a visit he paid to Uncle Bill Richardson in Rotherham. Uncle Bill had got hold of some shop-soiled shoes and was selling them on the quiet. Uncle Bill lived in a house with connected cellars. One night as Joe Bennett called, he heard a copper up the echoing passage as he was approaching; he was questioning the neighbours about the whereabouts of the Richardsons, and whether they had offered them any black market shoes. Joe shot round the corner and tapped on the kitchen window of the Richardson home to be let in. He told them of the advancing copper. 'There's a bleedin' flatty outside, trying to capture you for sellin' shoes. Hide them, for Christ's sake, otherwise you'll get nicked. The Old Bill are on their way!'

The whole family, men women and kids, shot down the cellar to move the stock of shoes. They lugged them along the narrow passages, shuffling and whispering, loading up armfuls, passing them along a human chain, hauling and carrying them through all the neighbours' connecting cellars, to a house at the very end of the block. They holed the shoes up behind some boards, completely out of sight. Quickly

---

25 balm (n)–yeast (used especially in Northern England)

they came back upstairs and settled themselves in the house to create a nonchalant family scene, ready for the copper's arrival.

When the copper knocked on the door he was let in and he stood in front of the fireplace, rocking on his heels staring at the assembled family.

'There's been a report of you selling black market shoes,' he uttered, gazing round at them, looking for any signs of shiftiness or guilt. Uncle Bill looked at him blankly and shrugged. The copper circled them.

'So none of you know anything about any shoes? None of you has sold any shoes from this house?'

There was silence. Then the copper spied a note on the mantelpiece, resting behind a candlestick. He took it down slowly, read it silently, peered at the group, then read it aloud triumphantly, enjoying every word: *'One pair of brown size fours for Hetty.'*

My father liked a drink, and during the war booze was on ration, so he did not have the opportunity to enjoy his favourite tipple as frequently as before. Being rather canny, he'd heard about the landlord of a pub on Leppings Lane who was scared of the German bombers and whose fear caused him to suffer badly with his nerves. Any sounds could trigger his anxiety, and there were frequent thuds, hisses or whooshes of the whistling bombs in the night sky which sent him scurrying down the cellar, waiting down there, abandoning his pub to all comers until the all-clear sounded. Leppings Lane was a couple of miles away from our house, but my father made frequent visits to this pub because of this particular landlord's character; like many people, taking advantage of the free beer on offer if he left the pumps unattended.

My father would walk into the pub in the early evening when it was quiet, taking off his Homburg and taking off his overcoat. The landlord was polishing the pumps, chit-chatting with any new arrivals.

He turned to greet my father. 'Evening Arthur. Is it quiet out tonight?'

My father shook his head and shivered, growling, 'Quiet! You must be bleedin' jokin'. I've just nearly shit myself!'

The landlord looked startled and jittery. He stopped polishing the pumps to listen to my father's tale, asking at the end, 'Any Gerries around?'

'Not half. I had to make haste to get in here, there's bleedin' bombers comin' down Leppings Lane, flying low.' The landlord started to go ashen, and visibly shook. 'Do you know they came so low, I could see the whites of their eyes,' said father, widening his eyes for dramatic effect.

At this the landlord started to reverse, making his way down to the cellar door. Father knew what to say to tip him over the edge. 'One came so bleedin' low I could see a blackhead on the end of his nose.'

The nervous landlord turned white, and scarpered down the cellar shouting, 'I'm just popping downstairs, I think a barrel needs changing!' There he stayed for the rest of the evening.

My father developed an arsenal of frightening sayings and anecdotes that could scare him down into the cellar on a regular basis. Even with beer on ration, he managed to get drunk frequently.

My father did not vary his routine much, even during war time. Most evenings we heard the chant, 'I'm off to t' Malin for a bevy[26]'. He'd brave any bombing, venturing out with only his hat and coat for protection, even when the sirens were wailing. Warning him of the dangers could not stop him. We might say, 'It's bad out tonight, Dad, best stop in. Gerries are at it.'

'Gerries, bleedin' Gerries. They're not going to stop me from doin' what I want to do; cobblers to them.' Out he'd traipse, slamming the door behind him in patriotic defiance.

One night during the war, we'd had to scuttle down into the air raid shelter. Father was out and we had no idea if he was safe during the air raid. When there was a pause in the shelling, a neighbour peered into the shelter, saying nervously, 'We've heard they bombed a lot of buildings down Penistone Road. Can somebody come... There's a dead body on the wall down here.'

My sister, Agnes, went out of the air raid shelter, creeping apprehensively down the street with the neighbour. Spying the familiar

---

26 bevy (n)-drink (slang, probably abbreviated from *beverage*)

shape of a figure, she started to wail, 'It's my Dad, my Dad. He's dead; he's dead!'

The neighbour ventured a bit nearer, prodding the weighty hulk draped over the wall, the face groaning and buried, leaning over into someone's garden.

'He's not dead, he's just bevvied[27]. He's snoring like a pig,' he said, grabbing him, straightening him up and manhandling him upright. He walked with him, half carrying and half dragging his lifeless frame, tipping him in through the front door over the threshold.

'Thank God,' cried Agnes.

'Thank God,' said the neighbour. 'God, he's a mad bugger, could have got killed.'

When he came round, Agnes rollocked him, still fighting back her tears, 'Where were you? Couldn't you hear the bombing, Dad?'

'Nah. The Gerries must have put silencers on their bombs. That beer made me go deaf,' he said.

---

27 bevvied (adj)-drunk, inebriated (slang)

-3-
MY FIRST PITCH

Mick Edwards, July 1945, aged 9

So have you had a look in your cupboards? Have you got any best bone china there? The chances are you may have bought it from a member of my family. My name's Mick Edwards, I was born in 1936, the youngest son in the Potty Edwards clan of that generation. My Dad was Arthur Edwards. My Mum was born Agnes Lockwood. My parents were married on 4th August in 1913 at St Philips Church, on St. Philips Road, Sheffield. I am from a large family. The oldest of my brothers and sisters was our Bib (we never called her Elizabeth as she was christened). Next in line came my eldest brother, Joseph, or Joe. In order of age then came Arthur, though his nickname in the family was Buck, then Agnes, and then John William, or Bill as he was known. There was ten years difference in age between Bill and me. I am the youngest. Purportedly I also had an older brother, who was born between Bill and me, named Henry, who died of pneumonia at the age of three. I have a hazy recollection of him. I remember him when we had a shop on Bellhouse Road. He ambled round the shop unsteadily, his dummy in his mouth. In those days people used to come in with an empty bottle and ask for a pint or half pint of vinegar, which we poured for them from a big wooden barrel with a stopper tap on it. Henry used to get into trouble for turning the tap on the barrel on and drenching the floor with vinegar. It stank the place out.

My sister, Agnes, told me I was a surviving twin; the other twin was supposedly stillborn. I am not sure whether there is any truth in this or not. But I always felt it gave me an air of romance, a grateful start in life. Perhaps I was meant to have a charmed existence, if my start in life was so chancy.

I always preferred the market to school; I spent a lot of time in the market. From the ages of six to ten I served my apprenticeship as a junior schlepper holding limited responsibilities, for I was not trusted to pitch as a very young lad and the tasks given to me were menial. I set up the joint ready for work and unwrapped the pure white reams of tissue paper from their brown paper covers, to be ready for a run on wrapping when we got busy. We packed everything away each night, as the market wasn't very secure, so it was my job to restore the displays, getting pots back out that we'd put away for safekeeping, and to carefully unpack tea chests full of new lines, wiping them off with clean tissue paper to get rid of the straw dust and to bring a gleam back to the glazed surface. I found this very dull, but I realised I had to prove that I could be trusted first, if I was to progress to the dizzy heights of salesmanship.

When you are the youngest in a large family, the older ones enjoy bossing you around and training you, as they've gone through it before. I understood this apprenticeship was just a rite of passage for me, and so I bore it with good temper. I also enjoyed observing a certain pride in the way the others approached their work; they had fun, but they were serious about selling gear[28] and giving the punters high quality goods. They were also serious about creating the best conditions for sale possible, sometimes thinking they could manage circumstances beyond their control. It amused me if it suddenly started raining, my father would bark orders at me. 'Mick, look lively, it's starting to parney[29]. It's getting dark, get those glims[30] on, and let's get the joint flashed up, otherwise the punters'll all scarper off home.'

28 gear (n)—wares to sell, products, merchandise (market slang)
29 parney (n)—water (n), rain (Indo-European, possibly Hindi or from pan`i—water (poss Greek rom),) used in this context as a verb-to parney (v)-to rain
30 glims (n)-lights (market slang)

Each day he set himself a sales target and he considered it a personal affront if he didn't reach it. He'd say, 'We'll give it another half hour, I haven't got mi wages yet.' With that he'd hang on doggedly, to wring a few more sales from the scuttling travellers making their way home.

My father was something of an entrepreneur; always quick to realise an opportunity, he could spot a seemingly useless product and convert it into a saleable line. One day my father opened the big wooden doors to the warehouse to reveal piles of plates spread all across the floor. Nodding towards me he said, 'Got a little job for thi,' then thrusting some tools into my hands, he added, 'Be careful as you go; don't pagger[31] 'em.' He taught me how to drill a hole, using a hand drill, into the centre of thick, large plates. I remember this as one of my earliest jobs as a child. I took up my tools a little reluctantly, rollocking[32] my father under my breath as I did this thankless task, thinking he was enjoying having invented a purposeless little job to keep me out of trouble. It was no easy feat, the drill kept slipping. My hands sweated and the plate slid all over the place, as I tried to use my knees as a vice to hold it in position. It was hard to get the angle right as I drilled a hole.

My father had twenty dozen of these plates, which he'd bought on offer, which the factors had been holding as a line for some time because they would not sell. He spotted them and had an idea how to make them more attractive; he had had some metal stands and handles fashioned and plated at a little workshop. He had a pal who was a 'Little Mester'[33]. The idea was that the stand and handle could be twisted through the hole I had drilled into the base, and be secured with a washer and screw. My last task after drilling the holes, was to slip the handles through and to tightly secure the bases. Thereby a relatively useless plate was converted into a comport[34], which was effectively a posh plate with a small three-footed stand and carrying handle. I made a sign for the stall stating: *English Comports - Half a Crown*, in my best handwriting. I found the idea of comports rather grand; they looked and sounded very sophisticated. My father's in-

31 pagger (v)-to damage, break, spoil (market slang)
32 rollocking (v)-to scold, reproach, tell off (slang)
33 Little Mester (n)-a Sheffield term for a self-employed cutlery worker
34 comport (n)-a large dish or plate(often of glass or pottery) used for serving fruit or sweets with a wide, shallow top with a heavy stem and foot; also compote.

stincts were right; it was a good line. We sold cotchells[35] of them.

Another of my jobs as a child was to sort plates. My father would buy dozens of assorted dinner plates, line ends, oddments, sometimes slight seconds; and it was my job to sort them into half dozens, finding the matching patterns from hotchpotch piles across the warehouse floor, then grouping them into half dozens or dozens ready for sale. I would line them up ready for taking up to the joint, (our term for the stall), and the area around the stall. Then back up at our joint, I lined them up on the floor at the side, where the salesman could easily reach for them or have them thrown up to him. There were many different goods for sale and the person on the joint selling, usually my father or one of my brothers, had the choice of different items. The salesman had to judge the buying mood of the gathered public, assessing their spending power by the look of them, their dress and how they were turned out, and assessing the likelihood of wares being sold in a particular season or weather. It was something of an art, and you needed some skill and brains for it. We weren't Yorkshire Puddings, you know!

As a kid I was desperate to have a go at pitching. All my brothers could do it, and I felt I had to prove myself too as the youngest. I'd stand soberly at the edge of the stall, my hands thrust deep into the pockets of my three-quarter length trousers, watching intently, itching to get involved. It was a holy rite of initiation in our family; I suspected if I could pitch, I would then be seen as a real Edwards. If not, well I might not amount to anything special. I might even have to get a 'proper job'. It was as if I had to prove that I was capable of going into the family business. One of the most basic skills I had to master was to be able to firstly 'pull a pitch'. This was the act of getting people in front of you in the first place, drawing them in to view your presentation. You might think it's a logical assumption to make, that if you have interesting goods for sale, that you will immediately pull a crowd; not so, sometimes they need a little more coaxing. You have to let them know that the attention is totally on you, and that you won't pick on them, embarrass them or bully them into buying. You have to convince them that you are a benign presence, and that it is safe to buy from you. It helps if you can get them to warm to you, and have some interest in you, to get them near.

---

35 cotchell, cochell–lots, loads (slang, probably Cockney origin)

My father and brothers had already mastered the art of pitch-pulling. Once people were drawn close enough to hear, they would start their spiel[36]. I loved the thrill of the crowd building round the stall, the patter and spiel of the lines, and the lilting cadence of the set pitch, which I knew by heart:

'Come on now. It's a fine bone china sugar and cream. It's got a lovely pattern, lined with gold...I'm not asking five-and-twenty-shillings, a pound or fifteen bob, fourteen shillings. I'm not even asking twelve and six. Stay with me, if you're interested... I'm not even asking ten bob. It's a lovely set that. Yes, ladies, it's fit enough for a vicar's tea party. Not nine bob, eight bob, no... Come here, let's be having you. Not seven and a tanner, not seven bob, or six bob. We've only got a few left now. We've got four lots. If you fancy one, I'm going to treat you. Come on, put your hands up, give us five bob. Come on, just a dollar[37] for the pair... You'd like one, Madam? Lady at the back. Thanks very much. There you go. Wrap them up for the lady. Just five bob now, come on. Put your hands up if you'd like one, ladies and gentlemen, I've only got a few left to treat you with. Don't be shy.'

My father liked nothing better than a 'sea of green' as he called it, raised hands waving with bank notes, ready to pay. The technical term for our selling technique is a 'Dutch auction'. This is when you start prices high and bring them down to your best price. As a child I sometimes helped with taking money and handing out goods. I stood in front of the joint to enable good eye contact with my brother or father, who'd be pitching. You had to be quick, taking the money and giving any correct change, dipping the notes or coins into the damper, or money bag secured tightly around your waist, and then making a mental note regarding who'd bought which item, and where they were standing, so you could pass their goods to them. I'd deftly wrap the goods in tissue paper, rolling the paper around them to protect them, bag them up in a brown paper carrier bag, and hand them to the customer with a smile and a 'Thank you, Sir,' or, 'Thank you, Madam'. 'Manners cost nothing' was drummed into us. Dad was always keen to get us to put the money into the 'Jack and Jill'[38] as soon as possible and he'd watch us to make sure we did so, glancing at us unobtrusively as we <u>worked. Dad liked</u> to use old-fashioned names for money, still calling

36 spiel (n)-patter, set speech (market slang, German origin)
37 dollar (n)-five shillings (market slang)
38 Jack and Jill (n)= till (rhyming slang)

two shillings a florin and referring to twenty-one shillings as a guinea. He also had particular names for denominations of money, and we adopted his expressions too. He called a half crown a 'tusheroon', five shillings was a 'dollar' or a 'caser' or five bob; ten shillings was 'half a nicker'. A pound was a 'nicker' or a 'quid'; a 'pony' was twenty-five quid; a 'stripe' or 'a long un' was a hundred; a 'bottle' was two quid or two-hundred quid; a 'monkey' was five-hundred; a 'grand' was a thousand. Some terms are well known, such as tanner for sixpence, or a bob for an old shilling, but Dad also referred to a sixpence as a 'cye' or a 'sprarsey' and called a bob a 'chip' or a 'dinah'. I soon became familiar with these terms and was able to follow conversations about money using the terms too.

One day I got my chance to pitch. I was probably about twelve years old. My Dad and my brother Bill were working together on that day. Dad decided to go to the toilet for a jimmy[39]. So with my father away, I asked Bill if I could try my luck. Reluctantly, but with some grudging interest, he said I could try. He shifted aside to let me through behind the joint, smiling to himself at my enthusiasm. I jumped up on to a little platform we had behind the joint: raised wooden pallets and boards, covered in flattened out cardboard boxes. This gave us added height to draw attention to ourselves, and in winter the cardboard was an effective barrier against the cold. If your feet or head got cold, you froze to death on the stall, so keeping warm was most important to enable you to keep working.

'Come on then, Mick, let's be havin' you,' Bill said, patting me on the shoulder. I jumped into the area behind the stall, squeezing through the opening to stand behind the front display table and started pitching. I banged the gavel to get some attention and started the sale. People turned to look at me — a kid selling pots was a bit of a novelty — and I soon had a crowd round me. I sold quite a few pieces, by aping what I'd seen my brothers and father do so many times before. My patter flowed easily and I even added the odd creative flourish of my own. I gathered what we call in the business 'an execution pitch': a massive crowd gathered to watch the sale, just as townsfolk used to gather to watch executions in the days when hangings were still popular.

---

39 Jimmy Riddle (n)-tiddle, piddle (rhyming slang)

Eventually Bill ushered me out from behind the joint and he then stepped in behind the stall and continued to sell to the crowd I'd gathered, making use of the assembled masses to move on up through a range of goods, to a few higher priced items. My father came back from his break and had to make his way through the crowd to reach us. He came up to the joint unabashed, though he must have noticed the throng. I was on tenterhooks to talk to him, to tell him about my success, wanting to report each detail. I couldn't wait.

'I've just had a pitch, Dad,' I said with pride, wanting to mark this occasion, my first proper pitch ever.

He looked at me, clearly baffled by my enthusiasm.

'Has tha? How much did you tek?'

'Seven quid,' I answered proudly. I paused, waiting for his praise.

He grimaced, looking singularly unimpressed.

'Mmn,' he grunted, 'I could have took that sat on t' box.' He meant he could have sat on the stall, selling quietly without actively pitching and could easily have taken more money than I had, thus doubting my presumption that my pitching dramatics had earned us any additional income. I don't think I did badly, for that seven quid of takings might have been equivalent to a man's weekly wage in those days. As always his praise was understated, and it only served to spur me on to do even better. Some people might have given up. Not me. I just thought, *I'll show you, you old bugger!*

My father wasn't completely unaware of my uses. When I was even younger, just after the war, sales were hard to come by. Often we'd be in the market where there were plenty of customers, but they weren't buying. Little actual trading was taking place. My father hated it when it was quiet; he liked to be busy, selling and taking money. When it was slow he'd get grumpy and scowl, 'This quiet's doin' mi head in. It's like a cemetery wi' lights on.'

There was considerable competition to get customers' attention and to get them to your stall. Sometimes they were present in the market purely for their own benefit; they were treading a little time, wasting an hour or two. They were not there with any particular purchasing intent, merely ambling around, handling things, and wiling away their day. Thus when it was slow, I was wheeled out as a human curio to grab their interest. More than once my father would get me to go out front to pick a fight with another kid, staging it right in front of the stall. There were no real injuries. Often my fighting mate was the son of another nearby trader, and both stalls were likely to benefit from the ensuing commotion. I knew what to do when he issued the order, 'Get thissen out front and start a feight, Mick!'

Obediently I went out to the front of the stall, nodded to a nearby chum and we started arguing, and putting our hands up in front of our faces like boxers. As we warmed up to a full altercation, the chant of 'Feight, feight, feight!' from the bystanders would soon ring out, and they'd gather to watch, crushing in around us, pulling in close to the action.

People would come flocking to see what the noise was all about. There was a lot of fancy footwork, swerving, dodging and dancing around with fists raised. Before too many damaging punches were thrown, my father would step out from behind the stall, like a hero, to stop the situation deteriorating, separating us and keeping us apart at arm's length, tutting at us disapprovingly; and with an announcement of: 'Ladies and gentlemen, gather round, the sale's about to start!' he'd gather the punters in and draw them close into the joint. Later when it was quiet he'd slip me a couple of bob, to go and buy myself some ice cream as a reward.

I enjoyed the cheeky confidence of my elder brothers who had developed quite a line in satirical patter. I particularly liked it when sales were slow and my brother Bill charmingly insulted the punters. He'd say, 'You're a tight lot today, just coming down here for a free show and buying nowt. I hope when you get home t' cat's got int' cupboard and brok' ev'ry pot tha's got! You're a bad lot and bad'll come to you.' Or he might say to them, viewing them blackly with a deadpan expression, 'Th'art a miserable lot, I've seen happier faces round a bleedin' graveside.' Fortunately he could get away with his complaining. They'd laugh and smile at one another at his gall. We might even get a quick surge in sales out of sympathy. I think they knew there was no malice in his effrontery; there was always affection there.

Our relationship with our customers was quite intimate. We sold things that you don't see in the shops today, such as chamber pots, known as 'potties'. They were used in many homes; people didn't want to go out into the back yard in the middle of the night for the toilet. Our colloquial name for them was 'laggers'. Using this term, we could call up for them, keeping their appearance as a surprise, using our private lingo. We'd ask for them from one of the schleppers, crying, 'Pass me that crate of laggers up.'

We varied the items in the sale, according to our assessment of the punters' spending power. Earthenware or bone china, we stocked them all and we had one for every pocket. If we had a largely elderly audience before us, perhaps as was usual on pension day, we'd bring up our robust earthenware potties for sale, made to last. We got the audience giggling even with this intimate subject. We'd say, revealing the item to the audience with mock surprise, holding the potty high above our heads, upturned, so we could read the bottom of it, 'Oh look at this, ladies and gents. This one's a posh un. Well I never; it's got a motto at the bottom!' and we'd pause with dramatic anticipation. Then reading supposedly from the bottom of the potty, we would announce grandly in our best poetry voice:

> '*Wipe me out and keep me clean,*
> *And I'll not tell what I've just seen.*'

They would laugh out loud, and a sea of hands would go up, indicating they wanted to buy. There was no embarrassment as they came forward to pay for their gazunders[40].

We liked to kid the punters that we were cultured, and offered up another poem if we showed willow pattern pottery for sale, saying out loud a well-known poem, describing the scene on the plate:

> '*Two pigeons flying high,*
> *Chinese vessel sailing by,*
> *Weeping willow hanging o 'er,*
> *Bridge with three men, if not four.*'[41]

---

40 gazunder (n)-colloquial term for chamber pot, so called because 'it goes under' the bed.
41 A second verse exists, though I did not know this at the time. The second verse is as follows:

> *Chinese temples there they stand*
> *Seem to take up all the land*
> *Apple trees with apples on*
> *A pretty fence to end my song.*

Whilst growing up, I enjoyed learning the trade from my eldest brother, Joseph Lockwood[42] Edwards. He had been grafting for so long he didn't realise what skills he had gained. I remember once seeing Joe work in the 1960s. For years he had a stall at Barnsley Market. None of us were academic types, it's doubtful that he could have articulated his knowledge, but he certainly knew about sales psychology. I watched from the sidelines as Joe held the audience enthralled. He was on the box pitching and he was banging his gavel and bringing up a series of

My brother, Joseph Lockwood Edwards, (Joe)

wares for sale. All eyes should have been on him. Even the schleppers at the side were meant to stay still and quiet. There was to be no fide-ing; all eyes had to stay on the main pitcher.

There was a well-dressed attractive woman in the edge[43]. You know the type; as my mother would have said 'she liked herself!'

She was one of those sorts who fancied herself; salmon-orange lipstick, gaudy earrings, tossing her back-combed, bouffant hair-do about flirtatiously; her whole demeanour screamed *please look at me*. Her nonchalance was feigned and she was one of those people

---

42 In our family some of those without additional middle Christian names often take my mother's surname as a middle name to honour the Lockwood side of the family.
43 edge (n,)-the gathered customers, crowd, audience.

who needed constant attention, whilst all the time pretending that she didn't care and wasn't seeking any notice. She was at the front of the crowd in full view of everyone. She primped her hair then she took hold of a lamp base. Then after placing that back in its place, she picked up a glass vase, boldly taking it from the front of the display. She held it up high, under the lights, seemingly to examine it more closely, but she was really vying for attention with Joe. She was starting to distract the punters. They turned to look her up and down, wondering what she was doing. He clocked[44] her and realised he had better take action, before she succeeded in gaining all the attention, and distracting the punters from the sale of goods at hand.

Deftly, but politely, he took the vase from her, wrapped it up in tissue, handed it back to her and held out his hand for the money saying, 'Thanks very much, love. That'll be a pound.' She looked at Joe momentarily, meekly took a pound out of her purse, paid him, packed the vase in her shopping bag and walked away. Afterwards when it had quietened down we chatted, and I recounted to Joe what a classic move I'd just witnessed from him.

'That was bloody good that,' I offered, praising his skill.

He shrugged and looked at me.

'What thy on about?' he asked with complete puzzlement.

'That vase; what you did with that woman.'

'What woman?'

He had no idea at all what I was talking about and had no conscious recollection of the event. He hadn't realised what he'd done. I had to explain about how he'd sold her the vase without her really wanting it. He'd been in control of the sale and she hadn't resisted it. She'd stopped messing with the vase and had meekly paid him. By doing that he'd got rid of her, and he'd got the punters' attention back, restoring all interest in him and the goods he was pitching. He looked at me quizzically, the penny dropping, then he chuckled and said he wasn't bothered about the money or the sale, but he certainly didn't like anyone taking the limelight from him. He said chortling, 'Well, you see, Mick, I'm the only bleedin' big-'ead round here. I had to stumm[45] her.'

---

44 clock (v)-to look, see, have a look at, spy (slang)

45 stumm (used as vb)-quieten, prevent from speaking or taking attention (German adj. stumm-quiet, silent, mute, dumb).

I learned a lot from my brother Joe. He had many tips for me; he told me if anyone asked the price to ignore them, and not to interrupt our patter by answering them. This might seem rude, but he was correct in asserting that some people would drift off once they knew the price, and we wanted to keep them in the edge as part of the audience for as long as possible, in case we had some goods that would suit their pocket. He told me to ignore their questions about the prices by saying, 'Sling them a deafen,' and, 'Bottle[46] them if they ask about the bat[47].' By holding their attention for longer, we built a little more drama and maximised our opportunity of obtaining a sale. It was best to tell them the price when we had come to the end of our stock patter. 'Bat[48] them at the death[49],' he said wisely.

The stallholders were a resilient lot, working through all weathers, through bust and boom, recession and depression, both economic and personal. What a way to get a living. The market was full of characters. There was Big Ada. She'd sit on a chair selling lines from boxes in front of her, at the top of the market, wrapped in coats and shawls, grappling with her leather money bag tied round her wide girth. She only ever had the choice of two lines, come rain or shine. She stocked whatever she could make money on, on that day. It might be celery and lettuce, lettuce and tomatoes, or cucumber and tomatoes, always just two types of goods for sale. Each day she worked out how much she could afford to buy, and her profit margin, which was probably quite decent as she bought seasonally and cheaply, making use of the gluts of produce. She was a big woman and she could chin any man if she had to, and she didn't stand for any aggravation.

Then there was the woman who owned the big red weighing scales at the top of the market. She was a little bird-like woman, but her small frame oozed confidence and she would try to guess your weight within three pounds either way, either under or over your actual weight.

---

46 bottle (v)–to ignore, disregard, desist from, cease, (market slang)
47 bat (n)–price (market slang)
48 bat (v)–to inform customers of the price, state the price (market slang)
49 at the death–at the end (slang)

Before you sat on her scales she'd look at you with piercing eyes and summarise your poundage, 'Twelve stone, three'. Then she'd sit you on the scales, clank the balancing arm, running weights across, checking the accuracy of her conjecture. She was stunningly precise. In the unlikely event that she was wrong, she'd reimburse customers their weighing fee of three pence, handing them a thrupenny bit, or three copper pennies. People queued up to be weighed, enjoying sitting on the seat with its heavy old-fashioned carpet cover with swinging tassels.

We saw her most mornings as we went down to fetch up new lines from the warehouse. She was used to us having a nobble[50] with her.

We'd shout a greeting to her in passing, yelling across to her, 'Morning. I'm comin' to have a sit on that in a minute, love. My missus says I need to go on a diet.'

She'd shout back at us, laughing, 'It wain't hold tha weight, you big bleeder!'

I believe that she eventually sold the weighing scales to someone in Australia or America. I wonder if they are still in use...

There was also little Long-Haired Paddy, the quack doctor who wore an old-fashioned black frock coat. He was light on his feet and he used to dance to pull a pitch. He sold medicines and remedies, home-made tablets, oils, poultices, cough lozenges, Epsom salts, ointments, tinctures and linctus, ridged bottles of liniment and camphorated embrocation fluid, balms and rubs, and dried pieces of orris root and mandrake root.

His patter was amazing. As soon as he had a crowd round he'd thunder with his booming, rasping voice, 'If you've got piles, blind, bleeding or itching, I'll cure them. If your wife wakes you up in the early hours of the morning and nags you, I tell you, give her the root, now give her the root, I say.' At this he'd wait and the crowd would shift, wondering whether to react or titter at his *double entendre*. Mostly they were silent, avoiding his gaze for they feared he might alight upon them, drawing them into some unwanted interaction. Then following this pause he'd lift a piece of mandrake root ceremoniously up in the air for all to see crying, 'Here it is, the white blood of the mandrake. When I pulled it from the earth, digging it up early this morning with my spade, prising it from the earth, it

---

50 to have a nobble-to have a laugh, to tease someone about something (market slang)

screamed. I tell you when I got the spade underneath it, dragging it from the earth, it screamed like a baby. Look upon it now, the pure, white root of the mandrake.' He'd then take a piece of mandrake root and rub it across his forehead, indicating its miraculous properties for banishing headaches. 'Ladies and gentlemen, for cuts and headaches use the white blood of the mandrake. Put a bit on your brow and within ten minutes they will be gone,' he cried, beckoning the crowd in to look at his samples.

In those days you had to pay to see a doctor, so if you could heal yourself with tablets, a lotion or potion, it might serve you well. He had remedies for cleansing the blood, for healing gout, for boils, blebs[51], pustules and cankers. He was not afraid to tackle some of the thornier topics, addressing the crowd about the dangers of venereal disease too. His tablets could allegedly sort any affliction, even gonorrhoea and syphilis. No one dared leave the pitch when Paddy was talking. If you left the pitch he'd shout and point at you, making the heads of the assembled crowd turn in your direction, hollering after you with his guttural tones, 'There goes a sufferer! That gentleman's got it!' and heads would turn to watch your diseased, syphilitic carcass rolling away through the crowds, as fast as your legs could carry you.

51 bleb (n)-blister

-4-
MY EARLY LIFE

I was born at a house in Cross Bedford Street, Sheffield 6. The house is not there any more and was pulled down long ago. That area of Sheffield was full of terraced housing. It was a very ordinary house, with no bathroom and no proper heating. Mam had to get up early to light the fires. We used to store our coal in a coal hole. One day Joe Bennett, then my sister Bib's sweetheart, went out to get some coal. He was ferreting in the hole with an old rusty shovel when suddenly he spied two little black eyes staring at him. Startled and scared, he ran back into the house shaking, saying he'd seen some big eyes looking at him from the darkness. My Mam and Dad laughed this off, thinking he was a soft ha'peth[52], but apparently a few days later I was sitting in my pram outside in the yard, when my mother saw a rat sitting happily on the pram, sunning itself with me! Soon after that we flitted and went to live in a house on Harris Road, off Middlewood Road. Mam was not willing to share our home with any 'long tailed uns,' as she called them.

I'm not surprised there was a rat sitting on the pram. My mother used to dip my dummy in Nestle's condensed milk to keep me quiet when I was a baby. She used to take herself off to the pictures one afternoon a week, to the Oxford Picture Palace, and she was soon mesmerised by the swish actors and romantic storylines; mechanically she'd be dipping the dummy into the can of condensed milk without looking at me, dabbing it vaguely in the direction of my mouth. I always had a veritable beard of condensed milk by the end of the flick. So began my life of luxury, and my early relationship with rich food.

I was born at home and christened Michael David Edwards. I was named after the doctor who delivered me, by all accounts, a Mr.

---

52 ha'peth (n)-literally half penny worth, used as a term of derision, i.e. silly or stupid person

43

Michael David O'Connor. He had his surgery at Parson Cross. It is told that the unfortunate fellow stumbled and fell down our stairs as he left, though he wasn't badly injured. My mother was concerned for him, asked him his name and named me after him 'to sweeten it' — to recover the situation somewhat. An act typical of her; she was a woman of great wit, warmth and charm.

The house at Cross Bedford Street was a terraced house with a warren of connecting cellars. In those early days we rented. When things were hard, people clubbed together to find the rent, taking it in turns in the yard to pay their dues, from family to family, week by week. Many avoided being at home when the rent man came by. Often families were seen at the dark of night doing a moonlight flit, to avoid rent arrears. Sometimes we had to hide from the rent man too, and lie low in the house, in case he nosied through the windows. Mam would leave a pile of coins on the sideboard in view, so it looked as if we intended to pay.

As I got older we became more affluent and we made various moves. We lived in various houses when I was a child: Burton Street, Harris Road. Then Herries Road for a while; we moved from there because we got bombed out during the war. The doors and windows had got blown out in an air raid. It wasn't safe as buildings all around us were in danger of collapsing. At first we went to live with my sister Bib, (who was married by this time to Joe Bennett), at their home in Watersmeet Road, Malin Bridge. I attended Morley Street School from this point on. [53] Then in the early 1940s we moved to a bungalow on Rivelin Valley Road. This was the first house that my parents owned. They had done well to purchase their own home. We stayed there for many years, and I only left when I got married and finally bought my first house, at the bottom of Stannington Road, in the early 1960s.

When we first moved to Rivelin Valley Road my mother sent for the Stores to come and decorate. In those days the Stores had their own decorating department, with a team of skilled craftsmen and apprentices. It was a bit high class if you had the Stores to come and titivate your house.

I think at the time just after the war, wallpaper must have been scarce, as painting techniques were the main art of interior decora-

---

53 readies (n)-money (slang)

tion. I remember they made a good job of the hallway; the background colour was cream and they painted tulips and daffodils as if they were growing out from the skirting board. I always liked it. No one else had this design in my circle and it was cheerful as you came in the hall. Painters and decorators were skilled in those days. I watched them as they worked; they did special lining and two-tone colours. We had a picture rail and below it they painted a decorative line. To get the measurements right, they had a bit of chalk tied on a string and they pinged it against the wall. It left a mark, which they used as a guide to attach the tape for lining out the inch-wide border accurately. We had lines with extra bits of fancywork as they went round the corners of the walls in dark cream and brown, fashionable colours in those days.

Moving to our own house caused some excitement. It signalled a period of prosperity and pride in our home. Mother kept her brass ornaments on top of the mantelpiece in the front room. No one had as much brass as she did and she used to polish it religiously once a week with *Brasso* and a duster. I often came home to find the dining table spread with newspaper and her glinting ornaments strewn across it. She also collected *Goss* ornaments and on any holiday or day trip we searched for a *Goss* memento to buy and bring home. The bungalow had a shelf cornice, about a foot lower than the ceiling, where Mam put all her china ornaments: little figurines, Toby jugs, small vases, old Victorian plates, china fancies and money boxes, which meant you could view them from any vantage point in the room. I particularly liked an old tin moneybox that was up there. It was fashioned in the shape of a Negro man's head and shoulders. You placed a penny on the flat of his hand and turned his ear, making him swallow the penny into his mouth. I was always asking for it to be fetched down for me to play with it. She'd sigh as she reached for the kitchen stepladder to haul it down, 'Blimey, you can tell you're a typical Edwards... interested in readies[54]!'

My mother blagged my Dad to buy a new parlour suite, costing eighty pounds. She also got him to buy some Utility bedroom furniture. They probably got them on the never-never. In those days if you needed furniture you got it on the weekly, and kept a book listing

54 readies (n)-money (slang)

all your payments. Dad was rather reluctant to get maced up[55], as he called it, for anything, unless it was for gear to sell. Investing in china to sell was never a waste of time or money in his book. However, he liked a quiet life and he didn't really begrudge my mother's spending. I think they bought the furniture from a shop on Hillsborough Bottom, where the Kinema used to be. Our few electrical goods came from Wigfalls.

It was at this time that Mam invested in our posh sofa, with its beech frame and horsehair stuffing. If you flicked an iron rod at one end, the sofa arm dropped down at an angle, flattening out, so you could lie down on it and relax your head, as if reclining on a chaise longue. The fabric was lovely, of a really good quality, and lasted for years. Mam always loved it and she urged us to keep it clean. She shrouded the back of it with little mats, antimacassars that our Agnes had crocheted, to keep the fabric in pristine condition.

As a child I was very happy with the move to Rivelin Valley Road. The location of the bungalow was perfect for me; I had the streets and gardens to wander through, the wildness of the river to explore and the wending woods and paths and tracks to ramble along. Our back garden rose up steeply; there was a lower area, partly cultivated, then up on the higher level was a patch of wilderness full of blackberries, stinging nettles and a gnarled apple tree clinging on to the bank by its twisted, buckling roots.

We were not great gardeners, but we enjoyed the studded, bejewelled tangle of unruly raspberries, left by the previous house occupants, and we picked the woody moss roses and old cabbage roses, which smelled sherbet-sweet on sunny days. I was in my element in this house with countryside and wildlife on the doorstep. My father was less pleased with the wildlife, as the house could be overrun with mice at some times of the year. Father was quick; he'd jump up and grab one as it scuttled up the bay window curtains. He'd grimace, growling at it, 'Come here, you little bleeder!' Then he'd throw it on the fire back.

I was quite untamed in my wanderings as a child and I was given the freedom to come and go and to roam that would not be likely nowadays. The hills and allotments around Morley Street were my kingdom. I explored the Donkey Woods on Rivelin Valley Road. I

---

55 to get maced up (v)-to take out a loan or hire purchase agreement to fund a purchase, borrow money (market slang)

hunted for adventures with my pals along the footpath's leafy tracks and ventured through the woods, exploring the teeming ponds in the valley bottom. I ventured far without any cares. My mother and father did not seem too concerned about me being out and about either. In those days they could be confident that it was likely any passing adult would haul me home in shame, give me a clip or a thick ear for any minor transgressions or cheek. In those days no adult would be afraid to tell you off for any misdemeanours, and would happily give you a public coating[56] or scutch[57] you across the head, calling you a cheeky little bleeder. When out in public it's fair to say we got away with a lot, but there was always the worry that any news would travel home to get you done. You could be in big trouble by tea time. It was no bad thing and it kept us in check.

Nature was my church. Rivelin Valley Road came to be my playground with its green-tunnelled roof of trees filtering a great arc of soft emerald light. I loved to be walking under the vaulted branches, under its arching leafy canopy with tree tips hanging over the road, meeting in the middle, light dappling through the leaves, sometimes yellow, sometimes acid green, shimmering in the sunlight; my green cathedral roof. I meandered for miles, taking in the sights.

There was something interesting to see at all times of the year and plants were familiar signposts on my roadmap. In late April and May, I loved the undulating mist of bluebells carpeting the donkey woods, pulsing and glowering in the sunlight and flickering cloud, like the powder blue embers of a dying fire. In summer, I enjoyed swatting the tall, frothing heads of cow parsley, topping the grassy verges like heads on pints.

Local people often kept pigs, and drove them down from the bole hills to the donkey woods to feed, exerting their pannage[58] rights, freely making use of the acorns, beech mast and plentiful holly. It amazed me that any creatures could find holly appetising, but pigs managed it, munching and grazing greedily from bush to bush. Hollies also grew abundantly up by the old churchyard at St Michael's Catholic church, opposite Rivelin Park paddling pool, the young hollies giving their name to Hollins Lane.

---

56 coating (n)-reprimand, telling-off (slang)
57 scutch (v)-to beat, hit, slap, tap (slang)
58 pannage-(n) pasturage for pigs in woodland or forest

My travels were punctuated by familiar botanical stops and halting places. Patches of dock leaves for rubbing on your nettled thighs and ankles, patches of Mother-die to avoid, and plentiful missiles – the ovate, woolly burrs from burdock plants and long sticky strings of cleavers woven through the hedgerows, always well placed for throwing mischievously at your pals.

Each venture held the promise of bringing edible delicacies home. In summer I took a strong paper bag with me, always on the hunt for bilberries. I knew my favoured patches year on year where the biggest berries were to be found on scraps of heathy, sandy soil up Rivelin, and even as far as Wadsley Common. I brought them home and Mam baked my favourite sweet dish - bilberry pie, oozing blue-black juice which turned your teeth dark. It was the favourite pie of all the family and I was reluctant to share it. After a bowlful our tongues were darkly violet-black, accentuating the gaping holes of our greedy, cavernous mouths around the dinner table. These amazing pies had us circling the table like cheeping chicks, hungry for seconds.

My mother would urge me to overcome my natural protectiveness of the pie, saying, 'Don't be piky[59], give our Bill another piece.' Reluctantly I'd shovel a sliver onto his plate and he'd grab the knife off me and jostle a bigger piece towards his plate.

'Tha's 'ad enough now,' he'd say. 'Tha'll be badly, these berries work like opening medicine tha knows.'

I still know where the best bilberries are to be found, but I'm not allowed to tell. My brother-in-law, Tony, guards such secret pitches desperately too, and we still value and seek out this food-for-free annually.

In autumn I knew where every cobnut hedge was to be found and I picked jumper-loads of the fresh green nuts, cradling them, eating most of them before I got home, feasting on the sweet, milky nut-flesh. It was a frantic time for a young lad and each day was concerned with finding the best horse chestnut trees and chucking up sticks to knock down the conkers. I'd take them home, to firm them up by soaking them in jam jars of vinegar overnight, hoping to develop a champion for conker tournaments in the school yard.

---

59 piky (adj)-mean, parsimonious, tight, stingy (market slang)

In winter it was often cold enough to skate on Micky's Dam, the ice a solid two or three inches deep. My friends and I did this, completely unaware of the dangers.

In spring and summer I ventured for miles on foot, with my wooden trolley, and as I got older, by trundling bike. I liked nothing more than to set off with a chunk of bread and butter and my trolley, ambling up through the arched trees on either side of Rivelin Valley Road, or following the route of the river, over the wall by the road, visiting the area known as Micky's Dam, where there was a house with a fantastic pear tree in the garden. At fruit harvest, I'd pop in to buy pears from the lady who lived at this house. She served me and wrapped them in a big brown paper bag, and I would settle down to feast on them with a couple of pals, pear juice dripping down our chins.

In summer my friends and I explored the land around the old mills and forges down by the Mouse Hole, messing around by the ponds, prodding and poking at the mud searching for creatures. We threw skimming stones across the surface, holding competitions to see who could throw them the furthest. We hunted for frogspawn or fished with makeshift rods and nets for sticklebacks and tadpoles, jumping froglets and assorted pond-life, bringing our finds home, slopping them around in jam jars with string handles. On hot summer days we liked to linger by the sluice, eyeballing the river watching for a dipper flitting and zipping by, curving dangerously above the surface of the glassy water. As nightfall came we'd hover, lingering in the sticky warm heat, looking up into the dusk sky to see if we could spot a bat sweeping by.

We stayed out for as long as we could get away with in summer, sometimes only returning home under a darkening sky, urged home by a cooling in the muggy atmosphere, sudden gusting breezes and fierce thunderclaps, heralding summer storms. I often returned home as dusk fell, to the sight of a family member hovering in the front garden, peering up the wide avenue looking for me.

I also spent a lot of time on the tip, at the top of Watersmeet Road, where there was a mound of ash and cinders. I don't know where such detritus and assorted debris came from, but we had some fun on it. We liked to make paper aeroplanes and stand on top of it, and fly them as far as the wind could take them. On a windy day they might be carried as far as the river, across into the back yard of Burgon and Ball's tool factory. One house tenant, whose back garden flanked Holme Lane, visible from the tip, kept pigs in the garden. We liked to watch him catch a paper aeroplane in his hand, looking round quizzically, wondering where the bombers had flown in from, musing on which denizens might be friend or foe.

In those days the wooden trolley was a young boy's preferred mode of transport. We all made them from a few planks of cheap pine, a cross bar made of old skirting, or 2 inch by 4 inch pieces of wood, a length of old washing line to pull it along, and salvaged pram wheels, which were a frequent find by allotments and on river banks. My brother Bill, who was nearest to me in age, (but being ten years older was an experienced trolley builder), helped me build my first trolley and it accompanied me on many adventures. There was always room for a pal on the back. You could sit or stand on it, freewheel down hills at great speed and it was light enough to drag up any slope. I took it to the shops on errands, and when I called for friends. It didn't have brakes, so most boys like me had scuffed shoes — if they had them at all — friction-torn with dried up toe-caps, frazzled by frequent blistering halts and emergency stops.

All my brothers and sisters were much older than me so I was always hearing stories of their travels and adventures, and I had little understanding that I was too young or vulnerable to do the same, I think I must have been listening to exploits about camping and backpacking when one summer at the age of five I was hassling my mother to let me go off camping. She rallied various arguments about how it was not a good idea, but I continued to mither. I'd caught her when she was busy. It was Monday, wash day and the house was littered with different piles of vestments, sorted by colours for washing. Across the hills of Walkley and up the Racker Way behind our house, gardens streamed with washing lines, garments flapping wildly in the wind; corsets, brassières, liberty bodices, trousers, balaclavas, shirts, blouses, cotton dresses, flailing in the breeze, billowing public ticker tape messages, announcing the news of private cupboards and drawers, streaming the latest stories across each and every garden. Mam was in the kitchen, ironing smalls and folding towels, her attention securely elsewhere, not concentrating on my chatter.

Finally, worn down by my chirping, she agreed a little half-heartedly that I could go camping some day, saying, 'Aye, go on then, stop pestering the life out of me. Get thi sen off,' she capitulated. My persistence had paid off it seemed; I took this to be the permission I needed and I gathered a few things in a canvas bag and an old tent from the hut and went off that very afternoon.

I hear all the neighbours were out looking for me by nightfall. She sent Joe Bennett (J.B.), Bib's husband, to look for me, and some-how he knew my favoured places, eventually finding me at the side of the railway track at Wadsley Bridge. I'd climbed up onto the rail-way embankment and had pitched my make-do tent there. He found me asleep, the tent falling down around me. I was hauled back home. However, I don't remember getting into that much trouble; I think mother was pleased the situation had not turned out badly, and any blame on her part had therefore fortunately been averted.

I was not often purposefully naughty and my mother's kind atten-tion offered me many opportunities to redeem myself, getting into her good books. There was my stock party piece for example, which always brought the house down. I had a lovely singing voice and big green eyes, and even from the age of six I had my own song, which I knew by heart. I had a well-practised rendition of *My Yiddishe Momma*. Anne Shelton made the song famous in the 1940s.

I don't remember how I learned it, but I did have one particular fan; my mother was friendly with a nice woman called Mrs. Patnick, who loved to hear me sing. I remember going round to her house with the grown-ups. They had a second-hand shop at the top of Burton Street where we'd visit them. With one eye on the shop counter and the other on me, they'd sit and chat in the back room and take tea. The atmosphere was always friendly and cordial. At any lull in the proceedings I'd be encouraged to get up and sing. My Mam would hearten me; she'd smile and look at me as I composed myself, getting up from my seat and taking up my stage position in the middle of the carpet or up on the dais. Sometimes an adult, conscious of the grand occasion, would do a fake drum roll and announce, 'Ladies and gentlemen, live from Sheffield, we present Master Michael David Edwards, who for your pleasure will sing *My Yiddishe Momma*.' There was applause, and I took a deep breath ready to start my song.

Even at that age, as I stood before the gathering, I was conscious of how to hold an audience, I'd wait for silence, then with their full attention, I'd launch into the song. I sang it sweetly and plaintively, lingering over the long vowels, emphasising the sense of regret and longing in the lyrics. Mrs. Patnick would sit looking at me, unable to take her eyes off my little face and chirping mouth. By the time I had finished she always had tears in her eyes and streaming down her face. She clapped loudly at the end, grabbing me to embrace me, planting a wet, sloppy kiss on my cheek in congratulations.

Encouraged by my early success in show business, my Mam enrolled me in tap dancing lessons. However, I soon kicked that idea into touch, sacking it in disgust. The teacher had us dancing around clapping our hands and waving like girls, which I did not appreciate. After a few weeks I refused to go, so it was clear I wasn't going to end up on the stage. On the other hand, my brother, Joe, was an excellent tap dancer. He'd had lessons years before me and never forgot the steps he'd learned.

My sister Bib was a good dancer too. She could do the Charleston, with fancy arm crossovers over her knees, and the kick-step. I thought she could dance and sing better than Ginger Rogers and Fred Astaire, or Anne Ziegler and Webster Booth. Bib was a looker too — with her luminous complexion, high cheekbones and sharp, blue-green eyes.

My sister, Bib

Mam was a real civilising influence, but she also appreciated my need for freedom. As I got older, I was quite used to fending for myself and was often given money to buy my dinner. This gave me the scope to wander round the streets and browse the offerings of the assortment of corner shops. Post-rationing, I could perhaps make sensible and savoury choices, and might have a pork sandwich with apple sauce and crackling, a chip butty, or a buttered bread cake or sausage rolls. If feeling more indulgent, I might buy a tea cake, a gigantic bag of mixed penny sweets, or a bag of spice[60], as we called them with pear drops, humbugs, gob stoppers, boiled sweets in the shape of little fishes, and various chews, perhaps a Sherbet dab or two, or bars of Cadbury's chocolate, or packets of biscuits.

When we stayed at Watersmeet Road at my sister's, after being bombed out, I attended Morley Street School, quickly settling in and making a band of friends. At dinner times I used to frequent many corner shops around Walkley.

Recently, (in my seventieth year), I met a chap who was a school chum of mine at Morley Street, Jack Dodd. He was in the swimming team and was a few years older than me. I looked up to him. He was a good swimmer. I think his best race was the breast stroke. He said an image was branded on his memory; he remembered us walking up through the gennels[61] and allotments of Walkley to a corner shop at school lunch time, and that I gave him the gift of half a packet of Lincoln Creams, to gorge on for his dinner. He said he'd marvelled at my generosity — until that day he'd never even had a biscuit and he could still taste them now. We had a good swimming team at Morley Street School. Yes, I remember Jack Dodd, Tommy Hudson, Brian Ward and Jack Ashforth. Happy days...

I occasionally had money to spend and might treat myself to a swimming session, or a flick. Sometimes at weekends I went swimming at Hillsborough Baths, and on my way home I'd call in at Daubney's Drink Shop for a refreshing glass of sarsaparilla. I went to the pictures too, to the Forum at Parson Cross, and enjoyed the films there:

60 spice (n)-(local S. Yorks. dialect), sweets
61 gennel, jennel, ginnel- (n) (Northern dialect)- narrow alleyway between buildings, snicket, often pronounced gennel in Sheffield (\'jen-əl\ ). Gennel is a local corruption of ginnel.

Captain Marvel, The Three Stooges, and cowboy films starring Roy Rogers and the singing cowboy, Gene Autry.

I had various companions and was never short of friends; however, my constant companion and best friend from a young age was Geoff Sanderson. Geoff lived near me in a small house at the top of Donkey Woods above Rivelin Valley Road, with his Mam and younger brother, Donny. By this time Geoff's older brother, Dennis, was married and lived away from home. Sadly, by our early teens Geoff's dad had died. Geoff told me stories about him; he'd worked as a haulier for Edward Box & Co, a heavy haulage firm. His dad had been a Chindit, one of the allied Special Forces, and had fought deep in the jungles of Burma behind enemy lines against the Japanese.

Geoff had never been too fond of school and from a young age he often went on the lorry with his dad, instead of attending lessons. Geoff's schooling had suffered, but he wasn't bothered. He was more interested in larking about and exploring. In the evenings and at weekends we'd play together.

Geoff was a few years older than me, but looked much younger than his actual age. He was spindly and gangly, and because of his interrupted schooling he never quite mastered the skill of reading and writing. I was no scholar, and if I had any intelligence it was of the pragmatic, common sense variety. For what I may have lacked in intellect, I made up in muscle, physical strength, and sheer front and self-confidence. I was stocky and solid in comparison to Geoff, even at a young age. I became Geoff's protector. He was a kind kid, he'd share anything he had, and really didn't go looking for trouble, but it seemed to find him. I was often called on, to weigh in, to rescue him from bullies far older than myself, which I always did with gusto.

I felt sorry for Geoff; he didn't seem to have a happy home life. His mother was a wiry, nervy woman and when we spent any time in his house, which was rare, he always seemed to be under her feet. She was quick tempered, which made him even more nervous and clumsy in her presence.

When she could stand him no more she'd wail, her voice rising in pitch to a crescendo, 'Now then, daft bugger, soft bugger, silly bugger, get aat. Daft bugger, get aat!!' This singular wail of hers would rise in pitch, along with her annoyance, and he'd dodge her as he ran out of the door as she made to plant a clip on his ear lugs as he scuttled by. Once she threw a plate of bacon and eggs after him and it slid down the wall. I felt sorry for him and could never quite understand just what he ever did that served to irritate her so much. But her moods didn't affect his feelings for his mother. He loved her dearly, and when he became a successful builder years later, he bought her a house.

Geoff never seemed to be very at home in his own home and preferred mine. He was always hungry. My Mam said he'd got hollow legs, but she liked him, declaring he was 'as reight as a bobbin'.

Once when we got back after some rambling adventure and found we had the house to ourselves he said, 'Now then, Mick, does tha fancy some beans?'

I didn't really, but this sort of questioning was always code for the fact that Geoff was hungry and *he* fancied some grub, so I often humoured him and opened our cupboards to him.

'Aaah, thee mek 'em,' I said, not being interested in cooking indoors; that was my Mam's domain.

So Geoff proceeded into the little kitchen at the back of the bungalow and sorted out our dinner. He rummaged in the back of the cupboards, grabbing some tins. I left him to it. He busied himself in the kitchen then came to join me in the lounge. We carried on with our games in the house for a while, when suddenly we jumped out of our skins. There was a whooshing sound, an almighty bang then clattering. We ran into the kitchen to see what was up. I looked up at an almighty orange mess dripping from the ceiling.

'Oh heck, now we'll cop it!' I said, dodging the baked beans dribbling down. 'What's that been doin', soft ha'peth?'

'Erm...I put 'em on to boil,' said Geoff shamefacedly, '...in the tin,' he added.

'Never mind, we'll clear up,' I sighed. 'I'll do us some bread and butter instead,' I said with resignation.

Poor Geoff had put the tin in a pan of water and left it on the stove to cook. This was a strange cooking technique, one that I'd never come across before. So we set to work and cleaned up.

'Next time, open t' tin before tha cooks 'em,' I suggested, belatedly.

I always knew right from wrong as a kid, but sometimes my longing for adventure and my natural appetites led me into wrongdoing. There was the time that I discovered a green-fingered neighbour was growing a grape vine in his greenhouse. I could not resist the temptation to sneak in and gorge myself on those sweet bunches of black grapes. I even doctored a pair of our Agnes's sewing scissors for the purpose of cutting off the bunches that were high up, from the highest branches bearing the sweetest prizes, which had caught the sun. I hunkered down amongst the garden paraphernalia and ate until I was sated. It didn't seem wrong, but of course I know now that it was. I can still taste them...

Business was in my blood. The whole family were involved one way or another in selling. My Dad and his brother, John Willy, sold pots in the market. My brothers Joe, Arthur and Bill were involved and even our Bib's husband, Joe Bennett, had been drafted in during their early courtship to work the network of pitches around the local markets at Rotherham, Barnsley, Doncaster and Chesterfield. It was always considered something of a recommendation, in my father's view, if you could graft.

I think I was about ten years old and I'd earned some pocket money from working the markets with my Dad, so I suggested to Geoff that we should set up our first enterprise. The plan was to get some chickens and ducks and rear them. Geoff thought it was a good idea and he was willing to act as my duck-man. We'd be able to sell them for meat, and whilst fattening them up, we'd also have some eggs to sell.

My parents had bought me a cinematograph for Christmas. It had a light inside that showed pictures, projected onto a wall. It didn't last long; part of the mechanism and pictures soon came adrift, but the container and light still worked. I suggested we should rig it up and it could function as a heat lamp for the fowls and chicks. We had it outside near the side passage, but someone told us it was too near to the window, so we rigged it up further up the garden; the trouble was we could not plug it into the electricity so we had to rig up a complicated selection of different wires of various thicknesses with connectors.

With great anticipation, after working on the links all afternoon, we plugged it into the mains. There was a fizzle, sparks and a big bang, and the whole thing fused, sending up a little puff of acrid smoke. That was the end of our home-made incubator. However, we were not deterred. We finally set up the outfit in our back garden. We had a coop in the shed to keep them sheltered, and an outdoor pen — from which they constantly escaped.

Every day when we got home from school we'd usher them across Rivelin Valley Road, shepherding them and shooing them through a hole in the wall, to enable them to go for a swim in the river. This could be rather tiresome and haphazard. We often ended up wet and bedraggled, as we'd have to wade into the shallows of the river to retrieve some duck that had made its way down the river to Malin Bridge, making a break for freedom and civilisation. I rather fancied myself as a businessman; the enterprise was growing and they were breeding fast. I took charge, feeling we needed to formally assess the success of the venture.

'Now then, Geoff, let's have a stock take,' I said to Geoff one day, handing him a piece of paper and a pencil. Geoff rather liked this authority bestowed on him and he licked the end of the pencil in anticipation of the process to come. It took him a while to write his notes on a piece of paper and I looked over his shoulder at what he'd written. In wiggly letters he'd struggled to scribe: *2 WIT COKS*.

'What's that say?' I asked, puzzled.

Geoff eyed me with a superior air. It wasn't very often I needed help.

'Two white cocks,' he said matter-of-factly, smiling to himself as if he'd finally confirmed that I was a bit daft in the head after all. I smiled back at him and said nothing. It wasn't my place to correct him.

I don't remember if we made much money from those ducks. I do remember them churning up the lawn and crapping all over my Mam's garden, which meant that our business was soon thwarted. I seem to remember we ended up selling them to the milkman.

I kept in touch with my pal Geoff regularly for many years, until his death in 2006. We called regularly at one another's homes for a chat and a pot of tea, always able to pick up on conversations where we had left off the previous time, and share our history.

Geoff and I had a largely wild, outdoor life, roaming for miles. This was not due to neglect on my parents' part, they had a healthy respect for my developing independence, and a trust in my worldliness, knowing I was capable of getting out of most scrapes. Whilst girls collected flowers and played at shops, mums and dads, or made slop-dosh pies, we lads prided ourselves on developing skills.

We each had a penknife on our person and used it for whittling and shaping. I'm afraid to say I carved my initials, M.D.E, on a tree outside the bungalow, taking my time to interlink the letters, leaving a child-height, monogrammed orison to posterity. We developed certain dexterity in wood craft; making wooden daggers, bows and arrows, walking sticks, sling shots and catapults, and weaving bits of willow and building dens and shelters. We also liked to find hollow sticks to make pea shooters. I'd pinch a box of Batchelors Dried Marrow Fat Peas off the pantry shelf, and we'd spit the peas at high speed at flotsam sheets of tin, air raid shelters, old windows and greenhouses. If I was spotted, I always got told off. 'Turn it up, you'll have somebody's eye out wi' that bleedin' thing!'

We also got involved in rudimentary engineering, just minor civil projects, like damning up the shallows of the river at Malin Bridge so we could paddle or send toy boats down it. We often played by the River Rivelin, passing Mouse Hole Forge. At one time the forge must have had a steam-driven engine. There were great belts and shafts, spiking up into the sky, which were still on the site. The forge was still in use and they specialised in making anvils. It is said they made the anvil that is at Gretna Green.

There was a great rusty sluice gate, which had once been used to let water out of the dam into the river. By this sluice was a deep hole where we could find varieties of newts, nestling in the muddy bed. We prized the crested variety in particular, looking fierce, frilled and dragon-like, and many a lad took them off home as pets.

The Mouse Hole was also home to industry too: Gold's Garage was down there, which was a big wooden shed, with their haulage truck parked outside. We also used to fish in the river for trout with rod and line, exploring the waters at Micky's Dam, and Wolf Dam further up Rivelin Valley Road. There was still a small steelworks with a water wheel at Micky's Dam, and a stone building with a water wheel up by the S-bend too. As I got older and was allowed to foray further,

I'd set up camp with some mates, across the river from the water treatment plant right up Rivelin, on the way out to Derbyshire. We'd drop over the wall and go across the bridge, to a good camping spot at the other side of the river. We set out nightlines to catch trout, and chatted in the candlelight until we'd caught enough for our supper, frying the fish in a little pan with a dollop of butter.

Sometimes we'd get hold of matches left around by an older sibling and use them to start a bonfire, nothing large or dangerous. We liked to make a little fire to do some cooking. I'd borrow a frying pan and get some bacon and eggs. There was nothing like indulging in the fiery glory of starting a little bonfire somewhere quiet. Food always tasted much nicer out in the open air, whether we had cooked it or brought it with us from home for a picnic, even if it was just white bread with dripping scrapings on it, especially the gravy from the bottom of the bowl. We experimented with melting marshmallows on sticks, with toasting bread, with an oven that was just a hole in the ground and we once tried to make our own charcoal in a pit. I preferred these outdoor woodcraft skills to woodwork at school, although I did make a pipe rack in woodwork class at some stage. I showed it to my father proudly. He took hold of it and turned it appraisingly in his hand.

'It's good that,' he said, 'Only one problem, I don't smoke a pipe. Never mind; don't worrit[62], I'll start!'

I also unwittingly became protector to Geoff's little brother. I sometimes went to call for Geoff and his mother would lumber us with him. The family always referred to him as 'Little Donny'. He was petite, pale and skinny, small for his age, rather fragile-looking, with big blue eyes that implored you to take him on travels. I liked him well enough, but being palmed off with a little kid slowed us down, and forced us to be mindful of dangers that we ignored when alone. Geoff never argued against his mum, so consequently Donny was a frequent companion on our adventures. Our ragged trinity tramped around the neighbourhood exploring, Donny tagging along at the back end, wailing because his little legs couldn't keep up with our pace. Tetchily we'd wait up for him, setting off again once he had caught up with us.

One summer's day we had ventured down to the river at Malin Bridge. Just over the wall, by the bridge at the bottom of Stannington Road, was a deep pool that was great for swimming. There was not

---

62 worrit (v)-to worry, to be nervous, to fret (local dialect)

much room, you could only swim for five or six feet, but it was deep enough and your feet didn't scrape the bottom. We sometimes damned up the sides a bit too, to get more water flowing into it, to create more depth. We grabbed old crates, prams, chunks of wood, cartons, anything we could find and banked it up to create a little whirlpool.

We stripped off our clothes and we jumped in repeatedly off the side, whooping and splashing. I also had a dingy and a makeshift paddle, that I'd crafted from a long pole with a saucepan lid tied at each end. We parked Donny on the bank, telling him to stay there and watch us. Occasionally we checked him out as he sat tugging at grass tussocks, chucking sticks in, looking bored. We'd jump out and stand at his side, chat to him for a while, dripping from the water, coyting[63] stones across, then we'd dive back in and splash one another.

Geoff and I were playing and were engrossed. Donny was wanting to join us. He'd found a big piece of wood and was pushing it across the surface of the water. He edged out into the middle of the water gradually. Suddenly there was a plop and he disappeared below the surface; he'd come from the shallow side into the deeper part of the water, where the side had given way to three feet of water beneath him. He dropped below the surface like a stone and was no longer to be seen. Geoff, who was at the other side, farthest away from him, had seen him sink and started to panic. He gesticulated and yelled wildly, pointing at Donny's shirt, which was to be seen bubbling under the water's surface.

'He's there, under t' watter[64]!' screamed Geoff, flapping his arms frantically.

I jumped into the dingy and quickly paddled to where Donny was last seen. I dropped off the back of the dingy, rolling backwards into the water, immediately grabbing to feel for him under the surface. I found him, pulled him up to the top, clutching him by the chin to keep his head above water. I then quickly swam to the side with him and hauled him out onto the bank. He looked wan and lifeless. 'Mi Mam'll kill me,' uttered Geoff with grey-faced terror, frozen in shock.

I hauled Donny out onto the bank, placing him on his side in the lifesaving position, clearing his airway. I finally got him to breathe

---

63 coyting (v)-to throw, chuck (local dialect)
64 watter (n)-water (local dialect)

again. I patted him hard on the back, until a torrent of water came sputtering from his mouth. He started to cry. He was alright.

'He's alive!' wailed Geoff. 'Tha's saved his life. Thanks, Mick.'

We huddled together on the bank in shocked silence for a while, with our arms around Donny's shoulders, willing him to get warmed up. Geoff sat cuddling him and I drifted off to find Donny's jumper, which he'd abandoned around the other side of the water. I gathered our equipment together. When Donny had got his breath back and had recovered, Geoff came over to me.

'Here, Mick,' he said, handing me a sixpence, 'have this tanner.' His bottom lip was trembling. 'Thanks for saving our Donny.'

Our eyes locked. I looked at the sixpence and looked up at Geoff.

'A tanner; if that's all he's worth, I'll cob[65] him back in!'

As always, humour saved me from a surfeit of emotion. Of course I didn't want any payment, but it was a generous gesture from Geoff, who rarely had any spending money. Geoff smiled at me, delivering me a friendly punch on the arm. We solemnly gathered our belongings and grabbed Donny by the hand. Feeling blessed and lucky, we trudged homeward a little more soberly that day.

I was never very conscious of what we had in comparison to others, but I suppose we must have been quite well off. I don't remember other people being unkind or envious. At one time there were only three people on our road with a car. Our next door neighbour, Mr. Gregory, had a car which he needed for his work as a musician in a band. He also worked in Milner's Music Shop in town. Mr. Pat Gold up the road also had a car, a Vauxhall, plus he had a haulage truck for his garage. My father had a Wolseley, then later he purchased a Vauxhall. Occasionally kids would knock at the door and ask if they could have a sit in the 'dicky seat' of Joe Bennett's car, which was often parked outside too. This seat was a small third seat in the back of the two- seater that unfolded out of the boot. The kids were harmless; Joe would let them sit in it for a while. If they were reluctant to go home, staying long past when they were welcome as dusk fell, my father would go out to them and they'd soon scarper. He wasn't known locally for his good humour.

---

65 cob (v)-to throw, lob (local dialect)

Vehicles were rare and any vehicle in a public place could draw a crowd. Even the rag and bone men and tatting men who drifted around the roads with their horses and carts, seduced a steady stream of followers on their travels. Kids would chase down streets after them, tardily trailing after them to hand over a bag of old clothes. Most rags in those days were made of natural fibres; they were pulped down to make paper, or cut in strips for rug making. The tatters rang a hand bell to attract customers. On hearing it, mothers would ferret through wardrobes to gather a brown carrier bag of rags as soon as they heard the bell ring out, sending the kids out to find him. The tatter could be two or three streets away by the time they caught up. The children ran alongside the cart, stretching to offer up their bag of rags to the driver, hoping to reach him as the horse kept moving. He'd thrust a piece of soapstone, for whitening the step edges, into their hands in fair exchange. A woman's housewifely skills might have been judged in those days by how she kept her front step. She was expected to rouge and buff the step with a brick-red paste before white-lining the edge of it. How times have changed. No one has time to white-line steps these days.

-5-
MAM AND DAD

To people outside the family my parents may have seemed an odd and ill-matched couple. My father, Arthur Edwards, appeared to be bluff and gruff, relatively unemotional, his emotion only seeming to stretch to bouts of criticism and bad temper. My Mam, Agnes Edwards (née Agnes Lockwood), was much warmer, a woman of quiet religion, self-possessed, serene and charming. She was a person safe in the knowledge of her place in the world. She was stable, protective and loving, with a good sense of humour. She was a well-built woman with a kind, open face with strong yet fine features and large expressive eyes. She had an ample, cosy lap and a voluminous bosom, like a shelf you could stack tins on.

Agnes Edwards —Mam

Mam was amused by simple things. On Sundays we'd hang out over the gate outside the bungalow, draping ourselves across it to gain a good vantage point, to watch the stream of ambling trippers strolling up and down. Our home was a bungalow on Rivelin Valley Road. In the 1930s and 1940s Rivelin Valley Road was a playground on Sundays. We christened it 'the monkey walk' or 'monkey rack,' as people strolled up and down in their Sunday-best finery, chatting, dawdling and chastely eyeing up the opposite sex. Mam loved to glue a two-bob piece to the path and watch the fevered antics of folk, as they tried to stand on it and fetch it up off the pavement to pocket it with self-conscious nonchalance. Another of her favourite Sunday pastimes was to wrap an empty box in brown wrapping paper, attaching it to translucent fishing line. Then she'd drop it in the middle of the pavement. The parcel was marked in a large, rounded script:

Private and Confidential
Property of Yorkshire Bank,
Hillsborough

We'd stifle laughter as people tried to kick the parcel into the edge of the causeway and manage it along in their path in frenzied desperation, thinking they'd chanced upon a fortune in fresh bank notes. We'd then yank the line, scooting the package out of reach, and chuckle at their embarrassment as we made the joke obvious. People were good-natured and laughed at themselves along with us.

When Mam was at home, the house was often full of visitors. They weren't so frequent when my father was at home. We used to think many of her visitors were a bit puddled[66], but she liked to make them welcome. We wondered why she encouraged them, but she was quirky like that, and her generosity was bountiful. The loveless could have a bit of love and attention, the hungry could have a bit of scran[67], and the lost might find some direction chatting to her. She felt sorry for them. There was Mary Ann who often called. Our Bill, who always had a creative and poetic bent, had further embellished her name, and we knew her privately as Mary Ann Tittybottle. She was a harmless woman who repeated herself. She'd say, 'I've been to Fred's, and did I tell ya I went to Fred's? I've been to Fred's and Fred's and Fred's, you know.' My mother would listen intently and feed her up with cake and cups of tea. Fred was Mary Ann's friend. He had a business doing up second-hand furniture and got a lot of old furniture from the Council which he did up and sold on.

I remember Mam used to also regularly make a chap welcome when he called. He had very little to say or offer, but she was amused by him. He was a Councillor and local bigwig, and he'd call in regularly because he had not yet mastered the art of tying a tie. Mam'd

66 puddled (adj)–daft, stupid, crazy, mental
67 scran (n)–food (market slang)

stand in front of him and quickly tie him a smart Windsor knot, and off he'd go on his way. She was highly amused by the incongruence of his grand public persona, and his private and unworldly lack of skill.

Harry Westnidge was another frequent caller who was amusing and entertaining. He could play the piano and he loved music, so he was often made welcome. He'd entertain us for hours playing tunes. My mother lapped up this private entertainment saying, 'He can play that Harry, oh and he's got a right face for radio.'

The house was always full of friends and callers. Only when Dad was home did people stay away. Harry's claim to fame was that he was a distant relation of Eric Portman, then a film star.

I'd always join in with a little ritual she always used to complete his visit. She'd call to me, quietly watching from the sofa, 'Mick, pass Mester a nice apple out of that bowl.' I would pass him a shiny apple and we'd both watch him eat it. His technique was extraordinary. The apple never left contact with his teeth. He'd swirl it round and round, adjusting it a half inch every time he rotated it through his gnashers, constantly snipping off pieces. Like a rabid rabbit he'd demolish it, and eventually hand me a spindly core. His visits ended like this each time. As she saw him out of the front door my mother would look at me knowingly and say, 'Look on.' However, there was really no malice in her. She was amused by such things, but I doubt that her hapless victims neither had any inkling of any disrespect, nor was any intended.

When we lived at Herries Road she once urged me to invite the Yanks into the house. One day I'd returned back home shouting with excitement, having seen all the American army trucks parked up all along Herries Road, down as far as Wadsley Bridge. I'd been playing out and had been mingling in their company. I liked to affect my favourite greeting with them, 'Got any gum, chum?' They'd smile and toss me a couple of slivers of chewing gum. I rushed home to show Mam my edible trophies, and told her they'd given me some chewing gum. 'Don't leave 'em outside. Where's your manners? Ask 'em in for a cup of tea,' she said. So I did. I courted a gaggle of soldiers outside the house and for one memorable afternoon we had a houseful of exotic Americans, chatting, laughing, addressing my mother as Ma'am, talking about their families back home, and drinking cups of tea from china cups and saucers.

Mam was fundamentally kind. I remember once as a young child just after the Second World War when I was out walking with her. I walked along holding her hand. We were just returning home across the tip at the top of Watersmeet Road. A woman, skirted by two filthy children, walked towards us pushing a baby in a pram. People were still very poor and didn't have enough to eat, or money to clothe themselves, and you often saw kids with no shoes or with flimsy plimsolls in all weathers, winter and summer.

I nudged my mother as she got nearer, whispering to her, 'Mam, that lady's crying.' I'd noticed her approaching and could see that she was weeping. As she got nearer my mother stopped level with her.

'What's the matter, love?' she asked with concern.

'We've got no bread,' she whispered breathily, still sobbing uncontrollably and struggling to get her words out.

'Haven't you got any at all?'

'No, nothing.'

'Here, have this,' said my Mam, rummaging in her basket, and then she thrust our bread into her hands. My mother had bought food that day and she handed over all the loaves which she'd bought that morning.

I was young, in no mood to give our tea away, and I was concerned at the prospect of my empty belly. Still weeping, and nodding her thanks weakly, the woman clutched at the food, and placed it on top of the baby in the pram and went on her way.

'Why'd you give 'em our bread, Mam?' I asked, screwing my face up, looking up at her, turning to glance at the woman heading off into the distance.

'Oh hush, we'll have more bread than we can eat by tea time,' she said consolingly, rubbing my head.

She was right. Later that afternoon, my older sister Bib arrived, bringing a rich supply of warm, crusty bread. I have no idea where it came from. My mother's unassuming and quiet belief in God meant she could trust in him to deliver what we required.

My mother had some funny sayings, that I still use to this day. If we asked what was for tea, she'd always utter, 'Three runs round,' or, 'A kick at t' cellar door'. She was very fussy about hygiene and if we ever picked up anything dirty off the street, as kids are wont to do, or handled anything out in public which we didn't know the origin of, she'd say, 'Turn it up; leave that. Give it a wide berth; tha'll end up wit' inco ponx o' t' rollerjacks!' I never knew what this was as a child, but it sounded grim and highly contagious, certainly scary enough to make me drop any treasure I'd found, quick-sticks.

She was equally superstitious about us being out with our heads uncovered in the rain. The slightest cough or wheeze would get her boiling up fresh lemons and honey, thrusting a hot mug of steaming liquid in front of me saying, 'Get that down thi, otherwise tha'll end up with gormerruttles.' In her opinion any rasping cough, wheeziness, or embryonic chest complaint was potentially the frightening prelude to the awful disease of gormerruttles! She was also worried about us sitting on damp walls, afraid that we might develop Farmers[68]. She'd warn us about sitting for too long with tales of people whose 'Farmer Giles' played up, causing them pain and embarrassment.

When Mam was in the house, it was so welcoming stepping over the threshold. She was a very good home-maker. There might be a saucepan of hash simmering gently on the stove, or a rack of bread cooling which she had just made. I might catch her in the early process of making bread with the tempting dough smelling sweet and yeasty, which she had kneaded hard and left to rise, covered with a clean tea towel in her big, yellow, pot pancheon[69] by the hearth in front of the fire. There might be a spiced loaf beckoning, with a glossy white top, dripping with icing. She often pottered in the kitchen listening to Radio Luxembourg on her *Roberts* radio. I was always hungry and I pounced on the baking as soon as I saw any, and she would pounce on me. I loved the taste of warm bread as soon as it came out of the oven and I'd tear big hunks off and feast on them. My mother always said, 'Turn it up, and let it cool a bit or you'll get belly ache.' To a kid with my appetite, bellyache was an occupational hazard, and my stomach had had a good training feast-

---

68 Farmers (n)-abbreviation of Farmer Giles (rhyming slang)- piles
69 pancheon (n)-large bowl, pottery bowl for serving or mixing (OE)

ing on plump, glossy hedgerow blackberries, allotment blackcurrants and thin sticks of fresh rhubarb, which I dipped in sugar and sucked. I was often gently reprimanded, 'That's enough, I think you've had your sufficiency.' However, my mother could not deprive me for long. I think it was probably the vestiges of privation during the war; if I was hungry she let me eat, and she liked to see me enjoy my food. If we'd got it, I could have it.

She was never one of these women who thought the children could make do with inferior quality food, only using the best stuff to feed up the men folk. I ate what my Dad ate: rump steak, sirloin steak, chitterling and bag, neck end, beast's cheek, hot pot, tripe, stew, hash, ox tail, boiled ham, finny haddock[70], rabbit, beef stew and dumplings, chops, and home-made meat and potato pie lashed with dark rivulets of Henderson's Relish. Mmmm lovely. I particularly liked pressed tongue, which she cooked from scratch around Christmas time, pressing the tongue under a heavy plate with big iron weights bearing down on it. Beast's cheek was probably my ultimate favourite. We had a relative, Gerty, whose brother, Jack, worked at an abattoir. He often brought us a beast's cheek down to the market, which we took home for Mam to stew up. The only food I refused to eat was boiled cow's udder. Mam cooked this occasionally, boiling the yellow flesh in a saucepan. I hated the smell and the taste, but others in the family liked it.

She was also a regular customer at Mann's Wet Fish shop on Hillsborough and we often had treats: cockles or whelks, or half a dozen best oysters. I liked to stand outside gazing at the slanting tablet of fresh wet fish facing the customers, piled neatly, dripping with ice, glistening on the marble surface. I peered in, trying to identify the species, flat and glistening with pearlescent freshness.

My father loved oysters and she would often buy them to get him in a good mood, giving them to him before his main meal. He'd sprinkle them with salt, pepper and vinegar and tip them down his throat, swallowing them whole, shaking his head as the acetic acid hit the back of his throat, as if taking nasty medicine, then smiling as they hit his stomach. She bought him a dozen best oysters one day. I spied them immediately when I got in from school and coveted one. She tipped

70 finny haddock (n)-smoked haddock, possible corruption of Finnan (Finnon/Findon) Haddock

some vinegar, salt and pepper on it and thrust it into my hands. As the afternoon went on, one by one, I kept drifting back to them, and gradually I ate them all. I confessed to Mam that I had eaten the lot, just before my father came in from work, and she said she'd cover for me.

'You'd better not say owt, you know your Dad can be a Noah's[71]. Leave it to me.'

My father must have been able to smell oysters as he walked in, but he sat and read his paper. Eventually he looked up and rubbed his hands, 'I'll have my oysters now, Agnes, love,' he said.

Mam looked at him blankly, shrugging her shoulders, 'You must 'ave 'ad 'em,' she said stone-faced.

Knowing his liking for them and the possibility that he may have eaten them without conscious thought, dipping into the kitchen to feast quietly on them, he didn't question her further, and meekly ate something else for his meal instead.

Food figured largely in my childhood, punctuating the year with seasonal treats, except for the time during the war. My father often brought goodies home from the market. He was in a position to scoop up bargains that had been sold off at the end of the day, still perfect for eating. He brought punnets of ripe strawberries, and at Christmas time he bought satsumas, tangerines and big navel oranges, all tightly cradled in purple tissue paper in close-packed cardboard boxes. The navels were so big you could hardly hold one in your hand. My Mam would bag them up and hand them round the family, as they were something of a delicacy and not an everyday fruit.

Sometimes he came in with bags of spice: Mint Imperials, fudge, or cough sweets. He once brought some woody sticks of natural liquorice, which I chewed on, enjoying the bitter black sweet pungency, feasting until the wooden sticks went stringy and sodden. I had to rush to the toilet. As I shot out of the room he chuckled to himself, laughing that I had enjoyed his 'opening medicine' so much.

When the end of the war was confirmed in 1945 I was nine years old, and I was looking forward to getting back to being able to eat some decent food. We hadn't fared badly during the war, but we had missed fresh foods such as oranges and bananas. I remember my brother Bill coming back home, and from his kitbag he unveiled a

---

71 Noah's (n)-Noah's Ark-nark (rhyming slang)

blackened and battered banana, presenting it to us like a treasure, which we fell upon greedily, cutting it up into slices so everyone could have a taste. We'd not tasted bananas for years.

In general, we had enough to eat, which could not be said of all families. Mostly we ate at home, but I was even treated to restaurant food after the war. Occasionally my mother went into town to do some shopping, which offered an opportunity for us to eat out. Her sister, Bib, often accompanied her. In those days it was the norm to get dressed up to go into town. You didn't know whom you might meet, and it was important to be well turned out. The occasion demanded clean, polished shoes, a decent handbag, a proper overcoat and probably a hat and matching umbrella in case of rain.

Mam and Bib were close. Our family relationships were complex: my father's brother, John William, had married Aunt Bib, my mother's sister. Joe Bennett's brother married my mother's other sister, Violet. People didn't appear to travel far looking for love in those days.

So we would walk down to get the tram from Malin Bridge from the tram sheds. Aunt Bib often brought her daughter with her, Betty. Betty was my posh cousin, a fair bit older than me and though I liked her, she had a knowing, superior air. I thought she was a bit toffee-nosed and we had little in common as children. Betty was bookish and learned; I was much wilder and lived on my wits. She made it known that she was well aware of our differences, and she made me feel as if I was a savage thing that she was in the process of taming. I thought of her as my posh cousin, and I didn't intend that she could civilise me.

We had a set route around the shops, and when my tummy was rumbling, I'd tug on my mother's sleeves and she'd suggest we go for lunch. The routine was always the same; we were creatures of habit, and ended up at either Tuckwood's or Davy's Tea Rooms. I had been well schooled in how to conduct myself in public.

Prior to going to town, Mam would always warn me, 'Now behave. Do as you're told; and no picking your wilk[72] in public. Don't lick your knife either; that's how the Queen cut her tongue.' I didn't need to be told, but she would keep on telling me. I knew how to be on my best behaviour and would not let her down.

My mother liked the staff at Davy's; you could ask for anything

---

72 wilk (n)—nose (local dialect)

off menu and they would bring it from the kitchen with good grace. It was quite a grand place to me. All the waitresses wore black dresses with crisp, white, starched aprons and a little frill of ribbon in their hair, fastened in with grips at an upright angle. They floated around the tables silently, taking orders with little notepads, placing menus neatly before their public with a flourish, smoothly serving, clearing plates, siding and setting tables. This café was posh, believe me. In most cafés in Sheffield you were lucky if the waitress avoided spilling most of your tea in your saucer.

I had a healthy appetite and was looking forward to my dinner. My mother passed me the menu and invited me to choose what I wanted.

'I'll have a boiled egg, please.'

'Alright, duck, how many?' she said. Betty eyed me warily from across the table.

'Two, please, with bread and butter,' I said confidently. Betty's eyes rolled and she pursed her lips, glaring at me with disdain.

'You can't have two eggs!'

'I want two.'

'You can't have two eggs. It's greedy!' she declared throwing me a withering glance.

'I'm having two, I tell you,' I commanded.

My mother ordered her meal and Aunt Bib's meal. Both Betty and I had chosen to have boiled eggs. Mam ordered for us, 'Egg and bread and butter; two for eggs, please,' she said to the waitress.

'Remember, please, I'm having two-all for me,' I piped up. The waitress scribbled the order down on her pad.

'Ugh, two eggs,' muttered Betty, enunciating every word slowly, as if to further exaggerate my gluttony.

I don't know why she sneered and turned her nose up. I couldn't understand why she was so sniffy about my eating habits. She was as hefty as the rest of us; it was the family failing, my mother said. I found it rather galling that she was trying to make something of my appetite; I resented the fact that she was implying my robust appetite was uncouth. My mother was unperturbed and didn't mind if I had half a dozen eggs, that was what mattered to me. I ignored my cousin, not speaking to her for the rest of the afternoon and ate silently enjoying every mouthful. We went to town together on many more occasions, and my hurt feelings were soon forgotten.

Betty grew up to be a confident and clever lady. She remained my posh cousin; she was very able and was determined to get a good education. She went on to be a bigwig in the Council, working for Social Services. I think she went to university too.

My mother indulged me, and looking back I can see that my father indulged my Mam too in his way. My father was not a yielding man, but it appeared to me that he was quite tolerant of my mother's quirks. Admittedly he wasn't easy to live with; he was often cantankerous and fussy about his needs. Their roles were sharply defined. It was her job to cook and look after the children. He liked his tea on the table when he got in from work.

My mother was not in any way downtrodden or resentful; it did seem to me that she exerted her own power in subtle ways. For example, when he got home from the market it was also her job to help him straighten out the money. In fact this job fell to any of us who happened to be around. He'd earned it, but he was less interested in the tiresome job of straightening and ordering the bank notes and piling up and counting the coins, putting set amounts in canvas bags which he got from the bank. He mainly liked the final count up at the end, licking his fingers to expertly rifle through the notes, totting up silently, stacking them in piles, then finally rolling them up in a rubber band and placing the roll in his back pocket and jotting his takings down in a little exercise book. He was as skilled as any professional bank teller. At intervals he engaged his friend, Georgie Smith, to do his books and handle his accounting. He was the headmaster at St Joseph's School, Walkley.

On such occasions counting the takings, I noticed that my mother liked to assert herself. She would regularly drop a bank note on the floor, and then she'd stamp on it with great speed, covering it fully with her foot. I often watched this dance between them. When he'd left the table she'd bend down to pick it up and pocket it. I know that he knew she was doing it, and she probably was aware that he knew about her trick. I think it amused him; she could have asked for anything and it is likely that he'd have given it to her. By most accounts we were well off. She had no reason to pinch money from him. I think they both rather liked this game, and they felt as if they were keeping one another on their toes.

Most of the time she was indulgent towards him too, but occasionally he irritated her; he enjoyed having us all run around after him and he was particularly fussy about his food. He had to have exactly what he liked, placed on the table in a timely fashion, with the appropriate condiments. He wasn't keen on bottles on the table either, whether milk bottles, Henderson's Relish or H.P Sauce. My mother placed a small amount of each accompaniment in a little glass bowl or cut glass jug for him.

He was very fussy about his vegetables too, particularly his peas. We were quite distrustful of tinned goods, so when peas were in season my mother would buy them freshly picked in their pods to shell. She'd sit by the back door shelling them, bouncing the peas into a colander, and then she'd boil them up until they were tender and serve them, topping them off with a knob of butter. This in itself was time consuming, but my father also insisted on having fresh garden mint on them too, with an extra knob of butter melting through them. Every time she served him peas he reminded her about the fresh mint that he liked so much.

Sometimes we just didn't have any mint growing in the garden, so my mother would whisper to me, 'Hop out and fetch me some privet for your Dad's dinner.' I dutifully would amble out to pick a few leaves from the privet hedge[73] and she'd wash them and chop them up and scatter them over his peas. He didn't come to any harm and he didn't seem to notice that there was no discernible mint flavour either.

He'd clear his plate and sit back patting his belly with satisfaction saying, 'Those peas were smashin', dead cushti, Agnes, I'll have my cup of tea now, love.' My mother always smiled and tried not to laugh.

With regard to bringing us up, he had a simple homespun philosophy, which could be summed up with a few aphorisms: Don't trust anybody; do your best, and if you are going to weed[74,] don't get caught. This isn't to suggest that he advocated thieving, not at all, rather he expected people to thieve from him and he was wise to all

73 WARNING. PLEASE DO NOT COPY THIS ACTION. APPARENTLY PRIVET IS POISONOUS TAKEN IN GREAT QUANTITY.
74 weed (v)-to steal, (slang)

their tricks. With his wisdom he always reckoned he'd got a start on them, and he always said he could smell it if someone was bent[75].

My father gave us all a good start in life. To my brothers Joe, Arthur and Bill, he gave a new lorry to each of them, stocked with a full load of pots, the theory being that if they could sell that load and buy more, they'd make it for life. This was both practical and generous and it set them up well. He also proffered us a designated patch of the local market territory, gifting us a pitch. Joe was allocated Barnsley Market. Bill and I had Sheaf Market in Sheffield; Arthur also had a pitch in Sheaf Market. My sister's husband, Joe Bennett, had Rotherham Market.

My father had encouraged Joe Bennett to learn the pot trade from him when Joe married my sister, Bib. Joe worked Rotherham for some time before going into selling insurance. Joe had no doubt seen my father stashing the takings in a carrier bag and he probably thought it was an easy option to get involved, but insurance sales soon beckoned where his income level was steadier and more predictable. When he moved on from Rotherham Market, the pitch was retained and we worked it too between us.

We valued all the markets as they were so busy and my father's greatest accolade for any market pitch was, 'Good gaff[76], good punters.' When he talked about new places where he'd worked, he never made any reference to the sites worth seeing — cultural attractions, or buildings of note — but he could certainly give you a run down about the punters, their preferences, spending power, market days, market rents, what toby[77] he'd paid, the best pitch to get, and most likely the name of the Toby Mush[78]. If he'd worked it in recent years he was also probably able to give you the amount he took on the last particular day of working too. He was a very practical man, and he didn't fill his head with miscellaneous knowledge which would be of little worth to him.

75 bent (adj)-dishonest, untrustworthy, dodgy
76 gaff (n)-market (market slang)
77 toby (n)-market rent, money paid for a pitch (market slang)
78 Toby Mush (n)-market superintendent, the official rent is paid to (market slang) (mush=man)

What we lacked in education, we made up for in natural confidence, which is no bad thing. My father didn't speak ill of many people, but his worst insults to anyone were: 'He couldn't keep his sen warm!' or 'He couldn't pull a pitch to save his life!' He used this most often about local dignitaries, councillors and officials, disliking them all, as he said they had no real talent or bottle[79] and criticised them for having jumped on the convenient gravy train of public life, which was not *real work* in his book. He admired any man who could graft.

He didn't like anyone who lacked generosity and he had his stock phrases about this particular personality characteristic too. He'd often say damningly of stinginess he'd witnessed, 'He's so bleedin' tight, he could peel an orange, one-handed, in his pocket.' If he spotted any niggardly tendencies in any of us, he'd growl, 'Don't be so bleedin' piky. Get thi hand in thi pocket.' He did teach us to buy good gear, saying, 'Don't buy any drek[80] for frumpence[81]; we'll be stuck with it. Buy decent gear.' Less choosy china sellers might have bought crates of lump: third quality ware, often damaged or spit, resulting in a grainy finish. This usually happened if clay was put in for firing whilst too damp.

Lump was all you could get during the war, but there was more choice after the war, and father thought our punters deserved good quality gear and they seemed willing to pay for it. He always urged us to buy good gear whenever possible, and thought it was false economy to sell anything schneidy[82].

Father was a man who liked his routines. He liked a beer and he liked his sleep. He didn't take kindly to Bill's burgeoning taste in music, as he became a young man. When I was a kid, I shared a bedroom with Bill at our house at Herries Road. At that time Bill was always out socialising at night, and my father was a right nark if you came in late and woke him up.

My father, Arthur Edwards

79 bottle (n)-courage, guts (slang)
80 drek, dreck (n)-poor quality goods (from German *Dreck*, filth, rubbish) (Yiddish, market slang)
81 frumpence (n)-little money, slang
82 schneidy (adj)-damaged, spoilt, broken, imperfect, dodgy

One night Bill came home late, having forgotten his house key. I was awakened from my bleary sleep by stones being thrown at the window. I eventually woke up fully, dragged myself out of my warm bed, and threw the window open to see what was making this clattering at the windows. I saw Bill down below, standing in the garden looking up at me.

'Let me in, Mick. Quiet; don't make a racket, otherwise you'll wake our old fella.'

Dad was a real curmudgeon and got annoyed if he got woken up. None of us liked to get on the wrong side of him. I watched as Bill dragged an old ladder up. He raised it up and rested the top against the window sill, then he carefully climbed up it.

As he dropped into the room, I said, 'Who's going to shift the ladder, Bill?'

'Ah, good point. Sod it, I'll shift it in t' mornin',' he said, pulling his tie off and loosening his cufflinks.

Bill was fresh from a successful night out and in a cheery mood as he made his way to the bathroom. He'd got into the house and there was no harm done; our old fella had no idea he'd come back late without a key. He crept along the landing on his tiptoes, congratulating himself on his commando-style entry back into the family home. Suddenly he got an almighty start, as someone kicked him hard up the arse. It was my father, who had heard the shenanigans, and wasn't best pleased about being woken from his slumber. Bill shot into the bathroom, locking the door behind him. My father, returning to his room, growled after him down the corridor, 'Get to bleedin' kip!'

Bill crept back into the bedroom, rubbing his backside. 'The old man's copped the needle,' he said, crawling into bed.

My father was often in a good mood at Christmas time; there was something about the season of goodwill that made him good-humoured, which we all enjoyed. He'd arrive home from the market with armfuls of holly, mistletoe, with wreaths for the door, one for us and one for Bib's house, studded with bright holly berries and festooned with red ribbon.

He wasn't given to romantic gestures, but occasionally he brought my mother flowers by the season too; Lincolnshire pinks in early summer, which she crammed into every spare vase or jug, filling the house with spicy clove scent, and long stems of locally-grown bloom chrysanthemums in autumn.

My father was not very involved in childcare, as was typical in those days for most working men. We even took some holidays apart as a family, my mother taking me off in the summer, just the two of us. We travelled on a charabanc to a guest house on the coast, while he continued to work the markets. He didn't like missing out on the possibility of earning money if it was there to be earned, neither did he like to lose a pitch or leave any opportunities open to competitors.

His one dispensation towards involvement in our upbringing was the reward of material items for good work. I had long given up the desire to get good marks at school, so I turned my aspirations towards sporting events. I was a good swimmer. I had a solid, muscled physique, powerful shoulders and a strong upper body. Morley Street School had a good swimming team and I was a keen member.

Competition between schools was encouraged and each school held a swimming gala, pitching the talent within a school against one another, before putting the best performers forward for the Sheffield Schools' Swimming Gala. I was determined to win and come ahead of the crowd. My best strokes were breaststroke and crawl. I was mithering my Dad to see if he'd agree to come and watch me at the swimming gala. It wasn't really his thing and he declined, but happily he did promise me a bike if I won. I would have liked him to see me swim, but he had a routine which he would rarely break, popping out after tea to the Malin Bridge Inn pub for a couple of pints. The school gala came around, and I journeyed home triumphant, having won two categories, breast stroke and crawl, to be named Morley Street Swimming Champion.

I rushed into the house and could not contain myself. Usually I was told not to bother him when he was eating tea and not to cause him his 'indigestion half-hour' by mother, but I hurtled in, stumbling over my words to relate my good news, 'Dad, Dad, I won my races. I'm champion now!' I spluttered. 'Can I have that bike you promised me?' He continued eating. 'Nitto, nitto, I'm having my tea here,' he said trying to quell my enthusiasm. 'Steady on. Go on then, tell me, what's tha won?' he asked, seeing that I was itching to tell him more.

'I won breast stroke and crawl, so I'm Morley Street champion, and you promised me a bike,' I garbled breathlessly. He continued chewing.

'Hold up, lad, I thought tha meant a bike for being Sheffield champion, across t' whole city, not just local champion!' he said shaking his head.

I sensed the dream of my bike was slowly disappearing from me. I was disappointed and felt he'd gone back on his word, shifting the goal posts now it was time to reward me. It seemed I'd have to try and win the races with the best of Sheffield swimmers, before the bike was to definitely be mine. Once again his lack of support made me even more determined, and I couldn't wait for the Sheffield Championship to come around. It was just a few weeks away. I swam well in the races, determined to win and was eventually named Sheffield Champion later that year. After winning my swimming races, I did eventually get that bike. I remember it was metallic green, a Dawes model, bought from a shop on London Road.

I loved the camaraderie of the swimming team. Much as I liked to win, I could also appreciate the skills of my teammates too. Tommy Hudson's best strokes were backstroke and crawl, and Jack Dodd was a big lad, built for breaststroke and powerfully good at it. Our competitive spirit drew us together, and we took pride in our athletic skill.

Admittedly I was quite well fed compared to some of them. We were a funny looking assortment of shapes and sizes; some spindly and thin, some tall, some well-covered, some stubby. We were passionate about our sport and we cheered on our teammates from the tiled side at Hillsborough Baths during practices.

On one such occasion one of the kids dived in for practice. He hit the water with a thud, cutting in at a good angle, disappearing under the surface. Then we watched mesmerised, unmoving as he surfaced, as we spotted his bony bottom, the cheeks popping up out of the water like the hump of an undernourished whale. We spied his threadbare trunks drifting back up to the surface. Of course the kids started laughing, and the poor shivering wretch realised he was trunk-less, and stopped swimming in a straight line, suddenly realising how he was exposed. He jumped out onto the side with great embarrassment, trying desperately to retrieve his trunks whilst hiding his bony, naked form. He finally grabbed them and stood shivering on the tiles. He grasped the flapping curtain from the tiled changing booths down the pool edge to cover himself, hopping around madly as one lad mischievously tried to whip his bare arse with a wet towel.

'Oy, oy, Tricky, we can see thi backside!'

He struggled to cover himself, trying to get dressed and keep his balance, along with his modesty.

'Look! Chuffin' elastic's gone in 'em! Reight laugh!' cheered the kids, tugging at his trunks, pointing at him and guffawing at his misfortune. He finally put them back on with difficulty, as the wet fabric dragged and squelched against his dripping frame.

This incident moved me. Could it be fair that each lad's trunks should indicate whether he was from a rich or poor family? It brought out my entrepreneurial spirit. It occurred to me that we needed to look more like a team, so I decided to do something about it.

My older sister, Agnes

My older sister, Agnes, was a dab hand at sewing. She had her own sewing machine, a sewing basket full of bejewelled little items: pin cushions; leather needle cases; mother of pearl buttons; steel and brass hooks and eyes; a myriad spectrum of coloured cotton bobbins; an assortment of Anchor embroidery silks; pairs of scissors and picks; tins of pins; darning needles; skeins of wool; crochet hooks and yarn, and Anchor embroidery booklets. I liked picking through Agnes's box of haberdashery riches. It was a treasure trove of strange objects, unknown to me. I pulled them out and she'd scold me for unravelling cotton from her wound bobbins. She had all sorts in there: bodkins; fancy edged hat pins; an embroidery hoop; press studs and coils of petersham stiffening fabric; glass beads and buttons; loops of different coloured bias binding; lace trimmings; ribbon, Broderie Anglaise edging; steel shuttles, spools and little attachments; and steel feet for her sewing machine.

You might think it's a bit strange that a boy could appreciate such things, but I knew they were her tools and she made lovely things from them. I've always been able to appreciate beautiful things. She was really talented, and could stitch her own designs and do fancy appliqué work. She'd just made a stunning cushion cover with an embroidered and appliquéd Iris motif on it, with petals of sapphire blue and indigo, and trumpeting speckles of yellow, fashioned from French knots of various sizes that jumped off the material, as if coming to life. She'd stiffened the petals with buckram and had embroidered it so it came at you, thrusting up desirous of being touched, the flower parts contrasting with the long, green, strappy leaves. I loved it and nowadays I often wonder what happened to that cushion cover. I coveted it.

She usually had a few pieces of fancy work on the go at once: tablecloths, tray cloths, a matinée jacket, cushions, tapestries, a sampler. I liked the way she prided herself on having the back of any embroidery being as neat as the front, so you had to struggle to see which was the right side. I liked to watch her as she did her work and I would ask repeated questions.

'What's that stitch?'

'Cross stitch,' she'd begin patiently.

'What's that?' I continued.

'Herringbone stitch.'

'What's that?'

'Stem stitch.'

'What's that?'

'A French knot.'

'What's that?'

'Bullion stitch.'

'What's that?'

'Whipping stitch.'

'What's that?'

'Chain stitch.'

'What's that?'

'Oh shurrup, you're mithering the life out of me. Look in t' book, it tells thi there! Read it for thi sen. Frame, lad.'

'Only asking,' I sniffed.

I'd sit still, watching her unperturbed, entranced by the dance of her dipping needle and thread. It never bothered me that the art of sewing, knitting and crocheting was part of the female world in our house; I was mature enough to recognise these skills as I watched her with fascination and fancied I might master them too.

'Can I have a go?'

With a patient sigh she'd hand the stuff over to me and watch as my clumsy fingers found it more difficult than it looked, stabbing and struggling to get my needle though the fabric, smudging the cloth with dirt with my grubby hands. Eventually she could watch my artless struggling no more, and she'd bat my chubby fingers away.

'Let me do it. You're making a pig's ear of it. Give it 'ere.'

I watched as her deft fingers swept up and down. I liked the way she did two neat backstitches then bit the cotton off with her teeth saying sagely, 'You are not supposed to do that, and you should always use scissors.'

Yes, Agnes would help. I was determined to ask her about it.

I chose my moment when she was relaxing and seemed to be in a good mood. I flopped down beside her on the sofa.

'Agnes, you know those old black-out curtains we've still got. Can I 'ave 'em?'

'Well I suppose so...,' she replied, laughing at me. 'What do you want them for? What're you up to?' She was used to my schemes.

'I was wondering if you'd make us some swimming costumes for the swimming team; we need some trunks and skull caps, all matching. We need to look like a proper team, you know. At the moment we look a reight mess, all in different trunks an' that.'

'Oh, go on, alright then, but you will have to give me their measurements, you know.'

I wasn't up to this level of intimacy. That sounded a bit complicated.

I thought for a moment, then I voiced my solution, 'Can you just make me an assortment of different sizes, some long shorts and some short longs?'

'Oh alright. How many?'

We agreed the number, and over the next couple of weeks I got used to the rumble of the sewing machine at all hours of the day.

She made us some wonderful trunks, made from black material with a white cord band, which you could pull, to tighten up the waist. The skull caps were black too with a sharp white stripe down the middle of the crown, and a strap which tied under the chin. We would look like a proper swimming team. We would look the business.

I arrived at Hillsborough Baths for our next practice with an over-stuffed duffle bag and a big brown paper carrier, crammed full with the new outfits.

The swimming instructor glanced over at me as I struggled in.

'You look a bit ladened up, lad. What have you got there, Edwards?'

'Costumes for the team, Sir. Our Agnes made 'em.'

The kids gathered round as I unpacked the bags. I took the assortment of garments from the bags and gave them out, holding them up against the kids to test sizing.

'Grab that,' I urged one of the lads. 'Looks like it'll fit thi.'

A great deal of swapping and trying on took place, but eventually all my teammates had a pair of trunks and a skullcap approximately their size.

Each time we lined up on the side of the baths at a meet we bristled with pride in our outfits, standing upright to attention, our puny backs like steel rods. We went on to swim in those outfits for a couple of seasons, until we wore them out. We did well in the league and won a shield for Morley Street, and thanks to our Agnes's robust waistbands, nobody lost their strides[83] diving in the water ever again.

I'm not unusual, and like every child I mused about my parents in their younger days. With my father's temperament I couldn't quite imagine him wooing any woman. I had often wondered how my parents met and married. Apparently they met through my Dad's brother, John Willy. He had married my mother's sister, Bib; her

---

83 strides (n)-trousers (slang)

full name was Elizabeth Lockwood. They lived at Abbey Lane for many years. I am guessing thereafter my parents probably met on some family occasion, and perhaps they started courting afterwards. I often wondered what he was like as a young man; I couldn't quite imagine him courting anyone.

My father and his brother were already selling pots in those days. I am not sure if they were independent traders, or if they had been drawn into selling china through the links with the families of the women they had married. It seems they had married well, for the Lockwoods were well off and had a thriving business. We had an old photo of old Mr. Lockwood, (my Mam's dad, we think), outside a shop with a *Glass and China Merchant* sign on the side of the shop window. From the style of the pots for sale it looked Victorian or pre-Victorian. The Lockwoods had been in the business a long time. It also seems that my Mam's grandfather, Henry Lockwood, known as Rag Harry, was originally a hawker of hardware. We have an old picture of him with his cart. Perhaps he then started buying pottery to sell. Legend has it that someone in the family apparently sold up and left this country to find his fortune in America, abandoning his wife and family. It is said he took all their assets to the States, settling in Manhattan, New York with his fancy-woman. Here is where the detail is hazy; either this man or his descendant was allegedly killed when a horse reared up on Brooklyn Bridge, and he died leaving a fortune — so legend has it. We are not sure who this man was exactly, or whether he was on the Lockwood or Edwards side of the family. This is possibly where the myth of the Edwards' millions started. It is a myth, and I can confirm that we are skint! One of my father's relatives, who was about the same age as my father, a Mr. Hudson, searched for this money during his lifetime, to no avail.

My grandfather on my father's side, was allegedly the owner of a brass foundry in Rotherham. He was originally from Rawmarsh. He died when my father was quite young, leaving the family in poor circumstances. Father used to have to do a sales round before he went to school, selling kippers around the gates of the steel works and knocking on the doors of terraced houses.

Father told me about how just after the war, when he was first trading, he used to employ a few ploys to get the punters to part with their cash. He used to travel over to Clowne to sell wares at the market there, and they had to tempt people out of their homes to buy with the promise of free bags of sugar. They could only afford to give a few bags of sugar away to the early birds, and when they were gone they were gone, but it brought people out of their homes to spend what little money they had.

My father cut a distinctive figure and was always well dressed, even though he was portly. I'm sure he'd been good looking when he was younger and that's what attracted my Mam. He always had nice suits, a pair of braces, crisp white cotton shirts, and a quality silk or tweed tie. His suits were always well cut, and he usually had them tailor-made with a matching waistcoat with silk lining. He kept a gold-plated pocket watch on a chain, slung across his waistcoat front and kept pulling it out to see what time it was. It was an American pocket watch, a Waltham, not an expensive make, but of good quality. He had it for years.

He always liked to wear a good suit jacket or blazer. In winter he wore a thick overcoat, tailored from good quality woollen cloth and he always wore a black Homburg hat. He took his hat off when he was pitching, but at other times he wore it.

He always had his suits made with extra fob pockets in the trousers, one extra pocket at the front and one really long one on the inside, double-lined with thick material that would last with a button for secure closing. This pocket was for his readies and he placed the notes close, next to his body, out of the way of dippers.[84] He knew of Rushy's misfortune, another market trader. He'd had his top chest pocket dipped. It was where he kept his roll of notes and he'd even had them secured with a rubber band and safety-pinned to the inside of his pocket, but a pickpocket got at them. He lost about seven hundred quid, a lot of money. Rushy had no recollection of how it could have happened, but he was extra careful after that incident.

My father's sense of style rubbed off on us too, and we all liked to dress smartly and have our suits hand-made. We always wore shirts and ties to work. We might have a new suit made each year, which started off as Sunday best and eventually would become workaday wear. In those days it was the custom to have a new outfit at Whitsuntide, for the church marches in the parks at Whit week. The tailors were also used

---

84 dippers-pickpockets (slang)

to making women's suits, and I often heard my mother making reference to needing to have another costume made, which was a suit, with a tailored jacket and skirt.

I picked up dressing tips from my older brothers. Bill was good at polishing boots. He taught me how to get a mirror-like shine on leather shoes by working the parade gloss polish round in little circles, spitting on it occasionally, buffing hard with a soft cloth and then polishing to a shine with a small shoe brush. Eventually the shoes or boots were highly glossy, and ordinary leather could look like patent. He even polished the bottoms of his shoes.

Bill also showed me how to polish brass blazer buttons, using a little gadget from his army days, which he worked round the buttons, which stopped the *Brasso* getting on the material. In my later teens I had a few suits made which deviated from the conservative norm — with bright silk lining. They weren't to my father's taste, and he sneered at them, saying I looked ridiculous.

He was so confident of his own personal style that he never detracted from making fun of anyone who didn't dress as he did. I remember being in the market once when a young kid came past dressed in the latest fashion, a suit with drain pipe trousers in vivid bright colours, with a bright jacket lining that flashed like a kingfisher as he swung by. He wore suede, wedge-soled shoes on his feet. His hair was modelled in a quiff at the front and it bobbed about as he walked. He was a world away from my father's classic suits of black, grey and navy. My father looked over at him inquisitively, chuckling at his crazy styling, shaking his head at his bottle to go out dressed like that each day.

'Ey up, what are tha, son?' he asked.

'I'm a bee bopper,' said the lad, grinning proudly.

'Bee bopper! Tha looks like a bleedin' tree hopper!' laughed Dad.

For a man who had little formal education, my father was interested in technology and the latest gadgets, whether it be cars or equipment that served him earning a living. My father used to boast how he and his brother, John Willy, had booked to work a fair at

Bowling Tide, Bradford and how they had stolen the show. This was when they first started pitching, probably just after he'd married my Mam. On arrival at the fair my father got into some altercation with another trader, who was gloating that he would be the first to set up and have a pitch that day. My father whispered to his brother, 'He'll not be having the first pitch today.'

They had brought along an innovative piece of kit, which they set up: a petrol driven generator, which in itself probably cost a fortune. They powered it up, attached the lights, or 'glims' as they called them, and the punters came drifting towards them, intrigued by the throbbing motor, their shouting and the sparkling china display shimmering under the lights. That was in the 1920s.

He told me it was a great fair and they took plenty of readies. After the fair they 'whacked it up' between them, and he bought a Chevrolet. Apparently it cost £350 at the time, which was a lot of money. He had it for about twenty years and used it daily, travelling round to the local markets and more widely to the fairs: Midsummer Common in Cambridge, Nottingham Goose Fair, Bridgwater, and Brixham Harbour in Devon, which my brother Arthur eventually worked annually. When my father finally got rid of the Chevrolet he sold it on to Coopers, the family with the scrap yard in Sheffield. He said they used it for another twenty years, to tow vehicles in after they'd broken down.

My father's father died when my Dad was quite young, so he was brought up with a strong work ethic born of necessity. He always worked very hard. He also used to like to tell us the story of how he got married, and there was no time off for a honeymoon for him. The next day he was out knocking on doors, 'on the knocker' as he termed it, selling goods, carrying his few pieces in a burlap sack. He'd got them on the chucky[85]. He used to get pots from his father-in-law, effectively borrowing them and going out selling, then paying for them the same week. After the wedding he got a load of brownware; earthenware casseroles, pudding basins and those deep, tight-lidded Lancashire hot pot dishes. Thereby he started to eke out an early living.

We used to sell a range of pudding basins too into the 1960s, in a range of sizes. They were made at a little pottery over at Chesterfield in

85 chucky-on a sale or return basis, borrowing wares to sell, paying for them later when sold (slang)

Derbyshire. I think the place was called Pearsons. It's not there any more. We used to go over every few months and load the van up, filling it with stock. We took a three-ton flat lorry over and we'd arrange them loose in the back in rows. We called this 'running them loose'. We put straw on the floor of the lorry, as a cushion to prevent breakages. Then we'd line rows of goods right down the lorry, packing the space between rows with straw; then we'd layer them up, building up the rows of basins and straw, until they were really high up. A load might have cost forty pounds and it lasted us ages. We'd pull them up from our warehouse to sell, as we needed them.

I also have a book of my father's indicating which potteries and factors he dealt with. He dealt with various different potteries: Gater and Hall; T. Wild & Co. which is listed simply as Wild's; Taylor and Kent; Shore and Coggins Ltd.; Royal Albert; Sadler's for tea pots, and Sowerby crystal. Occasionally he'd buy Thomas Forester's Majolica ware: novelties such as planters, jugs, flower pots and decorated fruit bowls. He also frequently dealt with factors named Harry Hill and Stan Simmons.

We also have some old record books belonging to our grandfather, Joseph Lockwood. His book of sales dated from 1914-24 shows he had purchased pottery from Guggenheim, Proctor and Johnson Bros. He'd spent £9.18s 8d at Burgess and Leigh (they still sell printed ware), and he had also bought gear at T.C. Wild, Belton's earthenware, Gater and Hall, Sampson Bridgwood, Clews and Co, Taylor and Kent, Allerton's, Collingwood's, Soho Pottery, and Adams. Adams made pale blue pottery, similar to Wedgwood's blue jasperware. My sister Agnes had some of it. Clews made ship's tea ware for liners; stacking designs capable of being stacked atop one another in tight spaces. He also bought Royal Winton Rubian Art Pottery during this period. We also have a record indicating that he spent £32.9d on Joblings glass in 1914. That was a lot of money, so he probably had a crate or two of best glass for that price. Some of the names mentioned were also familiar to us, trading right up into the 1960s: Midwinter, Barratt, Sadler, Adams, Beswicks, and Aynsley. Many of the surnames listed are also likely to be factors whom he dealt with, names too many to mention.

In the 1950s my father also traded with the British Anchor firm at Longton. I particularly liked their *Cottage Green* ware. They made lovely old fashioned mixing bowls, rolling pins, pudding basins, and milk jugs — all in a lovely cottage green stripe. It looked so fresh and cheery, with the emerald green, and black lining the white ground[86]. Our Bib had the whole set in her kitchen, and it was well used over the years.

Although my father was sometimes cantankerous and pernickety, he was rarely angry with me; however, I learned to anticipate and allay his dark moods. My mother taught me how to stay out of his way as a kid if he was in a bad mood, and she and I had a code where we could talk and understand one another. One thing my father detested was to have strange kids in the house playing when he got home. He liked his peace and quiet; and liked to settle down to his tea, without any inane chatter from strangers. If he arrived home and I had a friend round, my mother would look at me meaningfully and say, 'Arper scarry arver char,' which meant, 'Scarper the kid,' 'Get rid of them,' which I duly did, avoiding any awkward atmosphere or open confrontation.

I only once saw him really angry. His anger wasn't directed at me; rather it served to protect me. When I was a child I used to roam all along Rivelin Valley Road and thought nothing of any danger or hazards. At the end of the road towards Malin Bridge there were some public toilets, built of stone. You went down some steps to get to the gents. Late one afternoon I had gone in to relieve myself on the way back home. Suddenly I felt a hand on me. Some bloke had grabbed me from behind, trying to catch hold of me by my shirt collar, pulling me towards him, making me lose my balance. I was terrified, but I wrestled myself free and tried to lash out to kick him. I then shot up the steps and out of the toilets, and pelted back home up the road, just a couple of hundred yards away.

I went flying in through the door, breathless and anguished. I was shaken, and anyone could tell something was wrong. My father was home that day, and I told him what had happened.

---

86 ground-base (n) pottery term for base upon which other coloured slips are added to create finished design

'Did he touch thi?' he queried, clenching his hands tensely. I shook my head. His face blackened with rage. He shot up from his armchair and ran down to Malin Bridge to look for the bloke, based on my scant description. He couldn't find him, and it's a good job he couldn't; he was raging and would have punched him. We didn't ring 999 in those days and wait for the coppers to arrive, or even bang on door of the police box at the bottom of Rivelin Valley Road, in the hope it might be staffed. If you had a big family and many people did, it was best to give somebody a quick tanning. They never bothered you again, and all concerned got their just deserts. Thereby local reputations were made and promoted. We always knew who the local villains and good guys were. Certainly most people my age knew not to mess with me, with my brigade of older brothers, all National Service trained, and packing a punch. Bill's theory was he was a stranger, not from round here.

'If he'd known who thi wa', he'd have left thi well alone wi' our mob,' he said. 'Next time tha needs a slash, come home; gi' t' toilets a wide berth.'

This unfortunate incident was a minor aberration from my safe and idyllic childhood. Thankfully I had come to no harm that day.

Father had a brusque demeanour, but he was a kind man. I remember once when I was a child I was suffering from terrible toothache. It was the week-end and I was in agony, hardly knowing what to do with myself as the pain drubbed through my whole head.

My father saw the pain I was in and reassured me, 'Don't worry, we'll get in touch with old man Ditchfield. I've got his home number. Don't worry, I'll word him up[87], and he'll see us.'

So he called him, and we went round to his surgery that he opened up for us especially, persuaded by my father's offer of ready payment. My father marched us in, explaining the trouble I was having. The dentist helped me up into the chair, quickly examined me and told us it looked as if the tooth would need pulling out. He quickly completed the procedure and I started to feel better at once, clutching

87 word him up-to persuade (colloquial, market slang)

my father's cotton handkerchief over my mouth to stem the blood. Before we made ready to leave, Mr. Ditchfield turned his attention to my father. I'd already noticed him eyeing him when he spoke.

'So, how are your teeth, Arthur?' he queried nonchalantly.

'Aye, cushti,' father said, slipping his set of false teeth easily out of his mouth, and waving them in the direction of the dentist for him to inspect them more closely.

Mr. Ditchfield gingerly took hold of them in his fingertips and looked them over, tapping at them and prodding at the pink plastic with a hooked instrument. Gravely he set them down in a kidney-shaped bowl, pulled a long serious face at my father and sighed, 'They've had it Arthur; you've bitten straight through the palate.'

'Well they feel alreight; they're comfy enough.'

'No, I assure you, they've had it, Arthur. You need a new set, top and bottom.'

'If you say so,' said my father, bustling over to the now-empty examination chair in sprightly fashion, jumping up into it. 'No problem, 'ave a proper butchers. Measure me up, Doc.'

My father had courage and could be relied upon to protect us when needed. He told me another story of how he'd been intimidated, during the depression in the 1920s, when a particular pair of fellows came to call at his home one evening. At that time a well-known family in Sheffield had the run of protection rackets, calling on businesses to persuade them to give a proportion of their takings to them for so-called protection services. Gradually they had worked their way around the thriving businesses in the market, demanding protection money, often with threats and menaces. During hard times it was an unfortunate situation that most people tolerated, though the victims didn't like it, or appreciate being bullied into giving up their earnings. My father knew members of this family in passing and would nod to them warily, wanting to avoid contact. For some time they had left our family alone.

One evening my father arrived home from work, bringing in cod and chips wrapped in newspaper for his tea. As always he was taciturn and a bit tired and grumpy. My mother bustled around him, unwrapping the fish and chips and dished them up on a china dinner plate. She mashed a pot of tea, pouring the boiling water onto the loose tea leaves, then buttered slabs of white bread, found him a spoon for his sugar, got the tea strainer ready, poured his brewed tea into big breakfast cups, and placed the cut-glass vinegar carafe to hand with the salt. There was a knock at the door. It was unusual for anyone to knock on the door at this time. Mother shot up to answer it, mumbling grumpily, 'Don't they know it's teatime?'

She came back in the room ashen, followed uneasily by two burly fellows in dark overcoats and caps.

'Evening, Mr. Edwards,' they said in unison, throwing a glance towards my father.

He coolly looked them up and down.

'I'm just having my tea. Sit your sens down,' he said, hiding the fact that they were needling him. 'I'll be with you in a minute.'

He glanced over at my mother, and a knowing look passed between them. Reading the emerging situation well, she scuttled into the kitchen and busied herself, staying there. The men remained standing, viewing him all the time whilst he ate. It was of course menacing in itself that they had come to his home and it was designed to be so, communicating a clear message to him, *we know where you live*. There was one of the chaps who was the spokesperson, the other one was obviously the minder, a big, lubberly hulk of a bloke.

My father bode his time, pacing himself, eating his meal slowly and deliberately. He had supposed it would not be long before they came calling. Many of the marker traders were 'big hitters' with good takings, especially the fruiterers, and it was inevitable that they'd be round to the Potty Edwards for money at some stage. Quietly and purposefully he ate his fish and chips, lingering a little longer over each mouthful, belying his ravenous hunger.

The two men were standing and had not seated themselves on the sofa as invited. Perhaps to have sat down would have made them feel uncomfortable; this was not a social call. Instead they shuffled and hovered uneasily in front of the fireplace, standing in front of a wire, box-shaped fire guard, which we used as a clothes-horse, which was full of washing. They stood there, looking uncomfortable and not quite sure how to continue the conversation. They weren't so certain what to do when someone else took initial control. They'd never been made to wait before. Eventually one of them leaned forward and said meaningfully, through gritted teeth, 'You know why we are here, Arthur. Give us what we've come for, or we'll give you a tanning.'

My father quickly jolted up from the table, sending the pots shaking across its surface, his face thunderously dark with anger and his neck reddening with every irate breath.

'You'll do bleeding what?! Give me a tanning, will you? Come here!' he said, grabbing the bigger and quieter one of the two men, manhandling the hulk, tussling with him and planting a punch on him that shifted him off balance making him fall, tumbling back towards the fire, becoming entangled in the smalls draping over the bulky, mesh clothes-horse. He lost his balance completely and toppled over, stumbling towards the open fire, collapsing in the hearth bottom, shaking ornaments from their positions on the mantelpiece. The hearth brush and tongs went clanking down off their little rack. He landed awkwardly, sprawled all over the floor on his back, his legs paddling wildly like an upturned beetle. The spokesperson fumbled and busied himself to try to get his mate on his feet again, discarding the pieces of intimate attire which littered his torso like confetti.

My father darted towards the standing man, lumbered up into his face, eyeing him steadily, now outraged, shaking his fist threateningly at him too. 'Now thee lag off an' all. Otherwise thy's goin' on t' fire back too, like thi mate!'

The callers gathered their scattered belongings, planted their hats back on and sheepishly bundled themselves down the hall and out of the door. My father stood on the doorstep, glowering after them and then slammed the door shut behind them.

Realising that the door slamming sounded the all clear, my mother came out of the kitchen. She threw him a black look as if to say *you shouldn't have done that.*

'What? What?' he said glaring at her, his voice rising in tone with each word in annoyance, 'What? So I'm here grafting my tockers[88] off so those schmocks[89] can come and take everything we've got? No, no, Agnes, think again.'

---

88 tuchis, tockers (n)-behind, backside, arse (Yiddish)
89 schmock (n)-idiot (Yiddish)

My mother was someone who rarely felt the need to swear, only swearing occasionally for effect, but on this occasion she was forced to, through sheer emotion and unanimous support for her husband's brave actions. She went back into the kitchen muttering, 'Cheeky bleeders!'

Perhaps he had been right to front up to them. They never bothered us again, and we were glad.

Hearing this story years later as a child, I was fascinated by how my father had kept his nerve, and how he had thought on his feet.

'Weren't you scared, Dad? Why did you stand up to 'em? How come your bottle didn't twitch[90]?' I asked.

He drew himself up and looked me stonily in the eye, preparing me for his wisdom, borne of life experience.

'Well, I've got a philosophy see. Never let anybody shit on thi. If tha does, then mark my words, they'll do it again....and again. And you see, the next time .....' he said, pausing meaningfully, '...well, they'll rub it in!'

His graphic elucidation makes me both smile and wince with disgust every time I think of it today; although now with more experience of life, I have to concede that sadly, he was right.

We had many happy times as a family. There were pleasant evenings at my Uncle John Willy's, where he and his wife would entertain us with card games, which we played for matchsticks instead of money. We loved the impromptu dancing too; we'd roll back the rug and have a dance to old 78s on the gramophone.

We also spent many pleasant evenings at my Uncle Bill Richardson's. He and his wife, Elsie, were great singers. He'd sit on the sofa and she'd perch by him on the sofa arm and they'd sing songs of the day. They were brilliant at singing proper harmonies. She'd sing, looking up into his eyes, romantically holding onto his forearm, their voices sounding out into the room to our great delight. Their party

---

90 bottle twitch-lose courage (slang)

piece was *Carolina Moon*[91]. The front room resounded to the lyrics, full of hope and sadness.

On long summer evenings we'd rig up the horse and cart, and go 'mob-handed' as we called it, for a run out to Bradfield. Mam, Dad, my sister Agnes, and my pal, Geoff and I were frequent travellers on such occasions. If Dad was in a good mood he might call in at a pub for us, bringing out bottles of orange juice with waxed paper straws and a packet of crisps each, with a little blue bagged twist of salt at the bottom. The combination of crisps and orange juice tasted good in the open air.

We used to have a laugh and chuckle on the way back. Dad might have had a couple of halves, which improved his humour. He used to take the micky out of the poor horse; the poor beast had some feat to make any progress with all of us in the back: father, mother and a bunch of kids with their friends in tow. He'd say, 'Bleedin' horse is strainin'. We're goin' uphill, lean forward now. Agnes, breathe in. This bleedin' horse is nearly collpasin' wi' t' weight on your lot.'

He'd even do an anthropomorphised mime of the horse, slowly turning round to look at us, as we leapt up onto the back of the cart ready for the ride. He'd buckle a bit, dropping lower and pretend to sink down under the load, bending his knees and sneering as if he were the bad-tempered horse. He'd neigh and his eyes would roll and he'd mimimoke[92] as if to say, *Why is it my job to transport these heavy-weights to Bradfield*? We rolled around laughing.

On one summer evening we went up to Bradfield with the horse and dray. Father was driving; he loved it, fancying himself as a real expert with the reins, quietly talking to the horse, issuing instructions. We had got as far as the Admiral Rodney pub at Loxley when there was a crunch and a grinding sound. The cart suddenly lurched and tipped over, leaning heavily over to one side, upturning and spilling us out. The pin through one of the wheels had snapped. We were hurled from the cart. Geoff and I were laughing, thinking this was great fun. Predictably my sister Agnes was grizzling[93]; the slightest thing could set off her crying.

---

91 Carolina Moon Lloyd, Michael. Lyrics © Warner Chappell Music Inc, Mike Curb Music
92 mimimoke, (v) sometimes pronounced as minimoke-(Sheffield slang, to mimic, ape, pretend to be someone)
93 grizzling (v)-crying, weeping (slang)

My father, as usual, was quick to blame others, pointing in the direction of Mam and Agnes. 'That's your two; too much weight over that axle. Tha's knackered it!' he said. Luckily there was a blacksmith right by the pub in those days, called Fletcher. He came out from his little forge and fixed a new wheel, putting a new cotter pin through the axle. Within half an hour the job was done and off we went on our way, enjoying the rest of the long summer evening.

For a man who didn't appear to be that good humoured, surprisingly he had quite a few friends; he had a band of pals in the pub and his gaggle of regular schleppers who worked for him. There was Uncle Tom Fish, or Fishy as he was known, with his long, tea-stained pickle tooth[94] and deep-set, hooded eyes. He was my father's right-hand man at the markets and was not only an employee, but also a trusted friend. He had worked for the family for many years. Allegedly when he was younger, Tom Fish's stepdad was a bit mean to him. One day he arrived at our house, sweating cobs. He'd nicked his stepdad's bike and had ridden all the way to our house, right across Sheffield. He was adamant he wasn't going back, and we put him up at our place for some months.

One day at the market Fishy spotted a roll of bank notes on the floor that a well-heeled punter must have dropped. He picked them up, taking them to my father.

'Now then, Arthur, just got hold of this gelt[95], these readies, found them on the rory[96]. What shall I do?'

My father eyed him.

'Take it down the nick and tell 'em where you found it..... in front of Edwards' pot stall,' he said levelly, watching the punters who had espied this conversation.

So Fishy went to the police station and explained how he had come to be handing in about a hundred pounds in used notes. He rather enjoyed handling such a large sum of money, announcing, 'I'm from Edwards' pot stall. We found this money on the floor. I think it might

94 pickle tooth (n)-long, single tooth (colloquial)
95 gelt (n)-money (market slang) from Geld, German -money
96 rory (n)-floor (market slang)

belong to a farmer. He was a bit bevvied[97] and probably dropped it. He'd just bought a tea set off us and was struggling to carry it all.'

The police officer nodded, took the bank notes, counted them, logged the find in his record book, and coldly thanked Fishy.

Fishy was reluctant to hand it over, worrying for its safety. As he was leaving he turned to the copper, wagging his finger sagely.

'Now then, put that where the bleedin' mice won't get at it,' he said.

'If you don't watch it, pal, I'll put you where the bleedin' mice can't get at you. Now get thi sen off!' said the policeman, glaring at him.

Fishy arrived back at the stall somewhat crestfallen; he'd savoured his self-importance, delivering such a large sum into safe hands at the police station and he had found the copper's blasé reaction a little churlish. Fishy had expected more grateful thanks. It put him in a bad mood for the rest of the day. He came back to the stall mumbling to my father, 'Someone needs to teach that Plod some bleedin' manners.'

There were other schleppers who worked for my father who were part of the regular scene. There was Tripey, so called because he loved tripe and ate it almost every day. He was a casual worker and did not work with us all the time. Then there was Tommy Diddy. My father once told me he was called Tommy Diddy because he had some gypsy blood in him; diddy was an abbreviation of diddycoy (didika), meaning Romany traveller. My father was not one to discriminate; he wasn't bothered about his background. What mattered was that Tommy Diddy could graft, and my father always said he was a good worker for a casual schlepper. Fishy was a regular worker and was employed on a fairly permanent basis. My father really rated him as a grafter and he could sell pots, which was his main recommendation.

My father's best friend was called Ernest Crookes. They had known one another for years. Ernest was a painter and decorator and had done some work in our house. He was a craftsman of the old order

97 bevvied (adj)-drunk (market slang)

and he knew how to execute paint effects, which no one knows today. I watched him do graining, where you paint a lighter base coat onto wood and then a darker scumble glaze (a translucent oil paint mixture), custom mixed to match in a darker tone. Then he used a rubber hand-tool with patterned lines on it, rocking it up and down the door to make the grained patterns like wood. He even put knots in at intervals. He then scumbled the door with a soft cloth, polishing it gently to soften the effect. When he'd done, the door looked splendid, as posh as Chatsworth. Ernest was a frequent visitor to our home, and a frequent drinking partner of my father's.

It seemed to me my father treated the grown men around him quite dismissively. They were paid well, but he liked to send them on errands and off to do his bidding, fetching him cigarettes, boxes of matches or cough sweets. It was all part of my father's natural arrogance. I was once at the bungalow when Ernest called. He must have been about seventy years old and I was about ten. My father sent him off to the shops at Malin Bridge to fetch him some cigarettes. I was just a kid, but I was embarrassed. I stood there thinking, *Send me Dad, don't trouble Ernest, he's an old geezer*. However, Ernest went to get the cigarettes without complaint. They all seemed to think the world of my father, much as they might have complained behind his back.

It is always surprising when you come across someone who knows your parents. They can tell you things about them that you never knew, giving you a new and different perspective. I often wondered how other people experienced my father. Were they as fearful of him as we were? Yet it was just this outward demeanour that was bluff, underneath he was quite soft. He perhaps had not found a way to express his feelings, nor did he see any reason to do so. My fear turned to admiration, as I grew older. I learned to judge him by his actions, not his words.

In my adulthood I occasionally came across people who had known him. I was once working at Louth Market in Lincolnshire when a bloke came up to me. He looked at me quizzically, pointing at me saying, 'Are you one o' t' Edwards?'

'Yes, I'm Mick, the youngest.'

'I knew thi father. He were a nice bloke… generous. I used to help him unload pots at the station. I always remembered him because he used to give me a tanner for helping. That was a lot of money, let me tell you. What a nice old fella.'

In those days my father would go over to Stoke on the horse and cart, choose pots and then have them delivered by train to Sheffield's Midland Station. He'd have to then go and pick them up from the station by horse and cart. It was a time-consuming business. He'd set off on Monday to choose the china, returning on Wednesday to pick up pots, which had been freighted by train.

He also used to travel to local markets by horse and cart. When my father was a young man starting out working the markets he used to work Barnsley Market. I'm thinking this would be the very early days, perhaps just before he got married, around 1910. Barnsley's not far, but imagine how much time that took, there and back each day. He told me the story about an incident as he came home one summer's evening, when he was stopped by two men.

My father was at the front driving the cart; his schlepper, Tripey, was sitting at the back on the tailgate, his legs hanging over, dangling as the cart swayed. The men came out from the verge, down the causeway edge, waving at him to stop. They strolled across the road to talk to him, putting their hands up to make him halt, standing right in the middle of the road. My father tugged at the reins and the horse stopped. One man came towards him.

'Alreight, pal. Has tha got a light?'

'Yes,' said my father, in a friendly tone whilst watching their reactions intently. He felt in his pocket for a box of *Swan Vestas*.

The stranger eyed him up, appraising him.

'Got a cigarette an' all?'

My father nodded and held out the packet towards him, tapping cigarettes up to the end so he could easily take one out.

'Sure,' he said eyeing him steadily.

'Ta. I'll take one for my mate, if you don't mind.'

'Help yourself.'

The man stared directly at him, weighing him up silently, in temperament, girth and size.

My father was older, but was a match for him. He had an inkling of what was coming, and his hackles were starting to rise as he sensed an undercurrent of threat and danger.

The second man was starting to walk round the cart now, poking under the tarpaulin to see what he had on it. The man who had done the talking came a bit closer.

'Have you got any money?' he asked menacingly. 'Give us it,' he growled.

It was a lonely road, the back road from Barnsley; there was no M1 in those days and very little traffic. There was no-one else around if help was needed. Father and Tripey were on their own. My father was aware that this situation could turn nasty, but he remained cool, casually gesturing towards the back of the cart, saying to them, 'He's got the money, the chap at the back of the cart.'

As the man made his way round to the back, my father had to think quickly. He chirped to Tripey in a jolly voice, designed to disguise his real intent, 'Tripey, old pal, have a quick shufty[98]. This gentleman wants summat o'er his crust!'

The men ambled round to the back of the cart, prodding the sides as they went along, fishing under the covering. Tripey had shifted his position, alerted by my father. He seized his chance. First he quietly snatched an object from under the tarpaulin, and he crept up on them. Then bosh! He walloped the main perpetrator over the head with a vase. The man fell to the ground groaning. The other one danced around panicking; then he busied himself trying to help his mate up off the floor.

'I've decked him, Arthur!' cried Tripey, dancing with shock and excitement.

'Nitto, keep stumm!' said my father.

The two men gathered themselves up, somewhat stunned and gave up on their hold-up.

Tripey jumped onto the back of the cart and my father grabbed the reins, yelling, 'Gee up!' and trotted off, urging the horse to get a move on, and set off as fast as it could safely go with the weight of goods on the cart.

Next day, as usual he was working at a market. He was busy demonstrating a set of half a dozen glass tumblers. He was using them to knock a nail into a bit of wood. He had a tumbler on each finger and one in the middle of his palm. He happened to glance up to see the dark uniform of a policeman in the crowd. Uncle Tom Fish had seen it too; he nudged my father saying, 'Oy, oy Arthur, we've got the Old

---

98 shufty (n)-look (slang)

Bill here. There's a flatty[99] out in the edge lookin' at thi. O'er there, that copper seems to be giving you the eye.'

My father looked up expectantly. The bobby beckoned to him, mouthing slowly at him, 'You. Come here.'

My father whispered, 'Who me?' and the copper nodded. My father was mid-flow with his pitch so he continued the sale and as he came to a natural break in the proceedings, he stepped out of the joint. The copper appraised him as he stepped towards him and glared at him coldly.

'Now then, did you have a bit of trouble with two men last night when you came back from Barnsley?'

Well it was obvious someone had reported him, he thought. He was going to have to cough it.

He remained calm and polite, answering thoughtfully, 'Yes, I did, there were two of 'em. They were going to try to rob me.'

'What happened then?' asked the copper.

'Well, Tripey, he's this geezer who works for me, he's a bit crackers and he coshed one of 'em o'er the nut with a vase.'

The policeman eyed him steadily, pausing to think. He twirled a pencil between his fingers, hovering over his notebook, lost in thought for what seemed like ages. Then, to my father's relief, he looked up.

'Well, you did reight, Mr. Edwards!' he declared finally, smiling. 'That bastard's just got out of the nick. He was inside for robbery. Tha did reight!' he said, dipping his notebook back into his top pocket, without having written anything, in happy conclusion of the situation. He then shook his hand warmly and walked off, turning to give him a cheery wave as he turned the corner out of the market. That was the end of the matter.

I suspect not long after, a motor vehicle was ordered as his preferred and safer mode of transport. Indeed he probably dispensed with the horse and dray as soon as he could afford it.

Although I remember my father as sometimes grumpy and grouchy,

---

99 flatty, (flatties plural) (n)-policeman (slang)

he was not completely humourless. He had a dour belief that all family members working with him would be tempted to steal small amounts of money from the takings, and I think he saw it as a form of sport, trying to court us into such misbehaviour, leaving piles of change around the house, temptingly. If he caught any of us adding to our already generous wages, he'd just smile at us saying, 'You're getting better; keep practising.'

This calm wisdom was deterrent enough and would stop us. Although he was not an emotional man, he seemed to evoke a great need in us not to disappoint him. We did not expect his praise, but to evade his annoyance was reward in itself.

I once had a conversation with him about the prospect of his workers stealing from him. He always referred to them as 'weeders' and stealing as 'weeding'[100]. The Edwards were known as good payers and we rewarded our workers well. Work was constant for our band of employees, but seeing so much cash around must have been a temptation for them. I am sure father knew exactly what went on; he knew small change was pilfered.

I tackled him one day and asked him if he'd considered raising their wages, if they were struggling to make ends meet and had resorted to nicking smash[101]. My father looked at me askance, as if I was a complete loon. I had mentioned one worker in particular who seemed particularly light-fingered.

'Up his wages?' he queried, incredulously. 'Art tha completely radged[102] and trying to skint me?'

I reasoned that a schlepper got four quid a week and if Dad would raise wages to twenty quid a month, none of the workers would ever need to resort to pinching money ever again.

'Why dun't tha gi' him twenty quid a month as a trial?' I suggested.

'Twenty quid? Twenty quid!' he puffed, '...if I gi' him twenty quid, he'll still weed; he bleedin' likes it, I tell thi. I'm telling you, son, everyone's bang at the Austin[103]! The world's full of ganefs[104]!'

---

100 weeding(v)-to steal (slang) derived from rhyming slang, Austin Reed.
101 smash (n)-small change, loose coinage
102 radged (adj)-mad, crazy, loony (market slang)
103 at the Austin-to steal, stealing (rhyming slang, Austin Reed, rhymes with weed).
104 ganef (n)-thief, scoundrel (Yiddish)

It seems he viewed such behaviour as a hazard, which any upstanding employer had to suffer.

Father could be funny without realising it; his sense of humour was quite dry. Once my father decided to have a day off, so Bill and I worked Sheaf Market for him. We'd drafted in my father's cousin as schlepper that day, Sammy Brown. Sammy came to help, but frankly was not really that used to working in the market, thus his approach was a bit dreamy and dizzy. He was not particularly on the ball, and the regular workers had to keep telling him what to do and prompt him after he'd already been given instructions.

As Sammy was so slow on the uptake, we told him to stand out in the edge as part of the audience and look out for punters who wanted to buy, and take their money, and come and get pots to wrap as required. He obediently took up a spot in the crowd. Sammy was standing about six feet out in the edge and was watching Bill pitch, enthralled and completely lost in thought, staring in front of him with a dazed expression.

A lady customer who was standing in the crowd next to him had just bought a tea set. It had been packed in a brown paper carrier. She stooped over, bending down to tidy up the contents of the bag, having a breather, before aiming to set off to renew her shopping spree. She was wearing a fur coat. The fur brushed against Sammy's arm. Thinking he had a big Alsatian dog next to him, Sammy absent-mindedly started to stroke her back, rounding his firm stroke gently down onto her rounded buttocks.

'Oy, oy, cop a load of Sammy. What a soft Freddie!' whispered Bill chuckling, nudging me and nodding towards him.

Whether the lady didn't know she was being touched or chose to ignore it, I don't know. Sammy continued to gently brush his hand down her back, drawing it softly down onto what he thought was the dog's backside. Rhythmically he continued his stroking and she didn't seem to mind or notice as she ferreted around in her bag.

Eventually she straightened up and moved off. Her sudden movement pushed Sammy's wrist up at an awkward angle and he jolted, looking up with surprise, suddenly realising what he'd been doing. He watched dumbly as the woman moved off. He sneaked a look around to see if other people nearby had seen his antics. We had of course noticed his behaviour, and we couldn't help gawking at him and laughing, losing track of our spiel. It was an awkward dilemma we faced: if we'd have called out to him, it would also have alerted others to his activity too and might have got him into trouble. Leaving him to it ran the risk of the lady discovering his absentminded wrongdoing and drawing others' attention to it. Unsure of what action to take, we left him to it, and we just hoped he wouldn't get caught. When we got home that night, I recounted this amusing story to my father.

'Did the woman tip[105]?' asked my father matter-of-factly, smiling faintly to himself.

'Nah.'

'Did she buy owt?'

'Aah,' I said, 'she bought a tea set.'

'Well,' he concluded philosophically, 'he must have stroked her the right road, then.'

On grand family occasions he tried to get involved, but births, weddings and funerals took him away from his beloved market, which is where he'd rather be. When Agnes was getting married we were all involved in the preparations. Father watched from the sidelines, bemused at all the plans. A wedding cake had been ordered and Bill volunteered to drive to fetch it from the woman who was making it at Wadsley Bridge. Geoff and I eagerly offered to go with him to help, excited at the thought of a run out in anybody's car who was offering. We went into the house with Bill to fetch the cake: a grand tiered affair that was packed in three big boxes. We carefully carried the boxes to the car and Geoff and I each sat with a cake box on our laps. We had been told in no uncertain terms not to mess about on the journey

---

105 tip (v)-to realise, understand (market slang)

back. We did Bill's bidding and were taking our responsibility seriously, when suddenly Bill slammed the brakes on as he drove down Herries Road, sending us hurtling forward. We had to grab the cake boxes to stop them from up-tipping. A little lad had shot across the road without looking. The lad froze in terror on the other side of the road looking towards Bill. Bill wound down his window and winked at the lad.

'Now then, watch your sen. Life's sweet, tha knows,' he called to the kid. It might have been Bill's philosophy: life was sweet.

We got back to the house with the cakes. After getting changed into our Sunday best clothes, we all left to get to the church leaving father and Agnes alone. My father was a person who didn't hold back expressing himself. He had a certain way of communicating; it was unusual; there was no spectacle or outright criticism, but with a few ill-chosen words, he could sow seeds of doubt in any situation. If he was in one of his moods he could rile even the sweetest tempered person.

My sister Agnes was known for her sensitivity, and when upset she would faint. We called this penchant for dramatics her 'dying swan' and she often resorted to this behaviour in my father's company. Whether or not it was consciously performed on her part, I'm not at all sure, but she was famed for it within the family.

Agnes's fiancé was John Metcalfe. He worked at Daniel Doncaster's and was a steel worker. As my father and Agnes were left alone in the house waiting for the wedding cars to arrive, it should have been a special moment for gentle encouragement, giving a few chosen words to support his daughter, but his words came out wrong as he clumsily sought some words to calm the anxious waiting. Agnes was flouncing around in the lounge, adjusting her veil and tweaking her bouquet. With an hour to go her nerves were getting the better of her already. My father glanced over at her saying wryly, 'It's not too late to change your mind, tha knows.' She burst into tears, did her dying swan, and hankies had to be found for her copious tears.

John and Agnes married without further ado. John occasionally worked with us too, if we were short staffed on Saturdays. He curried favour when my father lost his best diamond ring. Father wore it to work every day, but one day when he got home from the market, he realised he'd lost it. The next day at the gaff we turned out tea chests, boxes, baskets and cartons in an attempt to find this ring. The schleppers were searching the warehouse, and turning the joint upside down and checking thoroughfares by the joint, kicking wisps of straw aside, gazing at the floor intently looking for anything shimmering or sparkling. John eventually found it in a basket of straw and handed it back to my father. He enjoyed a brief period of favouritism. My father was so grateful that he gave John five pounds as a reward. He didn't like the thought of losing a groney[106]. We reasoned it must have slipped off his finger when he was unpacking some pots.

My father's generosity occasionally extended to other people. He knew a lot of the market traders, and inevitably their fortunes went up and down. As someone who was relatively successful, he was often tapped for small loans. He once lent a fellow fifty bob. He'd not seen him for a good few months when he walked down the market. My father hailed him and the chap hurried over to chat.

'Ey up, Arthur, I know I still owe thee that fifty bob. Can I gi' thee this instead?' he asked, taking out a polished wooden snuff box from his coat pocket, handing it to him.

'Aye,' Dad said, accepting a small round wooden container box that was being thrust into his hand. He turned the treen over to examine it closely and unscrewed the top. It was an old wooden snuffbox with an aged, scratched George III shilling inlaid into the lid. Inside he saw a clutch of small, pure gold watch keys.

'Now then, what you giving me these for? All this gold, must be worth thirty quid. Here tek 'em.'

He handed him back the collection of keys, which the fellow duly pocketed, strolling off down the market. Thus the debt was settled, and he rather came to love and treasure the snuffbox, which he had unexpectedly acquired.

---

106 groney (n)-diamond ring (market slang)

-6-
SCHOOL DAYS

I was not always schooled at Morley Street School. My earliest memories are of Parkside Road School, Hillsborough which I attended for some time in the infants and juniors. We lived on Harris Road at that time. Mother sometimes walked me to school, but as I grew in confidence I used to make my own way there. My mother knew a woman who was moving into the area, and she had asked if I would call for her son on his first day at his new school to accompany him. I duly did this and we walked to school together. I was only six or seven and I tried to chat to him, but he was shy and hard work. We arrived in the playground and I told him he'd have to wait until they called him, as I didn't know what class he was in. He was hopping from foot to foot. I realised he needed the toilet and was about to explain to him where he could go when suddenly he undid his flies, and I looked on in horror as he went on to drop his trousers. He pulled out his willy and did a Jimmy Riddle in a corner. Even I knew it was bad manners to relieve yourself in public. I wasn't very happy that my mother had lumbered me with him that day. Poor kid; perhaps it was nerves that got the better of him. I told her about the incident when I got home and she was amused and a bit shocked too. This lad and I became friends, and I soon forgot about my embarrassment and his first day at school.

I wasn't a natural choice for teacher's pet. I had an air of confidence and self worth that teachers didn't easily warm to. I was a strong, practical child and it was in the practical tasks of school life where I could shine. I might be milk monitor, or in charge of putting out chairs or stacking them after assembly. I wasn't often tasked with things of an intellectual nature, so I felt it was one step up when I was tasked with the highly responsible job of filling up the ink pots. This job usually went to one of the more academic kids who was interested in school work, thus I had little experience of it and welcomed the opportunity to prove myself to be reliable. At that time the ink came in powder form, and it had to be mixed with water in a jug and poured carefully into the ink wells on each desk. I felt quite pleased I'd been entrusted with this and I was determined to make a good job of it. The teacher chose a classmate to be ink monitor with me and we set about the task. I assigned my classmate, who shall be nameless, with fetching the water in an empty bottle whilst I stayed in the classroom. I was rather enjoying my new-found power and I marked his card, explaining how to make up the mixture. He went off to get the water. Meanwhile I spooned the powder into the jug ready for mixing. I heard the trip of his steps down the corridor, noting that he had come back into the classroom quickly from his errand, which made me suspicious; he'd been quick, too quick to run to the other end of the building to the toilets.

'Where's tha been?' I asked.

'We ran out o' water,' he said grinning. 'There wasn't enough to mix it.'

'So, what's tha' done?' I asked, carefully tipping a measure of water from the bottle into the jug, giving it a stir with an old ruler. He smirked at me. Something suggested to me that I should distrust him. I sniffed the bottleneck suspiciously and realised from the awful smell that he had peed in it. 'Ugh, that pen and inks[107]!' I cried. He snorted smugly at his trick, laughing and flailing about with mirth. 'Th'art a dirty chuff!' I bellowed.

He was still dishevelled, his trousers undone where he had unbuttoned his flies. He was dancing around with glee, enjoying my displeasure. I was livid and hit out at him, my hand still holding the ink jug. My hand slapped him and I scotched him, accidentally pouring ink down his shirt as it slopped out of the jug. Aggrieved at my sudden authority over him, he gave me a heavy shove and ran off. He obviously went straight off to the teacher to tell on me. I suspected I would be for it. I determined to complete the task I'd been set and busied myself with mixing up a batch of new ink anyway, enjoying the last minutes of my authority in the quiet classroom, whilst I listened to the kids playing outside. The sound of the hand bell being rung ushered them in and I straightened myself up in readiness for my punishment. The other children filed back into the class after playtime. After a while the

---

107 pen and inks (v)-stinks (rhyming slang)

teacher entered, and the hubbub died down. She scanned the room looking for me, her eyes eventually resting on me. Her face settled into an unfriendly stare.

'Get out to the front, Edwards,' she barked abruptly, grabbing me and swinging me round roughly by the arm to face her. The kids giggled nervously, enjoying the fact that I was in big trouble and was in front of the whole class for a public telling off. He was skulking nearby, unkempt, red eyed and nervy. I could tell by her thunderous face that I was for it. She raised her eyes heavenward and launched into a speech about how, as usual, I could not be trusted; I'd been a bully and would no longer be given any responsibilities in the classroom. I was not happy about my power being so short lived. Finally after a brief tirade she gave me an opportunity to speak. She leaned forward and eyed me disdainfully. I felt her hot breath on my face.

'What have you been bullying him for?' she thundered.

'I've not been bullying him!' I retorted.

'Tell us all now, why did you hit him?' There was silence as I wondered how to handle this. I leaned in towards her saying quietly, 'I'm afraid I can't tell you why I hit him in front of the class, Miss. I'll have to whisper to you.'

She glared down her nose at me and reluctantly bowed down to let me whisper in her ear. I told her exactly what he'd done in great detail, being careful to use proper language indicating how he'd relieved himself in the bottle. Slowly she raised her head up. Her eyes nearly popped out of her head as she turned to glare contemptuously at my unfortunate classmate. His face collapsed, as he realised he had been found out.

'Ugh, you dirty boy,' she sneered, her lips curling in disgust. Then she turned towards me indulgently, smiling, 'Edwards, pick a new ink monitor!'

My shamefaced helper quivered in front of the class, his face reddening with embarrassment. She signalled to him to take his seat and he shrank down into it, all eyes on him. I did pick a new monitor, taking my time to choose someone with more personable habits.

My reputation as a responsible citizen was not to last long. In the winter I was also tasked with taking a band of helpers up onto the low roof of an outbuilding at school to sweep off the snow. It had a habit of piling up and then falling down off the edge, dangerously at risk of burying some kid down below in the playground. The teacher issued us with shovels, with instructions to stay away from the edge and to shovel the snow off gradually, taking care to see that the outlook below was clear before we tipped it over the edge. I was put in charge, as one of the strongest kids. We took some time to get up there; and as soon as we were just starting to tackle the task one of the smaller kids came to me red-faced and tugged at my jumper.

'Mick, I need a poo,' he said. I sighed and wondered what to do. 'There's nowhere up here to have a kack[108], tha should have gone before tha started. Hold it in,' I suggested hopefully.

He shook his head and I noticed his reddening face. I could tell from his bulging eyes that he wasn't going to be able to hold it.

I shrugged my shoulders and said, 'Well, you'll have to drop your keks[109] then and do one up here.'

The kid had no choice. He squatted down, undid his trousers and crouched down, heaving in a corner. The other kids cheered and laughed at the sight of him, though I tried to quieten them. Eventually he had done a poo and carefully pulled up his trousers. I bade him cover the poo with snow, in a corner away from where we were working.

'Thy'll have to wipe thi arse when we get down,' I said, as he continued his work shovelling, somewhat more bow-legged than before. 'Smother that Thora[110],' I directed. He looked back at me blankly. I realised he did not understand the lingo. 'Cover that up,' I said pointing to the faeces, and he biddably complied with my request.

It wasn't the end of the matter. The other kids began to show interest in what he had produced, ferreting it out from its hiding place, tossing the turd around on their shovels, hurling it as a missile and trying to hit one another with it; dodging it, screeching in disgust when it nearly hit them, screaming and yelling. I tried to calm the situation down, but had lost all authority over them. Our shouts drew the attention of a teacher in the staff room and unbeknown to us,

108 kack, kak, cack (n)-poo, shit (possibly Yiddish)
109 keks (n)-trousers (slang)
110 Thora (n)-turd (rhyming slang Thora Hird= turd)

she was making her way out to supervise. Suddenly a joker swung his shovel up into the air, hauling it high, tossing the faeces off the end of it, sending it flying off, spinning high then falling down below with a dull thunk. We heard a brisk clap of hands and a barking shout from the teacher below who had come out to check on our progress.

'Stop that this instance. Which dirty boy did this?' she shouted up to us, with her arm curled around some poor mite who had been a hapless victim of our games and had been shelled by some flying turd. There was silence. No-one was going to say anything. We were marched down from the roof and shamefully lined up for questioning in the yard. She glared at us.

'I shall ask you all once more. Who was responsible for producing this night-soil?' A collection of blank faces gazed back at her, struggling to understand her grammar-school euphemism. There was a long, awkward silence.

'Well, he did a shit,' piped up one lad, pointing vaguely in the perpetrator's direction. He was then nudged and poked for being a snitch.

She stared at us, waiting for a proper confession, but none came. There were no kids who were willing to admit their fault in the matter and thus as the leader she chose me to admonish. I was reprimanded and was disgraced. My period of leadership was short-lived; once again I became known as the kid who ran physical errands, considered incapable of being in charge of others.

School was always a mixed blessing. I liked the camaraderie and friendship, but I wasn't one who found great pride or satisfaction in excelling. However, I was good at mental arithmetic. This was borne of my Saturday boy experience working at the market. I could see the point of maths when it was concerned with working out what amount you had bought stuff for, and needed to work out the profit margin. I could easily work out the profit on a gross of teacups bought for 2d each and sold for 4d, no problem. I could work out total costs of gear and percentages of profit. I could work out the profit on takings by minusing the costs of china from the full takings, and if you asked me to split the profit between four brothers, (not that we ever did that), it was not difficult. That was useful maths to know and practical in application. I couldn't be doing with those silly maths puzzles they gave us at school.

For example:

A farmer is able to transport one and a half tons of flour in a boat across a river in any one crossing. He needs to transport twenty-six tons across to his farm at the other side. How many trips across the river does he need to make to complete the task?

I didn't get it. Was he a pillock or something? Why was he using the river? Couldn't he borrow a big lorry and do it in one journey by road? My Mam had always reassured me there were different ways of being brainy and I had intelligence of a different sort; I wasn't destined to be a university type, but she had always said I would excel at the university of life.

I tried my hand at Sunday School too, going to a chapel at the bottom of Wadsley Bridge. It was a funny little black church of sooted stone with a bell tower in the roof. For a while I took my little niece, Anthea, too. However, Sunday School did not prove to be very exciting, though I was conscious that Mam wanted me to learn things there. Sometimes they got crayons out which livened it up a little, but this shining habit soon waned.

Though I wasn't an obvious scholar, I did pride myself on my handwriting, which I had learned from my brother Joe. I loved to see him write and I wanted to be able to do it myself, to the same standard. My writing wasn't as well formed as his, but it was still special and nobody in my class wrote like me. Sometimes a teacher would discourage my individualistic flourishes, but I always reverted to this style, enjoying the craft of perfecting letter formation, adding hooked ascenders and descenders. I thoroughly enjoyed being different.

Mam must have got her money's worth sending her kids to Barton Academy. They all turned out alright. I always thought she'd made the choice of school on its potential academic repute, but later I learned it was the only private day school locally that my siblings could reach without crossing any major roads. My sister, Bib, and brother, Arthur, also went to this school which apparently cost 1/-6d a week for each of them.

All the family seemed to have a certain confidence. We all revelled in being different. I don't know where it came from; it was a funny mixture of conceit, ego, good humour and humility. To sum it up, I'd say we went around holding the views: *Don't mistreat us; we won't stand it. Don't take liberties with us; you'll not get away with it.* My mother was the same, though her temperament was essentially calm and measured, and it took a lot to get her riled.

She once got hauled up to junior school about me when I was young. I don't remember what I had done, certainly nothing serious; it was some minor misdemeanour. My mother trudged up to school expressing some misgivings. She knew that we were quite well known and she suspected that the teacher was curious to have a look at her. It got on her nerves when people thought we might be uncivilised or rough, just because we worked in the market. She was also irked by the fact that she suspected the teacher might be thinking himself above her.

I was not present and had been told to wait by the headmaster's office, whilst my mother met my class teacher. The other children in the class were playing in the yard at lunchtime. She walked proudly into the classroom, smiled at the teacher politely and sat down, after he'd invited her to take a seat. The teacher spread out his notes and the class register in front of him. Confident in his superior education, he proceeded to scold her for her parental shortcomings, and mistakenly shook his finger at her and pointed at her.

'Excuse me, please don't point your finger at me,' she said. The teacher continued with his speech and pointed at her again, waving his finger near her face. 'I asked you not to point at me, it's rude,' she said calmly.

Again the teacher continued, launching into a talk about my unruly nature, pointing at her again. My mother would have been the first to chastise me if I had been out of line. She could not stand pettiness, and this pointing at her was getting on her nerves. 'Young man, stop pointing; it's rude,' she said glaring at him. 'If you do it again, I'll bite your bloody finger off. Where are your manners?'

The teacher stopped short, stunned at her forthrightness and at her bad language. He fell silent. She took this to be the end of the conversation, stood up and walked out of the room.

I saw her striding down the corridor towards me. She was agitated. She never liked to have to swear, but she'd felt provoked. 'Come on, we're off. I've sorted laddo!' she said, bustling past the headmaster's office, grabbing my hand.

I was grateful for her courage. She always taught us to 'front up', as she called it: face your troubles and meet them squarely. The teacher now knew that if he was going to complain about me, it had better be over something major, and worth his while.

She was not trying to make herself superior; she taught us to feel equal to anyone and superior to no-one. She also used to advise us to be pleasant to people on your way up the ladder, because you might meet them again when you are on the way down. I admire that adage and recommend it.

In the late 1940s I was conscious of the atmosphere shifting in the house. Mam was weaker than usual, tired and not as good-humoured, seeming to be distant and not quite with it. Father was grumpier than ever and I learnt to keep out of his way with his fraying temper. They had both been upset by our Joe's arrest. He'd been involved in a serious car crash.

Mam had a weeping sore on her stomach, and people tried to hide the fact from me that she was in pain, but I knew. I'd seen them traipsing around with bandages and cotton wool dressings, which made the air smell of *Lestrol*.

I sometimes would creep into her bedroom to see her. She made an effort to smile, and lift her head up from the pillow to have a look at me. She'd try to shift herself up the bed putting her weight on her hands, but every move made her scrunch up her face in pain. She only cuddled me tentatively these days, holding me away from her a little, as if any contact might hurt her; I knew something was up. As she took to her bed, a quiet hush took over the place, and adults scurried down the hallway talking quietly. The doctor had been to call and Father enforced a respectful silence on us. I played outside as much as possible, well away from the house, so as not to disturb her.

Bill was also home to see Mam. He'd arrived from his current home in South Shields, where he was away working selling pots on the markets around Durham and Newcastle, crashing and banging through the house again and twirling me up in the air. For a while it was joyous again, but even our Bill, who was usually so cheerful, settled into a dour mood.

One day he sent me down to the grocer's at Malin Bridge to get our soda siphon exchanged for Mam. I was often sent down there on errands, mainly to Zerb's, the grocers. They sold lovely thick boiled ham, which they carved off the bone when you went in to buy a quarter. The soda siphon usually rested on Mam's bedside cabinet where she could reach it; she was off her food, but could still manage a drink. I obediently tripped down to the shops at Bill's bidding on this errand, but as soon as I turned to cross the road to the shops my heart quickened as I spied a herd of lads. I knew this group as the Stannington mob; all these boys were much older than me and they had a dubious reputation. They were led by the unlikely maverick figure of a vicar's son. They had gathered outside the shops and were bantering with one another, hanging around aimlessly. As I hopped up the kerb and tried to get through the shop door, they turned on me, jostling and poking me, trying to grab at the empty soda siphon, which I was holding tightly, peevishly snatching it from me.

'Let me through,' I urged. 'Mi Mam's ill and she wants this exchanging. I've got to get it back to her.' I tried to hold back my welling tears for I knew they'd pounce on any weakness.

'Ahh diddums, is he getting some soda for his Mummy?' they teased, prodding at me.

They enjoyed shoving me around, nudging me from boy to boy round the circle as they harangued me. I tried to hold back tears. I looked up, glanced across the road and saw Geoff hovering by the police box at the end of Rivelin Valley Road. I was grateful to spot him. I called to him desperately to get his attention. Seeing him made me feel much braver.

'Geoff, fetch our Bill! These pillocks are stopping me from getting into t' shop. Go and fetch our Bill!' Then turning to address them, I added bravely, 'He'll come and chin the lot of 'em!'

The lads continued to tease me, unimpressed by my threats; they'd heard it all before and most often big brothers failed to materialise. Geoff pitched around and pelted off, sprinting back up Rivelin Valley Road.

I knew that I could endure the teasing a bit longer, knowing that our Bill would soon be down to rescue me, and I soon spotted the familiar figure of him, running down the road towards me, already shouting at the kids before he got near.

'Leave him alone!' he yelled, looking resplendent in a smart, sports coat, already unbuttoning his jacket in readiness for any aggravation. The kids halted for a moment, looking at him. He skidded to a halt, his shoes scraping the pavement.

'What's up, Mick?'

'They're stoppin' me gettin' into t' beer-off to refill that siphon for mi Mam. They're bullying me.' Bill eyed the gang coldy, gazing round the line-up.

'Which one?'

'Him!' I asserted, pointing at the ringleader, accusing my main tormentor, who towered above me, a good foot taller than myself.

There were now four lads standing nearby, the others stragglers in the gang had drifted off into the background and started to saunter away. They'd assessed the situation and decided they didn't want to be on with any fighting.

'Him, there?' said Bill nodding, starting to take off his jacket and roll up his sleeves. 'No problem, thee feight him and I'll feight these three,' he said pointing at the lads.

I raised my eyebrows at Bill, trying to silently indicate that this lad he'd paired me with was much bigger than me and I was about to get hammered, but he did not seem to realise my predicament.

'Th'art not givin' much weight away,' chirped one cheeky chappy from the gang defiantly, looking Bill up and down in his civvies, determined not to be impressed by his military demeanour, and quibbling and moaning at the odds Bill had set up matching the fighters.

'Look at size of your[111]. It's not fair. Feight two on us each!'

I gulped.

'Reight th'art on. Thee count thi sen in, clever chuff,' retorted Bill. 'I'll feight thee and he'll tan both on them two there,' he said exaggerating my ability, and confidently gesturing towards me. 'Let 'im go first, then I'll chin thee.'

I quivered and edged forward miserably. Bill was supposed to come and make it better. He'd be scraping me up off the pavement in no time. I had no choice but to start scrapping with the two big lads

---

111 your- you plural-you lot, (used informally to indicate all members of a group)

coming at me. I hit out wildly, punching desperately in all directions, kicking and tussling, but I was soon losing. Bill stood on the sidelines watching us. One of them had grabbed hold of my jumper. He pulled my jersey so hard that it ripped at the seams and came apart, the front hanging down. The kid who had piped up with all the cheeky chatter was issuing a running commentary all the while, and he was enjoying the fact that I was coming a cropper. I looked towards Bill hoping for rescue. I was getting tired and couldn't keep this energetic wrestling up much longer.

Bill turned his attention to him now, jibing, 'Tha lot should know better, picking on him, you prat. Look at size of him, and look at size of your lot.'

I looked on, relieved, realising that Bill had finally copped the needle, and I was about to be rescued. Bill chipped a punch towards the gobby one and it landed on his chin, jolting him backwards, making him stumble. He fell, then turned away, backing out of trouble, holding his hands up in surrender, realising defeat was nigh, trying to remonstrate with Bill now.

'Ey, listen, I don't want any trouble.'

'Dun't tha? Then tha'd better keep thi gob shut in future.'

Bill did a sudden spin round like a hero from the cartoons and popped a testing punch on each of the others lined up too, sending them reeling back. Bop, bop, bop, down they went, three in a row, stumbling back onto the floor. They didn't look so tough now.

People had started to gather round watching to see what the trouble was, and at this point I saw Raymond Crampton gawping at us in the crowd. He lived near us. A few moments later Raymond's father rolled up, wearing a white mac. He bustled up towards the front of the fighting and squared up to Bill.

'Now then, what's going off?' he questioned, like the sensible adult that he was.

Bill, who was still wound up, turned round to take a look at him, wondering whether to chin him too. Then he grabbed him. Mr. Crampton was a good ten years older than him. He drew him up by the lapel, creasing his white mac and picked him up threateningly. Half lifting, half throwing him, he dropped him back on the ground a couple of feet away.

Raymond shot through from the back of crowd and blundered forward, spitting out breathlessly to Bill, 'Don't hit him. He's mi father!'

Bill dusted him off apologetically and turned round to hurl one more verbal parting shot to the lad who was ringleader, who stood nearby looking dishevelled and crestfallen.

'Tha should keep thi gob shut, thee; clever chuff. It's plain for all to see tha can't feight. All tha's gor is a big gob, which gets thee in trouble. I should keep stumm from now on, if I wa thee, pillock!'

With that, Bill accompanied me into the shop and we filled the soda siphon. By the time we came out, the sorry band had scattered. Bill put his arm around me and walked me back up the road home.

'While I'm home, remind me to give thi some feightin' lessons,' he said, giving my shoulder a squeeze.

I tried extra hard not to get into any scrapes, or cause Mam any additional stress, during her illness. After school I'd wander around the neighbourhood with Geoff. Sometimes we'd drift up to Bib's and she'd always feed us. My morning routine was much the same each day. I got myself ready for school and helped myself to any breakfast food I could scrabble together. If Father was in a good mood, (which was rare), he might cook me some breakfast. Each day before leaving, I'd nervously pop into the bedroom to kiss Mam goodbye. I trudged to school on my own, weaving up the hill and through the allotments, looking forward to the mind-numbing morning ritual of assembly, that helped me forget any cares: hymn singing, readings, notices about school events and the usual fable or story.

It was usual to listen to music as we filed in. The pianist plonked dramatically on the keys as if she'd missed her true vocation. She only faltered when she paused to turn a page, stumbling to find her place again in the rhythm of the piece. As she changed from one tune to the next, she'd flap around with handwritten cards and put up an educational sign on top of the piano indicating what she was playing: *The Blue Danube, Fingal's Cave, Peer Gynt* or *The Nutcracker*.

Assembly was a peaceful time, you could sit in a reverie, letting your thoughts ramble, tamed by the fall and rise of teachers' voices. It wasn't necessary to listen to the detail, there was no danger they might fire a question at you to see if you'd been listening. I liked the stories from the children's bible, the clashes between good and evil, and the tales of triumphant dominion of the weak and powerless over the ill intentioned. They chose readings from a familiar selection: the story of the Good Samaritan; the rising of Lazarus; the five loaves and two fishes; or Noah's Ark. The bible stories were comforting, read aloud to us in lilting sing-songy voices. If you weren't attentive enough to reap the benefits of the Christian message, then the teacher's voice might relax you for a few minutes or put you to sleep. Eyes drooped heavily with the monotone sound rolling across the gathered masses. Girls ducked low in the rows, mechanically plaiting one another's hair in long braids. I watched Joan Garvey picking at her long dark plaits, swatting them over her shoulder to enable the girl behind her to play with her hair. Boys picked fuzz off their jumpers, or picked spells out of their fingers, lulled by the readings into a quiet and peaceful stupor.

On one such cold January morning in 1949, I filed into assembly with my class group. The teacher urged us to sit cross-legged in our rows. I flopped down and soaked up the heat of the close-knit bodies. I gazed up at the high Victorian windows. It was one of those wintry, crisp mornings when the sunlight is particularly white and piercing, sending shafts of bright light streaming in through the windows, high-lighting the churning dust motes in the air.

The assembly hall was at the centre of the school, with wide cor-ridors leading off from it in two directions, north and south, opening onto wide corridors at either end where you could see anyone ap-proaching. The hall was well used for morning assemblies, music and singing, country dancing and P.E. We children sat on the worn her-ringbone parquet flooring, cross-legged, dabbing our fingers around in the dust, seated in our class rows.

The pianist played a musical interlude before the teacher stood up to address us at the front. A boy was called out, and we sang *Happy Birthday* to him as he stood fidgeting. He made his way back to his row blushing, and flopped down again cross-legged with his classmates. We then sang *Praise my Soul the King of Heaven* which was followed by notices and school news.

I sat daydreaming, gazing out of the high window. From the corner of my eye I spied the familiar figure of the head teacher, walking down the corridor towards the main school hall. I watched him intently, curiously. He paced sedately down the corridor with grim resolution. He hovered at the entrance to the hall and then confidently strode in, walking towards my class teacher, who was sitting on a chair at the side of the assembled gathering. They whispered together and then the teacher turned to search through the children's faces in the rows; her eyes wandering up and down, finally settling on me. She then beckoned me out to the side. I stood up slowly, shaking off my pins and needles and walked unhurriedly towards them. Children shuffled aside to let me through. *What do they want me for?* I wondered.

The assembly continued and the introductory bars of the hymn *Morning has Broken* rang out. There was a pause and a rustle of pages turning and a few coughs, then the pianist started into the first verse with gusto. A gaggle of children's wavering voices fluttered to join the piano playing, catching up, and straining to reach the high notes in the first line. I usually would sing along too; I liked the first verse with its promise of the new day, but I was concentrating and trying to understand why I had been called out. They continued singing through the verses as I slowly made my way out of the hall, heads turning to watch me and wondering at what could have called me away from my schooling that day. I followed the headmaster as he marched down the corridor, hanging back a little from him. The quiver of singing voices faded, as we walked down the stone steps to the headmaster's office.

I looked ahead all the while. We turned the corner and my stomach lurched to see the figure of my brother, Joe. He was dressed in a smart suit, but he looked thinner in the face, and he was flanked by two big policemen. I was afraid and worried. Joe was linked to one of the policemen by a set of handcuffs. I tripped towards him and he bent down to greet me. He gave me a wan smile and steadied me, his hand brushing my neck. The officer uncuffed him and the policemen stood nearby watching him, but they allowed us to walk together freely out of the building, hanging back a little behind us.

Joe took my hand, squeezing my warm little palm in his, leading me down the corridor. He stared ahead. As we walked together, he put his arm around my shoulder. We emerged from the building into the bright sunlight, the singing voices echoing, more distant now, the sound drifting out of the high windows and trailing away. We came to a halt and he turned me gently to face him, taking hold of my forearms. I saw that his eyes were wet. He bent towards me, and told me that my mother had passed away earlier that morning. I blinked, feeling the lump in my throat growing. I was fighting for breath, my heart racing, and a lonely sense of panic was rising in my chest. He hugged me, but it was no comfort. We walked back home silently to the hush of a house that was no longer a home, without her cheery laughter. It was January 18th 1949, and I was just twelve years old.

–7–
MY TEENAGE YEARS

My Mam had died when she was only fifty-three years of age. Dad used to say she'd aged by more than ten years during the war, with her sons away. We were all devastated to lose her, but I felt especially robbed of her presence, still being a child. When my Mam died, Father told me that she had a five-pound note in her purse. He gave me the fiver, telling me to buy myself a gold ring, in remembrance of her. I duly bought a ring and had the inside engraved with the word *Mam* and wore it daily.

Father did his best, but he could not fill the gap. Mam had always been warm and loving, whereas my father was awkward when it came to the expression of any feelings, and had no idea how to comfort me, or talk to me about his loss or mine. We lived together in the same house, rubbing along together a little clumsily, wondering how to communicate, and often avoiding it. My brothers and sisters were married and lived elsewhere, so we were forced to get along as best we could. I often cooked for myself and sometimes cooked food for him too. Neither of us was particularly interested in housework and we cleaned haphazardly by necessity. Eventually he employed a house-keeper, who worked for us now and then, Mrs. P. or Old Lass P., as Bill named her.

Father and I spent our leisure time apart. He reverted to his routine of going for a drink and a game of dominoes with his pals at The Malin in the evenings. I took to the comfort of roaming and hanging around outdoors with my pal, Geoff.

In our family having a vehicle was a necessity, and vehicles were practically the only large purchases we ever made, so it rather surprised me that my father started to express an interest in owning a television. Nobody in our road owned a television, and they were something of an expensive novelty. On questioning him further, it became apparent that he was keen to watch the racing on the telly from the comfort of his own armchair, rather than having to catch it on the radio in the betting shop. He liked to gamble and have a little flutter, and he was looking forward to seeing the racing and outcomes of his bets from a comfy seat in his front room.

My father wasn't one for shopping, so although I was only thirteen at the time, he instructed me to go and research it and have a look round for one. This was not unusual; he used the grown men who were his schleppers as his 'band of errands men', and he often sent them off on errands or to buy him things that he couldn't be bothered to sort out. He had such an aversion to shopping for goods that he had even sent Uncle Tom Fish out to the opticians to buy him a pair of glasses.

Uncle Tom tried to protest saying, 'I think tha should go, Arthur. They need to test thi eyes.'

My father grunted and batted this idea back at Tom, 'It'll be reight, tha sit the test for mi.' Thus my father wore glasses with a prescription made out for Uncle Tom Fish.

I wasn't that bothered about a telly, but I did want a radiogram. I loved music. Our Bill used to have a record player in his bedroom, but he had taken that when he married Madge and got his own house. He was always in his room playing particular songs over and over again; *Shout, Brother, Shout* by the Ink Spots, and *Don't Fence Me In* by Bing Crosby, which became known to me after as 'our Bill's tunes'. The music got on my father's nerves. Bill would play that same record night and day. Father couldn't stand it, and would growl down the corridor at Bill, 'Pipe down, pipe down wi' that bleedin' racket! Come to bed. Come to bed!' he'd bark. 'You're up all night and sleep all bleedin' day!'

So my father sent me off to search for a television with a blank cheque. I went to Cann's on Dixon Lane; Cann the Music Man. I found a model I liked. The man in the shop demonstrated the television functions, which I skipped over quickly; it all seemed to be working fine. I then went into much more detail about the radiogram, checking all the possibilities. I was excited; we'd be able to get music on it, roll the carpet back and have a little dance when he was out. I finally settled on a model made by *Bush*, top of the range, a combined television and radiogram, encased in a polished wooden cabinet about five feet high, with four doors that you could close, hiding everything away so it just looked like a big lump of furniture. The screen was about seventeen inches. I thought he'd like the telly at the top with its enclosing doors, and handy storage at the bottom. He could look up at just the right angle without craning his neck. It had a set of big push buttons in cream at the front just below the screen for operating it. It would take up quite a bit of room, but the wood was good quality and I thought he'd like it. It was expensive, but I was convinced I was making a good choice. I handed over the cheque.

It was soon delivered to our bungalow on Rivelin Valley Road and I set it up ready for his arrival and inspection. It was installed and took pride of place in the corner of the lounge. When he first saw it, I quickly leapt up to demonstrate all its features, rattling through what it could do. He nodded, standing with his hands on his hips, staring at it.

He didn't seem that impressed, but as I soon realised, he was building up to asking me the major question he was interested in. 'Well, what's the damage, how much was it?'

'Four hundred quid,' I stated boldly.

'Chuffin' 'ell!' he said, aghast at the cost. 'That's a bit batty[112]!'

Televisions were at the vanguard of new technology in those days, so understandably they were very expensive. Four hundred pounds was a great deal of money; it might be equivalent to a year's wages for many people.

'Couldn't you get one cheaper than that, for Christ's sake?'

I could see I was going to have to do a bit of a selling job.

'It's got a big screen so you can see it easily. You won't strain your eyes,' I added hopefully.

'Even so, it's a lot of money that,' he puffed, shaking his head.

'Well, I could have got a smaller one,' I offered inventively. 'But you see, the bloke told me at the shop that with the little uns, there's a bit of a problem. You can't get the racing on 'em.' I knew he had no idea about technology and would swallow my story.

'Oh well, tha's done reight, then!' he said brightening a little, satisfied with my explanation.

---

112 batty (adj)–expensive (market slang)

That telly and cabinet served us well for years. If there was anything unusual happening which was televised, we'd get neighbours coming round to see if they could watch it. It was quite a sociable thing. My Dad's pals from the Malin were often round to watch the racing. If I was home when they arrived, I'd get the kettle on and hand cups of tea around. He'd sit and watch it for hours with a couple of bottles of *Double Diamond* beer. I'd often come into the lounge to see him sitting there engrossed. When I came in he'd not even move and would continue viewing, getting me to make him a sandwich, saying, 'Now then, Mick, open a tin of salmon and make us a banjo[113].' Let me elucidate, *banjo* means sandwich. It's a strange slang term that my family (and probably lots of other market traders) use to name the humble sandwich.

Of course as a new and prized item, the telly was treated reverently for some time. He had Mrs. P., our cleaning lady, polish the cabinet, and he didn't like you to mess with the controls, but eventually as it became familiar it was treated with more commonplace irreverence. Sometimes in bad weather the reception was poor and he'd bang it on top. The screen fizzed and sputtered and you could only make out dim figures, as if everyone on screen was battling a snowstorm. I'd bought it, so naturally I got the blame. He'd hammer the top of it with his fist, crying, 'Look lively! This bleedin' thing's gone on the blink again. Tha's bought a demick[114].'

I tried to stop him banging it hard, crying, 'Leave it Dad, you'll bust it.'

I'd jump up and twiddle the knobs in desperation, trying to get the picture back for him. We had it for years and eventually the telly broke down, though the radio still worked. When it was time to let it got for a more up-to- date model, a friend of mine took it off our hands. My pal, Ronnie Mellhuish, had it; he made a cocktail cabinet out of the wooden carcass, and kept it for many years too.

One day when I was in my early teens my father announced he was going off to the races for a few days and he wanted to leave me at home. He wanted to know if I could cope. I thought, *Too right I can cope. Yes, cushti. We'll have a little party.* So I asked a few friends round to the bungalow. It had three bedrooms with a large through dining room,

113 banjo (n)–sandwich (market slang)
114 demick (n)-faulty item, not perfect, a seconds item, slightly damaged in manufacture, (market slang)

kitchen and bathroom. We'd recently had a proper bathroom suite fitted. At the party I suddenly noticed a lull in the proceedings, and found myself sitting alone. I hunted round to see what had happened to my mates, and I found them huddled in hallowed silence in the bathroom. There they were, staring in stunned homage, gawping at the bath and touching the taps. I ushered them back into the front room. I suppose at that time most people had a battered tin bath hung behind the cellar door, and if you were the youngest you probably ended up bathing in everyone else's scum. Our Bill said I'd missed a trick and I should have charged each one an entrance fee.

Father was a strong man, but he seemed a little lost without my mother. He had mellowed, not quite having the same fight in him after my mother died. Mrs. P., our housekeeper, came in daily to do the chores. I tried to like her, but found her hard to get on with. She bustled around the place, looking busy, but in reality I found it difficult to see what she really did to make our home comfortable. If you came in and she was unaware, she was often to be found on the sofa knitting, or having a crafty smoke by the back door, gazing into the distance.

She played a good game in front of my father, talking to me with some warmth trying to be motherly and nurturing, but when he wasn't there I caught her looking at me, as if I were a specimen to be examined and guarded against, as if I might sting her, and she wasn't sure if I were friend or foe. Her cooking was awful. I had a good appetite, but often had to leave her meals, pushing charred bits round on the plate. Mam would have said she could burn water.

Likewise her housekeeping and cleanliness were nothing much to write home about. I took to aping our Bill's moniker for her, calling her Old Lass P. (behind her back) and though I was brought up to respect my elders, I found it difficult to hold her in any esteem. I had long suspected that she was a bit light-fingered. Little things seemed to disappear from the house. My father was not someone who noticed these little trinkets, but I noticed as they had belonged to my mother and therefore, although not to my particular taste, they were especially precious to me. I noticed little *Goss* ornaments started to disappear one by one from their usual places. Emboldened by her success and the fact that no one seemed to notice, she became braver and more courageous. My Mam and

Dad always had nice bed linen, good eiderdowns and Egyptian cotton sheets, bright white, heavy and cool to the touch. For winter he had flannelette for extra warmth. I noticed that greying, moth-eaten, threadbare sheets with tears and holes in them gradually replaced our good cotton sheets.

My father must have noticed, for she was brass-necked enough to put them onto his bed too, not just mine. I had often come a cropper putting my toenails through the thin sheets, tearing them; the material had no body in it. I knew they weren't ours and she was gradually swapping them, taking our good sheets and bringing her cheap and tattered replacements from home. I wondered why oh why didn't my father confront her. I didn't take kindly to sleeping in these threadbare bits of tat.

My father was usually blunt and sardonic, so I just couldn't understand why he would tolerate this. He was the first one to point out my faults if he thought I was lacking in courage, and he often criticised my brothers for mishandling their love affairs, snarling disdainfully, 'Tha stands for t' egg under t' hat!' at any soft-heartedness.

Perhaps he thought that as a young lad I needed a woman's presence. His tolerance of her irritated me, and on my mother's behalf I was incensed at her cheek. My mother's words rang in my ears: *I can't stand liberty takers!* She never could stand what she called liberty takers: anyone taking advantage, or getting one over on you out of pettiness. I didn't like the fact Mrs P. was getting a living from us *and* pinching from us. My Mam's voice sounded in my head, the memory of her still sharply defined. I could hear her now, and Old Lass *was* taking liberties with us, of that I was certain.

I resolved to take the sort of action my late mother would have advocated, but I needed to bide my time and look for an opportunity. Open warfare wasn't an option. She was wily and had my father in a good position; he knew I got into scrapes and she would dismiss any direct confrontation from me as wilful fantasy or boyish capers. I aimed to be as canny as she was in my methods. For some time I'd been spying on her. I'd seen her go into the pantry to pinch eggs from us, just before she left on her way home. She'd sneak in and drop them down the side of her shopping bag loose, in ones and twos, as she left. Eggs were still hard to come by, perhaps they were even still on ration at the time, and she enjoyed these little gains over us. We weren't poor and we could get extra items and barter things. The irony was that if she'd have asked, making her plight known, my father would have gladly given her some food or some money to buy some.

One day, trying to be helpful as she gathered her things to leave, I passed her shopping bag to her. It was a big, tawdry bag with two handles.

'Don't forget your shopping bag,' I said sweetly. I'd seen her pinching our eggs from the kitchen earlier that morning.

Then I grasped the bag roughly, crushing it between my elbows, holding it up towards her so helpfully. Smack went my hands with a thud, thumping my hands together on each side, crushing the bag together in the middle. I pictured the wet, gelatinous mess dripping inside and gave her the sweetest, most innocent smile that I could muster, 'Ooh, careful, it's heavy. Thanks, Mrs. See you again next week. Thanks for coming.'

As she went out of the door, scowling, no doubt thinking about the mess she'd have to clear out of her bag when she got home, I muttered under my breath after her, 'Bleedin' liberty taker!'

Having older brothers and sisters who had courted and married, inevitably got me interested in the opposite sex during my early teenage years. You couldn't avoid the comings and goings and sheer otherworldliness of the fairer sex with their tight-bodiced dresses, coifed hair, wafts of exotic perfume and deep red lipstick. So as Geoff and I approached our mid-teens, we inevitably became interested in girls. Our usual weekend routine was to go to the Memorial Hall at Hillsborough, or the 'Memo' as we referred to it, on Saturday nights, where kids from thirteen to eighteen or beyond would hang around chatting and dancing to the latest tunes. We'd been going here for some time with varied success, both attracting and repelling the girls in equal measure, so I took it upon myself to suggest fishing in a different pool. Although I was younger than Geoff, I took the lead and tried to bring him round to my way of thinking. Instead of going to the Memo, I reckoned we should go for a drink up Bradfield.

Geoff squirmed at the thought of this variance in routine, looking at me askance, asking, 'Bradfield. Why Bradfield? It's chuffin' miles away.'

'Well, trouble wi' t' Memo is these townie birds, they're a bit wide,' I reasoned. 'Bradfield's full of country lasses. They're a bit thick, aren't they? We might be able to do what we want wi' 'em.'

Geoff nodded, convinced of my strategy. The night came when we were aiming to try our luck in Bradfield. I suggested to Geoff that we should set off on this new adventure well prepared.

'Let's get a packet of three, in case we get lucky,' I said. Geoff coloured up at the thought.

'Thee get 'em,' he said.

'Nah, thee get 'em,' I urged.

So our argument continued. Taking a coin out of my pocket, I resolved we should toss for it.

'Thee call,' I said, nodding towards Geoff.

'Heads.'

'Oh... it's tails,' I said, masking the coin with my hand. 'Th'art getting 'em,' I said with relief.

Geoff screwed up his face. I am not sure how much he knew about the birds and the bees, but he was reluctant to lose face in front of me, so reluctantly a little later we found ourselves outside a chemist's shop. We hovered outside, prodding and poking one another. I gave Geoff a gentle nudge towards the doorway.

'Get thissen in, go and get 'em.'

'Thee get 'em.'

'Nah, nah, tha's lost t' toss. Thee get 'em. Look lively,' I piped up, adamant that I was not going into the shop.

Grudgingly Geoff opened the shop door and went in. The shop bell tinkled as he entered, and I saw a female shop assistant in a white coat sweep out from the back room to serve him. I was lurking outside, trying to see what was going on, without drawing too much attention to myself, stifling laughter as I watched the back of him, easily able to picture the nervousness on his face and enjoying his discomfort. Geoff was a nervy kid at the best of times, easily reddening and flushing at the slightest embarrassment; he was bound to be sweating cobs in there now. Just after Geoff went into the shop a formidable-looking, middle-aged woman followed him in. This made me laugh all the more, envisaging his embarrassment with this tall lady behind him in the queue peering at him, scrutinising his every move. He twitched and I saw him turn to glance at the woman. His eyes were practically level with her chest.

A few minutes later Geoff exited, red in the face, holding a paper bag and ambling dejectedly.

'Has tha got 'em? Are we sorted, then?' I asked expectantly, bounding over to him to inspect the purchase.

Geoff shuffled, pausing, not wanting to meet my gaze.

'Nah, got two ounce of Kilfof™ cones instead,' he said. He squinted at me and held out a small paper cone of cough sweets. I slowly took one and threw it down my throat, puffing at his poor performance. This was now likely to be my biggest thrill of the evening. Dolefully we walked along.

'Bleedin' 'ell, we're goin' to have it spark off at Bradfield tonight!' I concluded.

Throughout my teens I was still working on Saturdays with my father or brothers in the market. I left school at fourteen and went straight into the market to work. For a youngster I was quite affluent. When I first worked for my father properly as a waged employee, I sometimes used to forego financial payment in favour of a piece of china instead. I'd say, 'Dad, instead of that tusheroon[115], can I have this piece of *Carltonware*?' He used to look over at me bemused, wondering what a young lad wanted with some pots. I suspect that secretly he was rather pleased at my appreciation of the fine wares we sold. In this way I collected a number of fine pieces, richly hand-painted, with burnished gold rims and edging. I wish I'd collected more; they would be collectors' items now, and I'd have amassed a fortune.

I sometimes used to work as a Saturday lad for Joe Bennett too, and I asked him for china instead of wages, collecting a lovely emerald green *Carltonware* china cigarette box and lid, with a matching grooved ash tray, pen trays, and good pieces of Midwinter porcelain. Joe Bennett particularly liked to sell *Carltonware* and had lots of *Rouge*

---

115 tusheroon (n)-half a crown (slang)

Royale pieces. Their small dishes sold for two bob or half a crown, not a great fortune and the buyer could delight in a little tasteful luxury. Joe sold *Rouge Royale Carltonware* ginger jars for a pound — they are worth over three hundred at today's prices. If anyone's got one out there, I'll give you a fiver for it.

Joe had a penchant for fancy glass too. He stocked *Knottingley Crystal* in white, amber, green and blue, made at their West Yorkshire factory. He also sold glass made by Chance Brothers and Co. of Smethwick, Birmingham. He stocked their slumped and pressed glass, *Spiderweb* set patterns, water tumblers, fruit sets, celery vases and designs such as *Lotus* and *Waverley*. He also bought glass from a wholesaler called Harry Hancock. I still have a glass mint sauce boat which Joe he gave me.

I had worked hard each week and was feeling rather flush with my earnings, and perhaps a bit cocky. One Saturday I came across some cheap rings in the market and bought a dozen for two bob. I fancied having some fun with a bit of tom[116]. They were gold plated, in the style of engagement rings. They weren't bad likenesses of proper rings; I thought I'd have some fun with them. I jauntily strode into the Memo that Saturday night, flashed up in my new Barney Goodman's suit. Dad had creased up when I put it on, as it had piping around the pockets and a pale blue silk lining.

It was far too unusual for him, and he laughed and ridiculed me as I left the house, saying, 'Th'art not goin' out in that, are tha? Tha looks like a meschuggy[117] bird. Get changed. Put something reem[118] on. Tha looks a right bleedin' cock bird in that thing!'

I ignored him and I went out in my suit and got 'engaged' to a few girls that night. Apparently my name was mud, as they huddled in the ladies toilets, arguing about me and blackening my reputation. I didn't dare show my face for a few weeks after that.

I avoided talking about anything personal with my father, but he <u>was a little more</u> approachable when it came to anything tangible,

116 tom (n)-tomfoolery=jewellery (rhyming slang)
117 meschuggy (adj)-crazy, mad
118 reem (adj)-right, proper, good, of good quality (market slang)

so I confronted him with my plans to beautify our home, as things were looking much shabbier these days. I was feeling rather flush and wanted to make the place more comfortable. As always I made any suggestion to him tentatively and politely; he needed careful handling. I approached him about getting Mam's best sofa re-covered. 'I think we should get that sofa done; it's lookin' a bit pony[119], Dad,' I offered cheerily.

'What's up wi' it? It's reight, enough for me. It's cushti[120]. Leave it,' he said.

I could see that I was going to get no joy from him, so I took it upon myself to sort it out. I got it re-covered at Wilcox's, on Hillsborough Bottom. I didn't really have the money, and took out a loan and paid them back on the weekly. It was delivered. Dad admitted he did like it, and it looked nice.

One night he eyed me, suspecting what I had done.

'Don't tell me tha's been bleedin' getting maced up. I've teld thi, don't buy owt, unless tha can bung[121] for it,' he chipped.

I shuffled uncomfortably, not wanting to admit my folly.

'How else could I afford it?'

'How much was it then?' he puffed with frustration.

'Eighty six quid,' I answered.

'Bleedin' hell!' he sputtered, practically choking on his tea. 'That's a bit batty!' he groaned, glaring at me.

I shifted uncomfortably from one foot to the other, expecting a further bout of bad temper, or a good telling off when he learned I'd sorted out an agreement and had arranged to pay the money back in instalments to the upholsterer. He grunted and scowled over at me. Shaking his head, he then reached into his back pocket and peeled off some notes from his wad.

'Here, there's eighty odd quid there. Get him bleedin' bunged[122] and don't get maced up again,' he said with irritation, dashing the notes into the palm of my hand. I paid the man off straight away the very next day. In his own curmudgeonly way Dad was a generous man.

I inherited the sofa. Some twenty years later I had it re-covered again with another lovely fabric, wanting to preserve it and keep it in

119 pony (adj)-crap (pony and trap, rhyming slang)
120 cushti, cushtey (adj)-good, really good, well, tasty, pleasant (Romany origin)
121 to bung (v)-to pay, pay for (slang)
122 bunged (v)-paid (slang)

the family, more for its sentimental value than intrinsic worth. The new fabric I chose had a beige velveteen background and muted colours with a dainty, cutaway flower pattern. You rarely see such fine fabric now; it was called uncut and cut moquette and the velvety flowers stood up, slightly embossed above the background fabric. I am still very fond of that sofa, and no doubt it will be passed down to the next generation. It has been re-covered twice again since that time and is still serving us well.

By my late teens I was still living alone with my father at the bungalow. Mrs P. occasionally came to clean the house, but we fended for ourselves cooking our own meals as much as possible, preferring our strange combinations of ingredients to her half-hearted culinary skills. Dad was semi-retired, having now given the pitches to his sons and spent a lot of time at home. I enjoyed my freedom. I came home to eat my meals and to cook for my father, but was out with my friends most evenings, drinking, dancing, going to the flicks and courting. I liked this freedom and felt my lifestyle had to be appreciated by him. It was an uneasy balance, as he could be an awkward companion; it paid to keep him sweet.

I was always keen to do his bidding and to keep in his good books. Sometimes a group of us played at cards with him and he enjoyed winning. We played quite gently, avoiding the heights of competitiveness, which we'd normally display. He had a winning streak. We had thought his run of good luck was particularly fortuitous, until he was playing with my brother Joe one night. My niece, Anthea, had come to call on us, and she hovered by the table watching us play.

Father was shuffling and dealing the cards and Anthea suddenly piped up, 'Oh I see you are playing with those marked cards again, Grandad!'

Joe tutted and swooshed his hands across the dealt piles, sending them shooting across the table.

'Thy crafty bleeder! That's it, I'm out if th'art playing bent!' he chimed.

It was the winning my father liked, not the cheating. He chuckled and rubbed his hands. He especially enjoyed a little one-upmanship gained over any of us. He meant no ill will. It was good to see him smile again.

My father had always advocated it would be good to own our own houses. 'Buy your own drum[123],' he urged all of us, as soon as we were earning any decent wages. Before I contemplated getting a house, I was keener on getting a car. As soon as I was old enough to drive, I got my licence. A car was a symbol of having made it, and I was determined to get one somehow. After many discussions, my father agreed that I could have a car instead of a lorry full of pots, which was what he'd given my elder brothers. At the age of seventeen I got my first car, which was handed down to me by my father, but I loved it. It was a 1936 Wolseley 14, a four-seater with a two-tone paint job, muted green and black. Dad had paid two hundred and fifty pounds for it when he first bought it, second-hand. He had used it for work, but it was in good nick and still rather grand as a hand-me-down. Relatively few people had a car, so I was lucky to have a vehicle. I used to adore the way the radiator light lit up when you switched the engine on. How I loved it. I would sometimes go and start it up and just sit in it outside the bungalow, enjoying the glinting paint work and the rev of the engine.

There had been one teacher who got my goat at school, and one late afternoon I resolved to drive back to Morley Street to give him a look at my car. I contemplated for a while before deciding on this action, hearing my mother's voice in my head. I knew she would urge me to turn the other cheek, but I was too headstrong to resist the urge to pay Mr. T. a visit.

I had never been very sure if the teachers liked me. I was brought up by my parents to feel myself equal to anyone, and I think this instilled a natural pride and self-confidence in me, which always seemed to be viewed as a challenge to teachers. I suspect they may have found it rather galling that my family's meagre wealth came from something

---

123 drum-house, home, flat (slang)

as basic and unskilled as selling pots in the market. I wasn't embarrassed by it, neither was I involved in promoting it. It was just a fact of my life, and not worthy of debate in my view.

Mr. T., a teacher who taught me when I was at Morley Street School, seemed to enjoy making negative reference to my family's business interests. Though I note his disdain did not prevent him from indulging in cadging ciggies off me, (or any other unfortunate kid who happened to come across him in quiet spots in the playground).

Mr. T. was one of those grubby types, smelling of stale tobacco, with a moustache, with dangling hairs up his nose. He always used to wear a faded jacket, with leather pads on the elbows where it was threadbare. He rode a bike and protected his shabby trousers with bicycle clips.

In those days teachers could afford to be mean spirited; it was in the days before political correctness when it was deemed perfectly appropriate to flick your ears, batter you with a flying board rubber or give you a quick clip round the ear hole to get your attention. I came in for some verbal stick from him just before leaving school. I wasn't stupid, and I was good at mental arithmetic; however, my skill was unappreciated and I never received any praise from him. He seemed to take pleasure in singling me out for ridicule. Mr. T. did not recognise any of my natural talents, and had already told me not to bother turning up for the school exams, as matriculation wasn't the expected path for me. He expected my path to be the same as many of the kids — out of the door at fourteen — straight to the Labour Exchange; or in my case, straight into the family business.

A month before I left school, in one careers lesson he was looking through the local newspaper, picking out certain types of jobs. With glee he suddenly announced to the class, 'Ah, look, here's one for you, Edwards. Mmn... here's one, look......pot washer!' He delivered this with a sneering and belittling emphasis on the word 'pot'. All the kids knew about my family, and of course our collective nickname 'The Potty Edwards' and they picked up on the joke with him. Peals of laughter rang out and there was noisy guffawing at my expense: the other kids were just glad and grateful that he wasn't picking on them. My classmates tittered and banged on their desks. He sat at the front, leaning back in his chair, throwing his head back, shuddering with laughter at the jape. He enjoyed showing me up. I never forgot that. It was rather unkind to vilify me, and undeserved on my part. I took it quietly at the time, and knew I would bide my time.

Every dog has his day, so they say. I left school and went to work in the market and didn't give this teacher a thought for some time — until I got my car! So one day I found myself parked up in it outside my old school, the engine running proudly. I was flashed up, wearing a nice new tailored suit, which I'd just had made at Barney Goodman's. I waited, and I soon spied Mr. T. as he came out of the gates wheeling his bike. He looked across, squinting at the car.

'Good afternoon, Sir,' I chirped.

He twitched a little at the sight of me, but came up to the car and eyed me, appraising me with some begrudging interest, leaning in towards me slightly to have a look inside the car interior.

'Mmn...it's you,' he said, unable to hide the fact that he wasn't particularly glad to see me. 'Hello, Edwards.'

'Hello, Sir,' I said, looking him up and down cheekily. 'You're still riding that bike, I see.' He wasn't going to answer me of course. 'Oh and I notice you've still got those leather patches on your jacket. Nowt changes much here.'

His lip curled silently. I hung my arm out of the car window and gently stroked the door's gleaming paintwork. I offered him a cigarette too, just to add a final insult, showing that I could afford to proffer him a few fags too. He took one and popped it in his top pocket, saving it for later. He eyed me sniffily. I thought of adding that I'd bought my car from selling pots in the market, but I realised there was no need; he knew that.

'Well, nice to see you, Sir. Better be getting off. Got a date tonight... got to pick her up.'

I switched on the engine, turning the key cockily with a little smile as I did so. I revved the engine and I pulled away smoothly. I looked in my rear mirror as I drove off. He was still gazing at me, clutching his bike. I know it was perhaps a bit childish of me to revisit him, but I wanted him to know I had done alright, and would amount to something after all. Family honour had been restored. However, my Mam would not have been impressed at me indulging in such *Schadenfreude*; she would have said it was unnecessary.

-8-
LUCK WITH THE LADIES

Mick Edwards at 19 years old

Having a car made me something of a catch, and my luck with young ladies was improving. At the age of seventeen I met June, who became my steady girlfriend. I first spied her when she was playing tennis in Hillsborough Park, and I liked the look of her and was very attracted by her thick, auburn hair. Subsequently we got talking properly one night at a dance at the City Hall. I gave her a lift home in the family lorry, as I'd left the car at home. We started dating. I even went for Sunday tea with her mum and dad, and think I passed muster during the rituals of cups of her Mam's *Brooke Bond* tea, and serving of sandwiches and cakes. Her dad was easy to please; if you took him to the pub and bought him a couple of rounds he could be your friend for life. June remained my girlfriend all throughout my late teenage years. She was different to the other girls; she was the type of girl who made you keep working hard to impress her. As our Bill said, she wasn't the sort you could fanny to. She had common sense, and a practical intelligence that matched my personality.

At the age of eighteen I was called up for National Service, which was then compulsory. There was a brief medical to check your fitness level and if that went well, you were drafted in. I was deemed fit and was sent to Kinmel Park, Rhyl for initial two-week training. Then I went on to Oswestry, for eight weeks.

My eldest sister Bib came with me to the station, to see me off. I've never seen Bib cry, but she wept as she hugged me that day. She wiped her face with her handkerchief as she waved me goodbye. It upset me to see her so moved and I tried to reassure her, 'What are you roarin'[124] for? I'm not going to get hurt, there's no bleedin' feighting now. Pull yourself together. We're just playing at it. It's like sending me off to Butlin's.'

I wrote to June regularly, and she wrote to me, and our relationship endured. I wasn't exactly looking forward to the rigour of army training; I'd never had a boss or had to take orders, so was unsure of what to expect. I wondered if I'd be capable of tolerating anyone in authority over me. However, I made some good friends and rather enjoyed the time when there.

One day I got chatting to another recruit. We'd been sent to the quartermaster and we got talking to one another as we lined up in the queue waiting for our kit to be issued.

'Alright there? I'm Mick.' I nodded towards the chap standing in the line next to me.

'Hello, Mick. I'm Peter. So what did you do in civvy street?' he asked me.

'I worked the markets.'

He suddenly changed, becoming instantly unfriendly and stared at me.

'I'm not embarrassed, you know.'

'Eh? What?'

'You'll not embarrass me, I'm not ashamed of it.'

'What are thy on about?'

'You are trying to wind me up, referring to my family, they work the markets ... Everybody knows. So what?'

'Turn it up. I'm not trying to embarrass thee. What's thi surname?'

'Leese. I'm from Nottingham.'

---

124 roaring (v)-crying (local/Yorkshire slang)

'Oh aye. I've heard of your family. There's a lady in your family, might be thy Mam or Gran, and she sits behind the stall smoking a clay pipe, doesn't she?'

'Yes. How do you know?'

'I just do. My name's Edwards. My family work the gaffs an' all; they sell pots.'

'Oh, I've heard of your family too. Sorry, I thought you were taking the mick.'

'No; why would I do that?'

We shook hands, laughing at the coincidence that we were both from market families, and were firm friends thereafter.

It was a pleasure to get into the army, and a pleasure to get out. I went in at the age of eighteen for two years from 1954-1956 as part of my National Service. I spent part of that period stationed at Belsen camp in Germany. I became the C.O.'s batman; this involved polishing his boots and leather belt, pressing his shirts and brushing off his suits and his B.D. (battle dress). I also had to scrape the mud off his gaiters if he went out on manoeuvres. It's safe to say I didn't get any useful experience fighting any battles; however, I did seem to spend a lot of my time doing the C.O.'s ironing. I couldn't wait to escape; I was itching to get back to normal life, as I had a good job already set up in the family business. I was not whiling away time like some young men, as I had had steady regular work awaiting me. I wanted to get back to selling pots on the market. I was demobbed after two years and was in the 54-14 cohort for demobbing.

When I came out of the army I went straight back into working with my father again, selling pots on the market. We got on quite well working together. I could read his moods and knew how to humour him. Home life was a little more unpredictable, but my father and I got along together somehow. I tried my best not to annoy him, and he did his own thing. We spent very little time together, apart from the occasional meal. He was hard to please. I sometimes cooked for him, and he always had something to complain about. After his meals he'd sit and read the paper, until it was time for his ritual pint down at the Malin. He never expressed much emotion. I lived with him in the bungalow at Rivelin Valley Road until my marriage to my girlfriend, June, in March 1959.

One night Dad came in from the pub. I heard him getting undressed as usual, pottering in and out of the front bedroom. I bumped into him as he made his way along the corridor to the bathroom, his beery breath wafting in my face. I stepped aside awkwardly to let him pass. He was stumbling, wobbly and a bit tight. I looked at him and I saw that there were tears in his eyes. He tried to turn away, and then he looked me in the eye. His bottom lip was trembling. Suddenly I was conscious of his age; to me he looked very old and tired, and I sensed his loneliness. His face crumpled and a tear trickled down his cheek.

'I miss your mother.'

I stood rigid, unable to show him tenderness or reach out to comfort him in my shock at his quiet display of emotion. I always knew he loved her greatly. He had a quiet respect for her, valued her views, and listened to her, despite his gruff demeanour and bossiness. Yes, I had no doubts that he loved her a great deal.

June and I were going steady and it seemed logical to move towards the next step of marriage. I proposed and June accepted. We got married fairly young. It wasn't the done thing to live together; going case-o[125] was frowned upon. When we were first married we lived with my father at the bungalow on Rivelin Valley Road. I hoped to follow Bill's lead and buy my own house. My other

**Mick and June Edwards,
March 1959**

brothers were making a good living, and I was conscious that I was lagging behind them somewhat, still living with my Dad. I wanted to be a good provider for my family. Living with my Dad grated with me somewhat and I wanted my own place, but I couldn't see a way out of it; houses were so expensive and I was nervous about committing to regular payments, being self-employed.

---

125 to go 'case-o'-means to live together outside wedlock (family slang), possibly a corruption of living over the case (suitcase)

As was usual in those days, youngsters often had to stay at their parents' homes whilst they saved up for a deposit for a house, or for a bond for the rent. We'd got a building society account and were saving hard. We just had to get along with my father. He could be cantankerous. June cooked for him, but he was always complaining, and he was hard to do anything right for.

Mick Edwards and his best pal,
Geoff Sanderson, March 1959

My brothers suggested I stick it out living with him. It was known that he'd bought them all a lorry each with a stock of pots for them to sell. I'd had a second-hand car. Bill urged me to stay, saying matter-of-factly, 'When he tails 'em, tha'll cop thi whack,' meaning that I was due to inherit the bungalow.

This was not why I stayed. I felt sorry for the old geezer and wanted to keep him company, but he was hard to love when he was in a bad mood, which was often the case.

June was itching for us to get our own place. She felt as if she was constantly walking on eggshells, trying not to upset him. Our daughter, Michele, had been born by the following autumn and though she was a peaceful baby, there were inevitably times when she wouldn't stop crying.

One night we tried everything we could to soothe her, but nothing worked. June had nursed her, and I'd taken her round the block in the pram, but she was still grizzling. He stormed down the corridor, bellowing, 'Can't you get that bleedin' thing to stop crying?

I'm trying to get some bleedin' kip!' Having had a drink or two had fuelled his bad temper.

This ended our stay at the bungalow. I was annoyed, but didn't argue back or challenge him. June and I went to bed that night, knowing we'd come to a point of no return. I said to her in hushed tones, 'That's it, we're leaving. I'm looking for a house to buy tomorrow.'

'Can we afford it?' asked June.

'We'll manage. We're not staying here,' I said.

We came downstairs the next morning to an awkward atmosphere. He apologised, knowing he had been a bit out of order, but my feelings had been hurt and I had stubbornly decided we were leaving. Our house-hunting began and I made an offer on a terraced house on Stannington Road the same week. I had no idea how we could afford it, and I had to borrow sixty quid off our Joe to afford the deposit.

I told father we were leaving. I think he knew he'd forced our hand a little, but he agreed. 'Ah well that's probably the best thing you can do. Leave here; she's roaring all bleedin' night.'

I agreed to pay Joe back the loan in instalments as I could manage them. Joe was keen for the money back. He came down to the market every week for some months, to see if I was able to pay him back.

'Has that got that there for me?' he'd chime.

'Tha can trust me. I'm not goin' to flit, Joe,' I'd say to him.

I hadn't got the money to pay him back for ages, but I finally managed to save it from my wages and pay back the debt. We moved out of the bungalow and Agnes and her husband, John, moved into it to look after father. Agnes got on better with him and they were better suited in temperament; she knew how to handle him.

We moved into the terraced house on Stannington Road, and enjoyed painting the rooms and slowly doing it up. Many of our friends, Joan and Ray, Jean and Ted, Cath and Gordon, and Keith and Elva were also in our position, buying their first homes and starting families. Our social life was quieter, and consisted of evenings in at one another's houses, the children sleeping in carrycots while we chatted. June and I set to work to paint the house throughout, listening to the radio or music on the gramophone while we painted, stopping off to dance to Chubby Checker's *Let's Twist Again* or Little Eva's *The Locomotion*.

My father was always matter-of-fact, and one night after he'd had a drink or two, he even predicted his own death, saying factually and plainly, 'I'll die when t' bluebells are up.' He pronounced 'die' as if it rhymed with 'sea', making the word sound even more bleak and mournful. He did indeed die when the bluebells were up, on the thirteenth of May 1964, at the age of seventy-two.

Bill and I went to see him laid out at the Chapel of Rest at the church on St. Philips Road, the same church where Mam and Dad had been married. As we went into the grounds, the rusty metal gate to the churchyard was hanging off its hinges, swinging precariously. We held it up as we went through it, then walked along the path towards the church building. The church was dilapidated and run-down, and we sensed it would not be standing for much longer.

We went inside. We stood side by side, silently looking at the old fella who was laid out before us. I felt so regretful that his final resting place was not grander than this. I welled up, feeling so sorry that he had gone, and sad that I had not been able to talk to him more easily when he was here. Seeing that decrepit old gate had really upset me. Sometimes you realise how much you love and respect someone when it is too late.

I always think of him whenever I see a carpet of bluebells...

–9–
TRIPS TO THE POTTERIES

I threw myself into my work after father died. Bill and I concentrated on the business. Agnes and John moved into the bungalow permanently after his death, making the place their own. They remained there for many years. June and I settled into our home at Stannington Road. I gained the confidence that I could earn enough to sustain a family, and by the mid 1960s we were moving again to a larger house.

I used to call in and visit Agnes regularly at the bungalow. She was an enthusiastic and accomplished baker. You could walk in to racks of steaming cakes: ginger cake, buns, Victoria sponge, fruit loaf, parkin, jam tarts, Bakewell tart, coffee and walnut cake, and my favourite, chocolate cake. I often called by to visit with the children, waving as we went in through the door to be greeted by the delicious aroma of home baked cakes, or the constant thud and rumble of the sewing machine, which she constantly had set up on the dining table.

She was always making something: kids' summer dresses, curtains, aprons, cushions covers, embroidered handbags for the grandchildren and sensational embroidered and appliquéd slipper bags which the children in the family cherished for years, long beyond their serviceable lifespan. Michele had a slipper bag with an appliqué washing line with clothes on it, embroidered pegs, dresses aprons and shirts flapping in the wind. My son, David, had a slipper bag with cars on it in different colours, with a road with a zebra crossing in black and white, topped with sunny yellow belicia beacons on top of black and white striped poles.

One day when I was alone I called in at the bungalow to find a freshly-baked chocolate cake resting on a rack, with chocolate icing dribbling down the sides. I called out, but it appeared that no-one was at home. Agnes must have popped out to see a neighbour. I eyed the cake and could not resist it. Hoping she had not baked it for a special occasion, I cut myself a generous piece and tucked into it. It was only polite to leave a note, after carving up her handiwork. I wrote on a piece of paper in big letters: *The Phantom strikes again!* I left the note propped up by the cake and crept away.

**My brother, John William Edwards, (Bill)
pitching in Sheaf Market, Sheffield**

My brother, Bill, loved pots, as I did. Pots are lovely, lovely things. There's nothing as beautiful as a bone china cup and saucer with a rim of burnished gold. I swear a cup of tea tastes far nicer in a china cup. If anyone had visited Bill at his home, it is likely they would have been served tea in a china cup with a matching saucer. The cup would most likely have been a big china breakfast cup with a narrower bottom, the side curving gently in a bell shape, with a wide top.

It is sad that people today balk at paying more than a couple of pounds for a cup of any sort, and would rather slurp their tea from a mug rather than from a well-turned, delicate cup. China is good value: if you were to work out how long a china cup lasts and how many cups of tea you can get from it, even if you pay a tenner for it, it's nothing and it will serve you well. Soon we'll have no potteries left, and everything will be made in China.

Pots should be used. There are people who store their prized dinner sets in cupboards and rarely make use of them, feeling they are too special for everyday use. I would urge you to use them and enjoy them. Often people keep their pots hidden away, waiting for special occasions, which rarely come. Wedding-present pots that are stored away in people's cupboards are often in perfect condition; however, occasionally they end up damp and crazed, with tiny veined cracks under the glaze, passing from beauty to tattiness, without constant use. Frequently they reach a sorry end, unused, unappreciated, finally left to fester in a charity shop, or dumped and smashed on a bonfire spoil-heap, after a house clearance by bereaved relatives. Treat yourself and buy some English bone china, and savour using it every day.

The Sheaf Market operated on Tuesday, Friday and Saturday each week. Our routine usually involved a trip to the potteries every Wednesday. Thursday was our unloading and sorting day, deciding what wares we'd bring up to the joint for market day. There was always a lot to do: unpacking them from the tea chest, wiping the pots to get dust off them and putting them in large oval display baskets filled with straw. We would also hang tea sets on racks to line the back of the stall for a flash, creating an eye-catching display, sorting oddments and bringing old lines forward to sell to shift them from the warehouse stockroom. It all took time and lots of schleppers in attendance to help lump the gear about. If we had a good day with everyone grafting well, we could clear the work and be on our way home by 2 o'clock on a Thursday.

Fridays and Saturdays were our best days for sales. If we had not had a good week by Friday, (which was quite unusual), we had a big push on Saturday to make good sales and shift a lot of gear, to make our wages up. We liked to make up any shortfall. If we were having a good week we enjoyed a busy Saturday too, pushing for sales, as any extra profit was a bonus.

Travelling to the potteries to buy pots was part of our weekly routine. Most weeks my brother and I journeyed over to Stoke-on-Trent to buy china and pots. I differentiate here with these terms because pottery and china are different. Pot usually refers to earthenware clay, made from a mixture of ball clay, china clay, flint and china stone. Earthenware is porous in its natural state and has to be coated with slip, (a liquid clay mixture with additives, often colours) and then glazed to create an impermeable coating to finish the ware. Then it is fired.

Bone china is made from a mixture of china stone and china clay with the addition of animal bone, which results in vessels with a pure ivory white, translucent finish. Bone china is a type of hard-paste porcelain. In my view bone china is altogether more fragile and beautiful, and in some ways more durable for all its fragility.

The potteries were once a flourishing industry, making the best bone china in the world, and exporting it to countries far and wide. What pleasure the potters must have taken producing those wares that were sent around the globe, and which many people used every day.

To drink your tea from a china cup is an affordable way of acknowledging everyday artists, those craftspeople who produce items which are both beautiful and useful.

There was one potbank[126], I think it might have been the Roslyn or Grafton works, where they used to wrap up each piece of china in tissue paper before placing it in the baskets for collection. I used to like this attention to detail, thrilled to reflect on what an amazing homage to craftsmanship this was, to value each discrete piece of bone china, wrapping it so carefully ready for transportation.

My father had been buying pots from the potteries for years and was well known. He had an excellent reputation as a good payer and as a good salesman. He told us it had been known for managers of potbanks to call up or send a telegram, asking if Mr. Edwards could come and buy some pots, as they needed money for wages when things were tight, especially just after the war. We were also able to trade off his good name, into the 1960s.

When I went to the market with my father he told us tales of what pots he had bought, and what factories had been producing in his earlier days. He told us he used to buy pots from Taylor and Kent, Thos. C Wild, Thomas Forester & Sons Ltd., Samuel Bridgewood — particularly *Indian Tree* patterns, and Empire Porcelain Co. He was very knowledgeable, and could tell you what factory had produced which pot by the cup shape, colours or decoration. In his day much of the

---

126 potbank, pot bank (n)-pottery manufacturer, refers specifically to the buildings in which pots were produced, workshops, factory

decoration was still hand-painted too, and he knew some of the decorators. The potbanks were housed in some interesting old buildings, with wide coach arches and great swinging doors.

Trade was good and our stock needed topping up regularly. At the back of the market in the Rag and Tag was our warehouse, where we stored our gear. It was down a steep roadway, we called it the catacombs, and behind great double wooden doors we had our stockpiles of pots, which we regularly bought from the various pot factors and manufacturers at Stoke-on-Trent. We stored them in tea chests, great square boxes which were lined with straw to keep the fragile pots safe from breakages. Some plates were lined up in dozens on the floor. They were not there for long, as we moved them up to the stall for sale. Pots don't store well in cold damp conditions, and it can cause the glaze to crackle, detracting from the look and value. We liked to shift them quick, as new stock came in regularly.

I loved going to the potteries and spotting a new line or new design that might sell, it always excited me. There was no better feeling than coming away with purchased treasures, lined up in dozens. We always worked in dozens; even when the metric trends came in, we worked in dozens and half dozens. The factors were the same: they'd often offer us a special deal on a gross of dinner plates or tea plates.

As a child I often accompanied my father to the potteries, but I remember most vividly journeying over the hills across to Stoke-on-Trent with my brother, Bill. We went into business together in the early 1960s, and were partners for some time, until we went our separate ways when it became more difficult to make a living in the new Sheaf Market.

Typically at busy times we'd go on Wednesdays and buy enough gear to stock all the stalls for the coming week. We traded with factors — middle men who traded with the manufacturers direct. This meant we could buy pots from various different companies without traipsing round to separate firms. In those days the journey to Stoke-on-Trent was an all day event; it was like going to Russia. We set off early in the morning with our rattling empty Bedford lorry, a big three-tonner. We never stopped en route; we always wanted to get there early, to have the pick of what was on offer. The Bedford was basic, but solid, with room for three in the front. The best seat in the Bedford was in the middle over the engine: your backside could soak up the heat from the metal engine cover, which was especially welcome in winter.

I always felt excited when we came down over the hills into Stoke-on-Trent, which were usually shrouded in mist. As we descended we saw the smoking, smouldering bottle ovens of the potteries, with their fat bases and conical spires pepper-potting the landscape. The canvas before us was a monotone scene: tones of grey and black daubed like a child's finger painting, clumsy smudges of charcoal black spiralling across the sky, and white clouds blanked out by great thick smudges of black smoke, softening as it drifted into up higher grey wisps. The tall, bulbous chimneys and bottle ovens were scattered in all directions; they crowded chock-full across the scene before us, sending teeming coils of polluting smoke into the sky.

It wasn't a pretty picture, but it was familiar to us and was an essential part of our livelihood. We came in on the old Weston Coyney Road (it was the only way we could find our way round) and we had a fairly standard round of calls to make. Stoke is confusing with its six towns which are linked: Longton, Burslem, Hanley, Fenton, Longton and Tunstall. The Stoke-on-Trent potteries sprang up because of the readily available natural clays to be found in those parts. The land was dug wherever clay was to be found, leaving open marl[127] pits.

By the sixties I often accompanied Bill to the potteries. It was a welcome weekly ritual. We were creatures of habit and our rounds to the factors and potbanks were nearly always the same, with little variation. One seller we always visited first was Arthur Mac, at Longton. I'm not sure what his full name was, perhaps Arthur Macpherson, for we always referred to him as Arthur Mac. You never knew what you might find in his warehouse. We had a reputation as good payers, so we were often proffered ends of lines or overruns on special orders, and we often picked up some lovely quality pieces. We might then visit Stan Simmons, another factor. We bought Paragon china figurines from him and Midwinter pottery, from their factory at Burslem.

When you bought pots, the rep from the company would walk you around the display room, showing you the latest designs. If you wanted any, they'd chalk a mark on a pile of pots with a special china pencil, marking them as part of your load.

---

127 marl (n)- clay, clay deposits mixed with other substances in the ground

Over the years we often could sniff out what we called 'a line', a good seller. We had something of interest for every pocket and to tempt every eye. Some might just make an impulsive purchase of a sugar bowl and cream jug (sugar and cream), or an earthenware pudding basin, some ornaments, half a dozen water tumblers or a vase. We might sell pairs of breakfast cups and saucers, or a half dozen best china teacups and saucers. Most people could afford something from us and we prided ourselves on the fact that we could always treat them. Some of these smaller items we called 'nailers,' as they guaranteed a customer's interest.

Arthur Mac also took special orders, so we could commission particular designs from him. He had a lot of white-bodied bone china stock that he would add your own design to, and your exact specification of coloured slip and gold decoration. This particular process of taking a white body and adding your own design in production was called a 'shine'. We liked to add a little burnished gold embellishment: a dash of gold down the cup handle, a line to the rim of the cup, to the lower body and to the outer ring of the saucer. When we spotted our pots in people's houses it gave us a little buzz of pride, as we all had our different designs and preferred colours, which we'd had commissioned. 'That's one of our Arthur's.' Or, 'That's one of ours,' we'd utter.

We brothers all had our different preferences and various suppliers, which suited the way we worked. In order to differentiate ourselves from one another, we stocked different gear and we each had our favoured lines. As my brother Arthur worked on the stall next to us, it wouldn't have been sensible to stock the same lines; we tried to appeal to different punters. He had quite a sophisticated, tasteful eye and was perhaps a bit more upmarket than us, stocking more decorative and ornamental pieces. He liked to buy Empire, Imperial, Regency, Coalport, Washington and Duchess china. He also liked to buy figurines made by Cauldon and Caverswall. My brother Joe used to buy Grafton and Balfour china. He also stocked sets of jugs made by Arthur Wood and Co, often in sets of three. Arthur Wood and Co. were known for their semi-porcelain teapots, creamers, jugs, pitchers, ewers, and *Lustreware*. Some were embossed, with fancy handles painted to resemble wooden branches or twigs. Joe sold three jugs for twenty-five bob.

Once we'd bought gear at Arthur Mac's we continued on our rounds. Next on our route around the potteries was Alec Dofsky at Hanley Glass and China Wholesalers, which moved to relocate in Fenton in later years. Then we'd go to J. and G. Meakin, a company memorable to many because of their *Bull in a China Shop* adverts. We bought dinner sets and tea sets from them. Some were fairly traditional, such as *Blue Nordic*. They had also started developing more geometric designs and modern shapes. I particularly remember their tall coffee pots, in designs such as *Eden, Maori, Aztec* and *Allegro*. Probably at that time a dinner set was six quid. I believe eventually Johnson Bros. bought them out.

When we went to fetch teapots they were potentially quite fragile to transport. We found the best way to get them home was to stack them on boards, packing them in quite closely, putting a bit of tissue paper around them to protect the spout. We layered them up: a sandwich of boards, a layer of teapots, another board and so on up to a safe height in the back of the lorry.

Sometimes we called in at Swinnertons; they were known for print and tints. At the factory grounds they had a massive tip, piled high with broken pots — splints, stilts, stems, and broken saggars, which were the shaped clay containers which selections of pots were fired in. The materials were not recyclable once glazed and fired, so the company was left with a lasting by-product.

If we were making good time on our rounds, we would then visit Plex Street Potteries, at Tunstall. Here we bought earthenware, finer dinner sets and tea sets. Plex Street Pottery was one of the first manufacturers to have electric kilns. This method involved the pots being fired through a massive oven, passing through on trays stacked on a long trolley. With the electric kiln the manufacturer could control the temperature, making it rise gradually. In the older potteries, which still used bottle ovens, the greatest risk to the product was when pottery was fired. If there was any miscalculation in temperature, a whole load could be ruined, and that meant lost profits.

We often would chat to a nice lady; she was something to do with the pottery, perhaps she was the owner. She was called Mrs. Rogers and she was in business with her son, Kenneth.

Kenneth had a nervous habit of whistling. It made us laugh

because it was a bit strange. He didn't really whistle proper tunes, they were scales ranging up and down. Our Bill joked that he was going radged[128].

We called one day and Kenneth greeted us. He stood on the threshold, whistling in front of us. He stood swaying and whistling, trilling up and down his scales, and gazing up to the sky, keeping us waiting on the step.

'He's gone doolally,' Bill whispered in my ear, nudging me, trying to stifle laughter.

We owed him about five hundred quid for pots we'd had on a 'sale or return' basis, and we'd come to settle our account. I looked at him whistling; his eyebrows were doing their own dance across his forehead in time with the music.

'I wish he'd lose his bleedin' memory,' I quipped.

Bill pissed himself laughing.

As we trundled round the potteries we could peep into the cobbled yards and see the craftspeople at work. In some yards pots and china were still made in the same way as they had been made for many years. There were the saggar makers, fashioning the containers that pots were placed in for firing, and a bank of women jiggering. This was when they placed a dollop of clay on a wheel and squeezed down to make a plate. We saw them trimming and grinding the wares, called 'fettling,' and painting the wares with coloured slip.

One day I noticed a sweet smell, and I asked one of the girls painting what it was. She smiled and told me it was aniseed, which they used to keep the colours open. This detail fascinated me. How on earth had anyone discovered that the addition of aniseed kept colours open, slowing down the drying time, keeping the paint workable and pliable?

We did not envy the staff their heavy work, lumping the oval saggars around, filling them with pots for firing, or emptying them once pots had been fired. I most liked to glimpse the skilled decorators painting on tiny flowers and swirls. They delicately swished their sable

128 radged (adj)-mad, crazy, barmy, nutty (slang)

brushes in the bright slip paints, adding a twist of greenery or dotted flowers, that stood out from the flat surface, brightly embossed, even brighter when fired. Most skilled were the gilders, adding flourishes, dots and twists of real gold with exquisite precision, not wasting any precious drops as they burnished the edges of cups or plates, sprinkling the surface delicately with sand to complete the burnishing process.

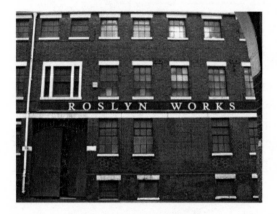

**Roslyn Works, Longton,
Picture taken 2006**

Once when we were in Longton, at the Roslyn Works, one of our helpers, Joss, stepped off the back of the lorry when he was carrying a basket (we called them kipseys) of cups. The works manager was a massive bloke; we'd typically call someone like him a *big sterricker*[129], for he was well built and strong and had the physique of a fighting man. He was eccentric and wore an old fashioned overcoat, and sported a tall hat with a big peacock feather in it. It was no stretch to him to twirl a basket up onto his shoulders and to lodge it on the tail of the wagon.

Joss was not going to be outdone, and when the bloke urged him not to carry the basket, as it was too heavy, he ignored him. Baskets were about three feet long, oval-shaped, packed with straw and china, and extremely heavy when full. Joss turned the basket up onto his shoulder and rested it against the tailgate of the lorry. He jumped onto the back of the lorry, then stood up, attempting to pick up the basket again, trying to heave it round onto his shoulder, but it was too weighty. His body twisted and buckled and the whole basket came crashing down at an angle, falling from the back of the lorry, cups tumbling and smashing, clouds of straw dust and china pieces rolling into the road. Joss went flying, losing his balance too and practically somersaulted off the back of the lorry. Workers from the potbanks came out to see what the noise

---

129 sterricker (n)-a big, heavy, fit man, capable of fighting (market slang)

was. We'd already paid for the china, so we had to stand the loss ourselves. It was just one of those things. We didn't like to reprimand him too hard; he was like one of the family.

My brother Joe had a good pal in the potteries, called Les Lockett. I occasionally went to the potteries with Joe. This was something of an outing as Joe was a good twenty years older than me, and a seasoned businessman. Joe was always a bit flash too, so travelling with him offered me the opportunity to see him showing off, which was always amusing. He could flirt with any bird from behind the wheel. Joe took me to Les Lockett's workshop and introduced me to Les and we shook hands. Les was probably a similar age to Joe. I'm not being funny, but to me, though probably only in their forties, they already seemed to be old men. I was probably in my twenties at this time, so anyone over twenty-five was knocking on.

Joe couldn't resist telling me about Les's war record. Apparently he'd fibbed about his age to get into North Staffordshire Regiment in 1937, becoming a distinguished serviceman, and he'd been selected to be a fighter in Churchill's elite corps and joined the 151/156 battalion. He was one of the first paratroopers who parachuted into Holland in the Battle of Arnhem, in September 1944, and he'd been dropped behind enemy lines on other occasions. Les served in Germany, Palestine and India. In 1945 he left the military and went back into civvy street. Once retired from the army, Les often returned to Holland, to recreate the 3,500-ft leap he originally made in Field Marshal Montgomery's operation in Arnhem, 1944, (Operation Market Garden).

Latterly Les had a workshop at Longton, finishing pots, decorating, and producing designs to customer orders. Les Lockett was something of an innovator in the potteries: he was the first one to introduce an electric intermittent kiln. Up until this time all bottle ovens were coal-fired and the firing process was unpredictable. Les came upon his innovative discovery through experimentation. First he built a working prototype on a farm, collecting old bedsteads and junk scrap metal for the casing. He then travelled to Sheffield to pick up elements for the electric heating part of the design. He built the firing box, got an electrician to rig up the heating elements and fired it up. The kiln worked! He then improved upon the design when he built a larger electric kiln in his factory, which is still in use to this day. Other manufacturers followed his example and adopted such designs.

Les had also discovered his own technique for making burgundy colours hold fast on china, adhering properly after firing. Until this time, working with burgundy slip could be difficult; it was very brittle and subject to cracking and flaking. Les found a way to keep it on the pots, making such decorated ware all the more durable. Others adopted this practice too.

We all got to know him gradually, as Joe had introduced us all to him. Eventually we added him to the round too and we'd all call to buy from him, enjoying being shown around his workshop, delighting in the latest designs to come out from his team. We had many dealings with him and his sons over the years.

One day Bill and I called in to see Les at his workshop. He came out into the yard to greet us, as we all knew him by now, and we stood catching up chatting for a while. He then showed us round and invited us to see his new lines. Bill couldn't resist emphasising the details of Les's war record to me. Bill was very interested in Les's stories too, as he had something in common with him, having been behind enemy lines himself.

I eyed Les, looking at this chap before me, greying, balding, with his rather portly, roundish figure. I didn't wish to be uncharitable, but it was difficult to square the man before me with the picture of this great hero that Bill had painted. Les nodded and smiled at me. He was very affable, and was not at all conceited about his war exploits. Bill told me how Les was dropped behind enemy lines. I nodded, trying to look interested.

As we talked we stood in the cobbled courtyard of Les's potbank and workshop. Around the open courtyard were long two-storey buildings. As was often usual, the decorating rooms were up at the top and the clay rooms were below. The decorating rooms were up high, out of the way of the dust and filth. In order to reach these rooms the decorators had to climb up a wooden staircase, which was fixed to the outer wall of the building. It took them up eight or ten feet, to a rickety wooden landing and the entrance to the workshops above.

Bill nudged Les, saying, 'Show him.'

I wondered just what this old chap could show me. Les started to dash up the stairs. At first he walked; then with some speed he shot up first few steps of the stairs, running, building the pace, and then he shinned up the set of rickety wooden stairs on the outside of the building. He seemed quite fit. I looked up, shielding my eyes from the sun. He was standing on the landing at the top of the stairs, leaning over the handrail, waving at us. He must have been about ten feet off the ground.

He smiled at me, waved again, and then like a rag doll, he just threw himself over the rail, dropping down off the top. I gasped, fearing for his safety. As he fell, his whole body seemed to soften and curl over into a relaxed ball. I watched him fold gracefully, his body twisting and turning with real poise. He suddenly finished with a commando roll, bobbing up in front of me, landing on his feet. I jolted and was amazed at his skill and fitness.

'Chuffin' 'ell!'

Les Lockett and Mick Edwards, March 2006

Bill laughed, slapping me on the back. He'd enjoyed seeing the shock on my face, as I thought Les was going to come a cropper.

'Good that, in't it? There's life in the old bugger yet. He's as fit as a butcher's dog, tha knows.'

I glanced at Les. It was a good lesson: Never judge by appearances alone.

I met Les again in 2006, when I was seventy, during a nostalgic trip to the potteries for my seventieth birthday. I'd not seen him for many years. By then he was probably over 80, still looking dapper and immaculately turned out with his pressed trousers with military-precision creases, smart blazer, crisp shirt and regimental tie and highly polished shoes. He had the look of a distinguished military man even then. He was still trading and had a thriving decorating business at his workshop in Longton, having now brought his family into the business too.[130]

We never ate very well in Stoke; it wasn't many miles away, but the food seemed very different to us. They ate oat cakes instead of sandwiches, and even the tea they made tasted foul. Everywhere we went they served tea with the addition of UHT sterilised milk, from long tall bottles with narrow stems, which we nicknamed 'monkey milk'. It spoiled a good cup of tea in our view. Every time we went to Stoke our schlepper, Joss, moaned, 'They scran[131] funny here.'

Occasionally we'd call for a bite to eat on the way home. One day, coming back from the potteries we called in at a little place, Millers Café, at Buxton. Joss deciphered the menu, holding it in his grubby hands and he announced that he was going to have 'Welsh Rabbit'. Bill and I ordered large servings of steak pie with chips and veg. We chatted as we waited to be served. The waitress flounced up with a tray heaving with plates and condiments. We could hardly see her face through the steam wafting up from hot piles of veg. We were famished. She set down the plates and we tucked in. Bill and I stopped eating, as we realised Joss was staring at his plate, poking at his meal with his knife. He pulled a face and started to slowly pick at his food, blowing on it, to cool it down.

'Nitto, don't blow on it. It's posh 'ere! Waft it with thi cap,' said Bill.

There was hell to pay when the waitress came past a minute later. Joss glared at her, chirping indignantly, 'Ey, up. I ordered Welsh Rabbit, love, not cheese on toast.'

Bill pointed out 'Welsh Rarebit' listed on the menu, but Joss wasn't having any of it. He complained bitterly all through the meal about how he'd been conned and he'd been looking forward to a bit of rabbit.

'Don't be a mardy arse, Joss. Get it down thi. It's grub in't it? Or does tha want summat else?'

---

130 Sadly Les Lockett passed away on 1st July 2009.
131 scran (v)-to eat

'I'll eat it. But I wanted rabbit! They need to sort their sens out 'ere. They've made a reight ricket[132] wi' my bleedin' order!' he grumbled.

Bill splashed a few chips onto Joss's plate to compensate him. He ate his food, harrumphing all the while.

'How's the chips, Joss?' I asked.

'Like bleedin' toe nails.'

Most often we'd drive home with our stomachs rumbling, saving ourselves for some good Yorkshire scran back home. The trip back was always long and slow, the big Bedford van much heavier now laden with pots, crawling up the hills, the engine labouring under the weight of the load. Often it was dark by the time we got back.

Sometimes in the summer, when it was still light, we might come home through Heeley, calling in at Taggy's Ice Cream; a lone house on a hill; an oasis of enterprise in a rather rundown area. Taggy's was a small operation, run from a place with outhouses and a yard, but they made lovely ice cream, pure white and rich tasting. Our Bill loved it. He said the same thing every time we bought it: 'I could eat a bleedin' bucket full.' Occasionally we arrived when they were just packing up, but they knew us and would open the door and serve us. Small, refined cornets were not our style. Bill used to grab pudding basins out of the back of the lorry, wiping them clean with fresh straw and handing them over the counter he'd say, 'Fill us them up, love. We're famished.' We sat in the lorry enjoying each mouthful. 'This is double reight[133],' said Bill.

On our return from the potteries we often spent the next few days unpacking tea chests, which was hard work, storing the pots in the warehouse, bringing the tea sets and combos up onto wire frames to display them, and choosing which items we would start sales with in the coming week.

---

132 ricket (n)-mistake, error (slang)
133 double reight (adj)- double right, exceptionally good (market slang)

−10−
IN BUSINESS WITH BILL

My father always used to say: 'Never go into partnership with anyone'. His favourite phrase in relation to this subject was: 'Partnerships are battleships'. I heeded this generally, but did not have any worries at all when I went into business with my older brother, Bill. In the 1960s we formed our business partnership, sharing responsibility for the running of the stall in Sheaf Market and the purchasing of goods.

Bill was laid back, good humoured, cheerful, calm, and was relaxed and unhurried about work and his chosen profession. Bill had done his bit in the war; he'd been in active service, had seen some real action and so he was entitled to be a bit laid back, in my book. After being something of an action man in his younger days, he settled into married life with his wife, Madge, and son, Robert, and was a home bird.

He was a man of quiet pleasures; he didn't drink, but would sip at a pint of lemonade; he liked to read books and he loved to write. He wrote saucy and witty doggerel poems. He told wonderful stories of his adventures, and could bring anecdotes to life with his animated face and sparkling eyes, expressive actions and irreverent gestures. He had a deep mellow voice, that you couldn't resist listening to with all your attention. In another life he could have been a writer or a comedian, but for now he was selling pots in the market. He liked to saunter down there to his work at 10 o'clock and go home to Madge and Robert promptly at teatime, sit down to his steak and chips and have a fairly quiet life. Bill even gave up some vices, such as his cigarettes. For many years he smoked *Three Castles* cigarettes, sixty a day. He gave them up when he lit up in his sleep and set the bed on fire...

Bill aged 18 (1944)

I noticed that Bill never went away on holiday, always preferring to stay at home, and I asked him about it one day, wondering about his reluctance to stray very far from the locality.

'Why don't you ever go away, Bill?' I chimed.

'I went away.'

'Where to? Where did you go?' I asked.

'I went away... from nineteen forty-two to nineteen forty-five.'

That shut me up. Fair enough, I thought. End of story.

We have two old photographs of Bill as a young man in his army uniform, with scrawled writing on the back, *Amiens and St. Albert, France*; both dated 1944. Mam used to pray that he'd be safe and he

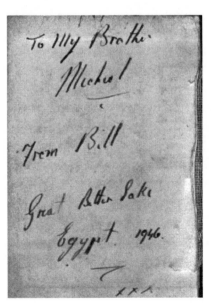

was, which was some feat as he was a corporal sniper, so presumably his life expectancy was not considered to be great. She bought Joe, Bill and Arthur gold crosses, and asked them to wear them whilst in the forces.

I always had a special relationship with Bill. He was closest in age to me and always looked out for me when I was a kid. I wrote to him so often, when he was away, that even to this day, I can still remember his service number, which I scribbled on every letter I addressed to him.

Bill brought me a bible back from Egypt, which I treasured. It had a carved wooden frontispiece and was inscribed with his lovely curlicue handwriting:

THE POTTY EDWARDS

To my brother Michael from Bill, Egypt 1946

When Bill first went into the army he was in the Royal Northumberland Fusiliers (RNF), then he was transferred to the King's Royal Rifles (KRRs). Bill had seen lots of awful things, which did not seem to dull his humour. He was very resilient, and self-deprecating, not one to sing his own praises, though he must have been very courageous. He'd seen friends injured, and had experienced a man being killed instantly whilst standing right next to him, when the bullet from an enemy sniper blew off his head.

Generally Bill put his war time past behind him, and adjusted to civvy life well. I asked him if he'd ever had counselling to deal with what he may have experienced during the war. He just raised his eyebrows and laughed at me. 'Counselling? Tha must be joking. We just got a kick up t' arse and were told to get on wi' it!'

His favourite saying was: 'If in danger, if in doubt, screw the nut and brass it out.' He once told me of the time when he was stranded down a drain-hole under a grate-cover, deep down a shaft in the ground, with a temporary camp of Germans around him. He spent four days down the hole, staying still and silent to stay alive, with only a tin of salmon for sustenance and no water to drink. There was talk in the family of him being awarded a medal by the Dutch government, Queen Wilhemina's Medal, or honourable mention in dispatches, but we can find no trace of, or any reference to either. Bill would not have made false claims about such a thing; we just wish we had more information.

Bill had been billeted with the Derieck family in Belgium, and he continued to correspond with them for many years after the war. The Derieck family were toy manufacturers, specialising in old-fashioned wooden toys.

Bill cited as one of his reasons for joining up, the death of our grandfather during the Blitz, on 15th December 1940. He never expressed much belligerence towards the Germans, but he was a little affronted by the bombing of our Grandad's home and shop, saying to me, 'They killed our Grandad. They dropped a bomb on his house at fifty-one Broomhall Street, where he had a china shop, warehouse and stables. They killed his horse as well. And the buggers broke most of his pots. I was not amused! I went a bit potty!'

It is said when Grandfather died on this night, aged seventy, he was found without a mark on him. He'd been killed when a beam fell across his body during the bombing. There was talk that he'd had a quick and painless death — which seemed fitting, as he was known to be a religious man — and had been spared any suffering it seems. He had a mission hut, and undertook charity work with children in the local area.

Before Bill went into the army he used to work for G.P. Wright's, a glass and china wholesalers, near Endcliffe Park. When an American bomber crashed in the park, Bill had been one of the first on the scene to give assistance.

Bill reached the rank of corporal, and was offered a commission to stay on at the end of the war, and he could have developed a good military career, but he wanted to sell pots in markets. He did not collect his medals after the war, feeling that for him to collect them did not effectively honour enough those who had been killed alongside him.[134] If Bill had accepted the commission he would have been retiring aged fifty with a good pension, but he preferred working the gaffs[135]. What a way to get a living...

When Bill was demobbed, the army gave him a set of clothes, a navy suit, shirt and overcoat. The first day Bill went out in his demob suit it rained, and he found that his crisp white shirt was streaked with navy blue dye, rivulets of deep blue snaking down his chest as the dye ran out of the fabric. The clothes were ruined and his government outfit went straight in the bin. He was philosophical about the cheap suit he'd been issued with, after fighting for his country, if a little irritated.

He joined father on the markets and soon had enough money to buy a new set of clothes. It was hard to get hold of gear to sell, but Bill had a good relationship with a factor called Clough, and managed to buy some of Meakin's *Celeste,* which kept him going for a while.

In spite of our differences in age and personality we got on well, and our characters complemented each other. I was ten years younger than Bill. I was chirpy and bouncy, ambitious, chippy, sparky, a bit of a go-getter. Bill was more laid back and philosophical, and brought me down to earth when I got too keen. The business went well, and

---

134 Bill's son, Robert, sent for the medals after Bill died in October 1997.
135 gaffs (n)-markets (market slang)

at one stage we had even branched out into having two shops. For a brief period we had a toyshop in the market too, at the top of the alley. We sold toys and cheaply priced goods. We could trade from two sides, and there was a fair-sized storage area at the back of the shop. Eventually we split it up, making two shop fronts, one facing each alley, and passed on one side of the shop, the best side, to Joe Bennett for a small rent, and he used it for selling his goods.

I valued Bill's opinions. Bill had more experience than I did on the markets, and over the years he had formed some views on how to spot crates[136]. These people were relatively harmless, though eccentric, and in the quiet periods we chatted to them quite happily, but when it was 'spark on', when punters were in a buying mood and we were taking money, we didn't like anyone wasting our time when we could be selling. Bill took it upon himself to mark my card regarding the physical attributes, behaviours and visible signs of such people.

He warned me not to get too involved gassing with any men with more than one pen in their top pockets. One pen was fine, any more, lined up, (often in descending size order) was most likely indicative of an obsessive personality. He also warned me against the frowsty women who wore more than one ring on their hands; those who wore a ring on each finger were definitely not compos mentis, and were capable of loose morals, insanity or extreme deviousness, in his book. In addition a stack of rings on each finger meant he'd advise you to give them a very wide berth, as they were a complete potty lot[137].

He dismissed such punters if they approached when we were busy, urging me to ignore them by whispering at me, 'Oy, oy, meshugenah[138] to the right. Bottle 'em!' By ignoring them, we avoided being drawn into their fatuous conversation. He was not a trained psychologist, but I have to say his observations have held true over the years.

His philosophical and psychological observations also extended to other areas. For example he believed he could predict character, as indicated by the colour a house might be painted (therefore never shack up with anyone who favours pink, purple or turquoise gloss paint); political affiliation as denoted by footwear (Loake's and

---

136 crates (n)-chumps, (rhyming slang-crates of lump)
137 potty lot-crazy person, nutter (Potty slang)
138 meschugenah, meshugeneh (meshugena, er) (n)-nutter, crazy person, eccentric person (Yiddish)

Church's Oxfords or brogues preferred, as opposed to sandals); and intellectual ability, as signified by hairstyle. Moreover, last but not least, he reckoned social class might reliably be indicated by the absence or presence of net curtaining.

He also had views on appropriate attire; his army training left him valuing clean and highly polished shoes and he'd glance down to check out someone's shoes as he talked to them. In his view, anyone who couldn't be bothered to polish his or her shoes was a drek[139].

He also had a theory regarding the cleanliness of hotels or letties, as we called them, suggesting that I might derive a clear indication of cleanliness from whether or not they had plants in the window bottom. He strongly advocated plant-free letties for an overnight stay, as they were cleanest. If there was little choice available and we had to plump for a room, they needed to be fully inspected and plant-loving establishments needed careful checking out. He suggested that ideally such hostelries were to be avoided, as they were often lacking in cleanliness throughout the whole place; for example, they might never change the sheets from one customer to the next, and the bed itself might well be schmatty[140] or chatty. If I had to settle on an overnight stay, he said I might stay somewhere where they had geraniums and mother-in-law's tongue plants on display, at a push; however, cacti of all varieties were to be avoided, as cacti lovers were dirty devils.

I had the opportunity to test this theory out during the 1960s, when we went travelling to sell our pots at various fairs throughout the country, and I admit Bill's theory had some predictive validity. Unfortunately the theory came a cropper when I went off to work in Germany in the 1970s, as many German hotels have cacti in the windows. Indeed you'd be hard pushed to find hotels there which don't host a regiment of plants, standing to attention, in every window bottom. Still, our Bill was busy winning wars on his travels abroad, and did not have time to develop any cross-cultural hypotheses.

Bill and I stocked a wide range of bone china, pottery and glass.

---

139 drek (n)-trashy person (Yiddish) from German *Dreck*-trash, dirt, filth
140 schmatty (adj)-dirty, very dirty as often derived from faeces (market slang)

We used to buy Enoch Wedgwood pottery; it was a blue and white print with country scenes. Typically sets consisted of six dinner plates, six sweet dishes, six four and a half inch tea plates, six cups and saucers; thirty bob the lot. We also bought Sadler's teapots, brown high glossed earthenware for everyday use, and Paragon bone china tea and dinner sets. We stocked a few figurines and ornaments: Radnor china fancies, Hammersley china, and Adderley fine china miniatures with their delicately hand-painted floral patterns. We had bone china dinner services and tea services from many manufacturers.

We always needed a few pitch pullers from the potteries — different wares at bargain prices that got people standing around watching with interest. We used Sylvac figures, little Wade animals, and any oddments we had, such as bone china tureens, which were already going out of fashion a little, even in the sixies. People didn't want to bother with heavy covered tureens, and open vegetable dishes were becoming the norm for serving hot food.

Our best lines in the 1960s were harlequin sets, six cups and saucers, which we bought from Les Lockett in Longton. He had white bone china, which he decorated in six different bright colours. They sold well; they were flying machines. He couldn't keep up with us. The colours were usually green, red, black, blue, yellow, and pink, but sometimes varied depending on what slips he had in stock.

Buying and selling could get complicated. You had to know what you were doing, tracking the buying prices and then working out sales prices. We noted everything down in a little logbook. Often we topped up sets with matching additions, so often dinner sets had vegetable sets too, if customers wanted to add to a collection. A veg set consisted of two vegetable dishes, uncovered, or two tureens with a lid, a sauce boat and stand, six soup cups and stands, six dinner plates of ten inches diameter, six fish plates of nine inches diameter, and six eight-inch breakfast plates. Confusingly we called the ten-inch an eight-inch plate, the nine-inch a seven-inch, and the eight-inch was called a six-inch plate. Veg sets also came with a large meat dish. Rarely could you get settings for six people; the accepted number of place settings was twelve for a proper dinner service. A very old fashioned traditional set might also include three meat dishes and a large turkey platter.

We also sold combination sets or 'combos' as we called them, which were a more modern interpretation of a dinner service, consisting of six ten-inch dinner plates, six nine-inch dinner plates, six oatmeals (dishes), six cups, six saucers, and six tea plates. A decent set from us might have cost you three knicker[141]. Popular sets were manufactured by Midwinter and Barratts of Staffordshire Ltd. We never provided a teapot with a tea service. That was something that you had to purchase separately. They were good sellers. People still used tea leaves to mash their tea, and you needed a teapot for when family came to call. We joked to the punters when we sold them, saying, 'Is the vicar coming round, love? He'll have a right flash wi' that. It's a lovely un, that.'

We both loved china, and sometimes we could not part with what we'd bought. We went round a factor's one day and I spotted a lovely hand-painted Paragon ornament of a young boy with blonde hair sitting on a dais. I turned it over to see the stamp mark and the name of the piece, 'David', my son's name. I had to have it and bought it for myself, knowing this fine piece would never get onto the stall.

Our father had been selling pots for years and not surprisingly he had developed likes and dislikes and irrational preferences. Bill and I once went to the potteries together on a buying reccy. We came back with a load of china that we'd bought quite reasonably. We proudly showed my father, thinking we'd made quite a trade, but of course we had forgotten to pay attention to the pattern, and he poo-pooed our purchase, criticising the unlucky birds on each piece. Dad had some funny peccadilloes; he hated any items with bird motifs, believing them to be great harbingers of bad luck. He'd glare at us if we brought pots or china back from the potteries with birds on, shaking his head and looking at us all as if we were idiots, saying, 'They're bad mazl[142]. What you got them for? They'll never sell. What's up wi' thi, ar' tha radged?'

Luckily the townsfolk of Sheffield were not as superstitious about birds, and we sold all the china and made a tidy profit. Since then I've noticed that many northerners are superstitious about birds as

141 knicker, nicker (n)-pound(s) (slang)
142 mazl (n)-luck, good fortune (Yiddish origin)

portents of bad luck. My mother-in-law used to say it was unlucky to have birds on your curtain fabric too. Perhaps it's a Sheffield thing.

We got stuck with some of Dad's old stock, notably meat dishes, which were piled high around the warehouse. Apparently during the war many china manufacturers still made meat dishes even though meat was scarce. They still had the patterns and moulds and were reluctant to abandon the investment they'd made in having them cast. Of course little meat was available so they had a stockpile of them, and they couldn't easily start to manufacture other wares that would be more popular with customers, instead.

When father went to buy pots during the war and just after the war, the salesperson used to let him have tea sets only on the condition that he would also buy a few meat dishes off them too. They needed to run down their stocks. He used to have to buy four or five-dozen meat dishes, to get his hands on tea sets. We couldn't shift the damn things either, and we ended up with a load in the warehouse. We only ever sold them at Christmas. A motley selection of meat plates were stacked high in our warehouse for years. Eventually we tired of waiting for them to come back into fashion and we sold them to Aaron Patnick. He had an antiques and bric-a-brac warehouse on Langsett Road.

During the war it was only possible to get plain white china or 'lump,' third grade china. The makers must have been prevented from adding coloured decoration, as it wasted materials and precious fuel during the firing process.

Apparently just after the war, pots of any sort were hard to come by, and you had to persevere and build good relationships with the firms to get your hands on any stock at all. Joe Bennett persevered with the works manager of the Midwinter factory. They got chatting and it turned out that his daughter was a nun at Notre Dame School, Hillsborough. Joe offered to act as go-between, ferrying letters to and fro on his travels, and he took small gifts to her. He particularly remembered her delight at the delivery of a small packet of biscuits. Joe's kindness and perseverance paid off, and as soon as the gent was able to release any coloured pottery of any note, Joe was offered a selection of the precious pieces. People were itching to buy colour-glazed pottery after the war, tired of the bleak utility mentality.

During the 1940s, the Midwinter factory worked hard to improve the ware and the quality improved immensely. Joe sold Midwinter's *Red Domino* pattern. He had a little morning tea set for two people, with two cups and saucers, two side plates, and a dinky teapot and sugar and cream. He sold a few to us and we christened it a 'love set'. We tried selling them at twenty-five bob, but then we dropped the price to a pound and they flew out.

Our Bill would chirp to the women buying, 'Watch yoursen wi' that, love, it's what we call a love set. Very nice. Serve him wi' that int' morning and it might get 'im at it. Pop down to Mr. Huntridge and see if he'll sell thi a few grams o' Bromide an' all.' The women would giggle, but Bill's cheek never put them off their purchases.

In our day the manager at Midwinter was Mr. Handley. The Midwinter firm also engaged popular decorators with excellent reputations, building the wares into something of fashion statements by the 1960s. Nowadays Midwinter is very collectable. They made lovely holloware, which was matte black. I liked their *Nature Study* design, which had delicate line drawings of insects, leaves and dragonflies upon it. I wish I had a full set now. Many Midwinter patterns were popular: *Cannes, Spanish Garden,* and their *Stylecraft* shape. The porcelain was glazed earthenware and was quite durable, being more substantial and weighty than bone china.

Midwinter made pottery for export too, and sometimes they had excess pieces, made in case any of the order did not fire well. We had a good relationship with them, and we'd buy the excess pieces, often at a fraction of the proper price.

I remember one of the best sellers of Midwinter was a design called *Happy Valley*. It was a cream body with a blue print of a village scene, a sort of modern take on the old blue and white ware. A whole set of it might consist of a dinner set, coffee set, fruit set, a set of three jugs, and a teapot. We sold the lot for twelve quid. In the shops in town it would have cost you twenty quid. It was a good seller.

If you've got a complete set as above, all sound and perfect, I'd love to see it again. I'd give you three times what you paid for it!

J. and G. Meakin made some good gear; we sold a lot of their tea sets. We bought on wholesale discount from them, as we were good punters and we bought an awful lot of their sets from them. Probably our best sellers of theirs were eighteen-piece tea sets consisting of six cups, six saucers and six tea plates. An eighteen-piece set might have cost you twenty-five bob from us. We had a lot of eighteen-piece sets, but sometimes we picked up twenty-one pieces, which were the same as eighteen pieces with the addition of a sugar and cream, and bread and butter plate. We usually married these up with dinner services, selling them together. Twenty-one piece sets might have been two quid from the shops in town. We probably sold a set for thirty bob.

Normally when my father used to purchase pots from the potters in Stoke-on-Trent he bought their finished designs. Bill and I branched out a bit and we built relationships with some small potteries that would do our bidding. In this way we developed what we called 'shines'; this was when we purchased cups with a basic white body and commissioned our own simple designs. Bill would pop into the pottery with a few scribbles on a fag packet, and a few weeks later we'd be collecting baskets of pots, with coloured decoration to our own designs, bearing our own patterns. We sold a lot of them. In the 1960s pastel coloured backgrounds were popular: pale pink, pale blue, pale lemon and pale green. We were sick of punters asking us if we had such and such a design in blue, when it only came in pink, so we had been noting what sold and we set to work. Our designs were pastel backgrounds with burnished gold trim, little dots or tiny gold stars, in a band of decoration on the outer top of the cup and in the middle of the saucer rim. It was great to get a schlepper to hand us down a tea set in a colour requested.

'Joss, hand us that pink set for this good-looking lady,' Bill would chirp. He reckoned it always paid to give the punters a bit of 'toffee'. [143]

Occasionally we got gear very cheap, and we always used to congratulate ourselves as we drove home from the potteries, saying how we'd 'spraffed' it or 'begged' it. Spraffing gear meant you had purchased it for a ridiculously low price. This meant we might be able to sell it for a considerable profit. It was good to get a bit of discount down to the 'old pals act,' now and then. I popped into Bridgwoods one day, and spotted a dozen bone china plates with a picture of a lad in a cornfield painted on them. I spraffed a dozen. I think most of my

---

143 toffee-flattery, praise (market slang)

relatives got a plate for their wall that Christmas. I still have mine, and enjoy looking at it, never tiring of the scene.

One time, I called in at a little sweet factory, next to one pottery we used to buy from. I think I was cheekily hoping I might tap them for a few spice. I got chatting to a lady potter next door who was making little jugs by hand.

'That's nice,' I said, offering her a sweet, and pointing to a little pot which was of brown clay.

'Oh, that old thing. You can have it,' she said handing it to me.

I took it from her and thanked her. I liked the fact that I could still see the thumb prints in the clay. I've still got it, and I used it as a shaving jug for years.

Bill liked to predict our potential sales as we made our way to the market each day. Certain cars were considered portents of poor sales. If we passed more than one Reliant Robin, his mood would drop and he'd bewail our chances of making any money, 'T' ruddy plunder snatchers are out in force today. That's two Robins I've spotted round Fitzalan Square. It's going to be a bad day, ah tell thi. We're going to tek nowt!'

Bill had some very amusing turns of phrase. He referred to plunder-snatchers as 'P.S.es', so he could refer to them when they were right by the joint wanting cheap bargains. They were the sort of punters who wanted the world for a penny or two, and always wanted something for nothing.

The types of women who bustled up in their jazzy headscarves, smoking a fag, who fired questions at him for five minutes, who then avoided buying anything, particularly amused Bill. He referred to them as Mrs. Altellas; (this is not a corruption of an Italian name). After he'd spent time and energy telling them about wares, they always started moving backwards to evade making a purchase, issuing their parting phrase to him, referring to their mystical absent friends, 'Ta duck, I'll tell her.' Mrs. Altella usually came with her friend

Mrs. Tisnice[144]. After each pot demonstrated to her, she'd warble, 'Mmn, 'tis nice.' They were harmless and we found them entertaining. You have to expect schnorrers[145] if you work the gaffs.

On the days when the market was closed, we were busy with our delivery rounds. If people bought tea sets and dinner sets, we always delivered the heavier items directly to their door, and we'd write names and addresses along with details of their order in a notebook with its dog-eared, duplicate pages. We knew most areas in Sheffield and you'd be amazed at the extent of our delivery round. On a full dinner set, (which comprised of a dinner set, tea set, fruit set and coffee set, which might cost twelve pounds in total), we'd charge two pounds deposit on the day of sale and we'd collect the balance on delivery. In those days even some of the poorest people had bone china in their homes.

Our Bill marked my card early on, telling me to always be polite to the billies[146]. (Bill often referred to punters as billies.) He told me to watch out for any vicious dogs, wipe my feet on the mat if there was one, and to refuse anything offered, tea or food. He said we had to move on and get cracking on the delivery round, and anyway at some of the places hygiene was something to be desired, we didn't want to 'cop[147] for something'.

We saw some sights: homes with no carpets and just newspapers or sawdust on the floor; tea tables littered with jam jars which where used as everyday teacups; homes where the cats and dogs had the complete run of the place, including some places where the animals looked much better fed than the people. Bill could not resist commenting to me on our rounds, 'Did you clock[148] how thin that geezer was? Looks like he could do with some meat and tatie pie down him.'

On quiet days in the market one of us might slope off to the warehouse down the steep roadway at the back of market, to our pot store. The market was overrun with mice. In the warehouse you needed carbon nerves to dip your hand into any box or carton. If you went

144 My daughter, Michele's comedy character takes the surname of Tisnice and is named in honour of such Sheffield womenfolk.
145 schnorrer (s) (n)-someone who cadges bargains, from *schnorren* to cadge, ask for small favours (German)
146 billy, billies (n)-Billy Bunter= punter (market rhyming slang)
147 cop (v)-to get, receive, obtain (market slang)
148 clock (v)-to see, look at, have a look at, spy (market slang)

inside into the darkness and you put the light on suddenly, you'd see them scarper everywhere. Mice we could cope with, but we hated rats.

Bill was very particular, and he didn't like to think of rats running all over any edible goods. We'd often nibble pears, apples, grapes as we worked, which we'd bought from our fruiterer chums. The fruit was top quality and keenly priced. We loved the stuff. If I picked up a bunch of grapes and started nibbling on them straight from the brown paper bag, Bill would often say to me, 'Wash that, you soft chuff, a rat might have lagged on it.'

I had a weakness for fruit and Bill would urge me to eat modest amounts, knowing it might affect my digestion, 'Steady on, take it steady. Stay off those oranges, otherwise tha'll need to leave the joint … Tha'll be leggin' it to the khazi[149]', he said.

When we'd been to the factors our stock was piled in lines. We'd look through the stock and sort plates into half dozens, or find teapots that needed to be brought up for sale. We never sold china teapots with dinner sets, so we often had assorted lines scattered around the warehouse. Some lines sold like dead men, such as soup cups and stands. We spent time marrying items up, preparing them for sale.

Sometimes we picked up unusual items and we had to develop a 'bit of a fanny', a story and explanation for the punters on how they might use these wares being presented to them. I was quite good at that: I had quite a creative bent. On one outing to purchase goods we came across some pretty bowls with a larger bowl and some servers. They were made by Crownford and were earthenware porcelain with a black and white pattern with embossed spots. I christened the collection a Swedish Salad Set. Most Sheffielders had no idea what Swedish salad was, neither did I, come to that, but it sounded sophisticated and otherworldly, and brought a little continental glamour to the Sheaf Market. What's more, we sold them.

Bill was a brilliant mimic and he had me in stitches pretending to be Sheffield punters with strong local accents, contemplating a purchase: 'Bleedin' Swedes comin' o'er 'ere swankin' with their posh pots. Think we don't eat salad. Well they can think again. Pass one o'er ere, pal. I'll 'ave one o' those bleedin' sets.'

---

149 khazi (n)-toilet (military slang)

Bill loved to 'tell the tale' as we called it, telling stories, mainly true accounts of things that happened to us. We made one another laugh and kept up our good humour, even when we had the odd bleak days and were taking no money. We needed to get along well as we worked long hours together, so it helped that we appreciated one another's sense of humour. After a busy day in the market, we could be delivering pots the next day all across Sheffield. We delivered to all sorts of places, hospitals, working mens' clubs, hotels, as we could supply Dudson's hotelware on special order. We delivered Woods' *Berylware* in green blue and pastel pink, so beloved of church halls and parish councils, and which is still in use today in some public buildings.

We were quite good employers back then. We tended to attract the likely lads, or the feeble-minded who had no work. There were many people who fell through the net of any social service provision; and there were no day centres in those days, so these unfortunates were often at the market whiling their time away as onlookers, or cadging occasional work from us and other stallholders. The atmosphere was benign and indulgent. We did have our regular schleppers, who were fairly reliable, whom we'd inducted in our trading habits. Many stayed with us for years. Some worked for all of us. Joss worked initially for Joe, then for Arthur, and finally for Bill and me.

We usually had a mixed crowd of punters visiting our stall. Ladies from the better suburbs would visit us to buy quality bone china. They stood out; they were the ones with matching hats, gloves and handbags. We tried to educate the lads to be polite, which they managed, but getting them to adopt higher standards of personal hygiene was something more of a challenge. Tom Diddy was one such schlepper. He had a lovely manner with the punters, but couldn't keep himself clean. He turned up in a suit each day, but look a bit closer and you'd see tides of grime worn into his shirt collar and cuffs. I was standing next to him one day as he showed a lady a teapot at the front of the stall. I recoiled in horror as I saw a big black bug, a 'steamer,'[150] walk up out of his collar and up the side of his neck. I froze, wondering what to do. Our slang usually meant we could chat without the punters understanding, so I said quietly, 'Uncle Tom, watch it, old pal, there's a steamer!'

'It'll be reight,' he said with little concern, '...it's only coming up for air.' He was quite indifferent to the bed bug crawling up his neck. Luckily the lady did not notice and the purchase was made without affronting her.

Our Bill used to tease Tommy after this incident and often made joking references to steamers. Tommy protested, 'We haven't got any bleedin' bed bugs at our house down Harvest Lane!'

Bill put him right, 'Thy has now. I came round last night with some of ours, and put a matchbox-full through your letter box!'

We also had a quiet chap called Albert, who worked for us for some time. He didn't say much, got on with his work, did our bidding, passed up baskets of china for sale, got baskets ready arranging tea sets in them and ran errands. One dinner time we sent him off to get fish and chips four times and a jug of tea, with a ten bob note. We often sent the schleppers off on such errands and they were used to it, and didn't argue about being sent anywhere locally. We kept bobbing our heads up and down looking for his familiar frame ambling down the market.

'Where's that bleedin' Albert got to?' said Bill.

This was an invitation to the others to fantasise about Albert's unlikely activity.

'He'll be maging[151] about with some bird!' said one of them.

'Ay, he's run off with a punter!' cried another.

'I wish he'd hurry up, I'm bleedin' famished,' said Bill.

We kept looking for him, and eventually it dawned on us that we were unlikely to see him again.

'He's bleedin' scarpered, I'm telling thi. That's the last we've seen of him,' summarised Bill.

The other schleppers drifted into bad moods, brought on by hunger and ill will, and envious frustration that someone had

150 steamer (n)-steam tug= bug (rhyming slang)
151 maging (v)-to mess about, to mess with (market slang)

successfully abandoned the stall and had set themselves up in a new life elsewhere with a ten bob note, away from this drudgery. Sadly we never got our money back, or fish and chips that day...

Bill and I had our band of regular schleppers. There was Jimmy Booth from Dewsbury who worked for us quite often. He was a lovely bloke with a personable temperament and a good work ethic. Previously he'd worked for our Arthur. One of the younger lads who worked for us in the 1960s was Keith Simpson. Keith was a likeable lad, friendly, bouncy, who got on with work, did our bidding and brought his good humour to work, which we always appreciated.

Keith had a complicated home life. We never employed book-educated types, but we did appreciate the ability to think on your feet and common sense. Keith had these qualities and he stayed with us for years. He was a good lad. We were upset when we heard he couldn't come to work because he'd had a motorbike crash. It was a bad crash and he was in hospital ages. He did come back to work afterwards for a while. The crash made a mess of his face, such a shame for a good-looking lad. He was philosophical and got on with life.

I have an abiding memory of a conversation we had with him one day. He came to work late one day, looking frazzled and told us that this sister was having trouble with her husband, who was a Pakistani. She hadn't been married for long. He told us there'd been a bit of trouble at home the night before and that his sister's husband was going off to Pakistan for a holiday. They'd had a big argument the previous evening and there'd been a lot of quarrelling. His sister's husband had packed his stuff in a temper and had gone off in the middle of the night, saying he was going back to Pakistan, ostensibly to see his mother.

Bill and I glanced at one another, worried on the girl's behalf. Bill said, 'It's t' last she's seen of him. I'll tell thi, he's schmeissed[152].'

'He's coming back, I'm certain,' said Keith confidently.

'How does tha know?'

'He's forced to come back.'

'How do you mean *forced to*?' asked Bill.

'He's left his bike,' said Keith.

Bill and I couldn't help chuckling.

---

152 schmeissed (v)-gone away, left, also to throw, (from German verb *schmeissen*, to throw, fling, chuck)

'He's not coming back for his old lass then?' asked Bill.

Some market traders have a certain appealing quality, which endears them to the general public. This is something which most of them are grateful for. On the other hand it has its drawbacks, so much so that a saying has sprung up amongst some grafters. They talk of someone being so successful at his job that he could and indeed would be able to 'pull a nutter in a desert'. No insult intended to those with problems here, this relates to the uncanny improbability that if you set up a stall, of any type, no matter how remote, how lonely the place where it is sited, it is guaranteed that anyone strange or eccentric will find it, and indeed you, and will engage you in conversation. My father always said, 'No matter where you set up, the first roll-up will be a crate[153].'

My brother Bill and I had this quality; without intending to, we drew people in and they hovered round to chat with us. Markets tended to attract the walking wounded, whether they were mentally, emotionally or physically damaged. We treated everyone with respect, interest and warmth, so not surprisingly we had a lot of visitors! This was sometimes amusing, sometimes unwelcome, and sometimes downright alarming.

One day I was busy setting up the stall in the Sheaf Market. I was carefully unpacking pots from the tea chests, picking strands of straw from them and dusting them off to bring up the colours.

I was absorbed in my task when suddenly I heard a loud voice ringing out, which seemed to be addressing me. 'Hello, Mister Michael.'

I glanced up from my work to see a woman I recognised. I knew her as Mary Ann. We had spoken to her before a few times before and she knew us both by name by now. She often came into the market, towards the end of the day. She always brought a core rake, a tool for raking out fire grates with her, which she used to reach under the joints to find discarded fruit and veg, which she then squirreled into her shopping bag. Some of the fruit was still perfect and it was these

---

153 crate (n)-crate of lump, chump (rhyming slang)

perfect pieces that she sought, they'd just rolled under the joint when the workers were setting up, and were still fine to eat.

She beamed at me revealing a striped smile, which gleamed with the twin tones of black and white. Her teeth were like piano keys. Her greying hair was tied in the fashion of a pony tail, but with wild strands straying all around her face. She brushed back her hair with her hand and scratched at her scalp fiercely. She spluttered and coughed and splat onto the ground. On her hands she wore a pair of finger-less, frayed gloves. I looked down at her plastic-coated shopping bag, its surface crisp with age, and saw that it was crammed full with old yellowing newspapers. She scratched at her armpit, and my nostrils caught a whiff of an unpleasant smell which wafted over to my side of the stall.

'How are you, love, are you alright?' I asked gaily, but with concern. She frowned and furrows trilled across her forehead. She clutched her chest and sighed.

'Oh Mr. Michael, I've been badly,' she said.

I leaned a little further over the joint to ask more. 'Have you really, love? What's been the matter with you?'

She glanced secretively around her and put her hand to her mouth to shelter her forthcoming utterance. She pressed her fingers to her lips.

'Sssshh, I've been in hospital,' she whispered, looking furtively around her.

I'm squeamish, but I felt obliged to inquire further.

'What for, love?' I asked.

She swayed and wiped her runny nose on her coat sleeve.

'I collapsed, you see. I had to have injections. I'm diabetic you know. Look, I'll show you.'

Before I could add anything further or protest, she'd turned with her back towards me and flipped her skirt up over her head to reveal her bare backside. She backed herself towards me to give me a better look. She had no knickers on, and her arse cheeks were marbled a dirty grey. Her chunky legs were streaked where trickles of urine had created cleaner rills down the backs of her legs, washing away the ingrained grime of many weeks. I jolted, a little shocked. She turned to look at me.

'I'll show you where I had my injection,' she added.

I narrowed my eyes in awkward anticipation as she hitched up her skirt an inch or two higher, to show me where she'd had her injection.

'Ooh you have been poorly, love,' I cooed. Then pointing across to our Bill, I said to her, 'See that mester over there? Well you go and show Mester Edwards what you've just shown me.'

She nodded, and I watched her toddle across the market towards our Bill, who was dusting china across at the other joint. I awaited Bill's reaction in delicious enthralment. I watched the scene as it unfolded, in slow motion. Bill paused, still keeping his feather duster raised where he was dusting pots on the top racks, and greeted her. Then as her skirt tipped up over her buttocks and she flashed her backside at him, he reeled, stepping backwards, his mouth a perfect 'O' of surprise.

Then he looked over at me, spotting my part in all of this, seeing me on the other side of the market alley, doubled up laughing, having to lean on the wooden block to keep myself standing up straight. He'd realised I'd initiated this treat for him, and he wagged his fist at me, but I could see that he couldn't help smiling. He recovered his decorum, and politely chatted to her for a bit longer and I watched as he eventually sent her on her way, with a free mug.

Bill came across later to have a cuppa with me.

'Christ, I thought I was going to faint when I clocked her Harris,' he said. 'I could feel the claret[154] draining from my brain. Thought I was going to hit the deck. Did you see her Hampsteads[155] an' all?'

Most days in the market were productive for us, but occasionally we had a few problems. It could attract a young rowdy crowd on occasion, and they used to see sparring and verbally jesting with the stallholders as something of a favoured pastime. They were usually young leery[156] lads who felt emboldened with any audience attention and a belly full of alcohol.

---

154 claret (n)-blood (slang)
155 hampsteads (n)-teeth, from Hampstead Heath=teeth (rhyming slang)
156 leery (adj)-alert, knowing, self consciously clever, confidently unguarded (local dialect, archaic)

One Friday dinnertime we were confronted by a ragbag of such lads, hanging around in the edge, drunk. They seemed harmless and were answering us back and mucking about, but we'd put up with them for about half an hour and they had overstayed their welcome; they were now affecting our sales. People were nervous, trouble was brewing and they wouldn't stand to watch us with them in the edge. One lad in particular had been offering a running commentary on everything we said, and was taking the micky mercilessly. It was our usual modus operandi to try to appeal to the one who was least drunk, in the hope he might persuade his mates to drift off. We needed to take action. Bill was still pitching, so I slipped out from behind the joint to chat to them.

'I'll sort these chavvies[157],' I said to Bill and he nodded back at me.

I stepped out and drew them into conversation, 'You've had a bit of fun, lads. Thanks for coming. You've got your wages this week, we need to work to get ours. Would you leave us now and let us get a living?' They stood listening to me quite biddably, and I was hopeful that they would heed my words.

Usually, one lad who might have been less drunk than others was more reasonable, and would manage to persuade his mates to leave and move on. Not this time. As soon as I'd walked back into the joint they started aping our patter again. They were intent on staying and would not leave.

Bill was usually sweet tempered, but they had pushed his patience. He snarled under his breath, 'That main mush[158] is needling me. If he doesn't stop it, I'm going to stick one on him. I'll stroke[159] him.'

They continued messing around in front of the joint. Bill's face suddenly changed and became dark and brooding. He handed me the gavel, stone-faced. 'Step in, Mick. I'm going to sort these godfers[160] out,' he said as he left the joint to go out to the front and I took his place. I watched after him. He approached them, took them a little to one side and they talked quietly. He beckoned them and moved them back a bit behind the punters. I observed as there was a bit of chat, Bill leaning in and forward to talk to them in a quiet huddle. Then sud-

157 chavvies (n)-kids, young people (poss. Romany origin)
158 mush (n)-man, male (Romany origin)
159 stroke (v)-to punch, hit
160 godfers (n)-God forbids= kids (rhyming slang)

denly Bill pulled his arm back and shot his fist forward and chinned the main perpetrator, planting a punch firmly on him, which sent him shooting under Rushy's joint, opposite. I put my head in my hands, this was all we needed, the punters seeing that Bill had stroked him, but I had to admit, it had been effective.

The lad lay under Rushy's joint, out cold. A few punters turned to see what the noise was and then turned back to us, unconcerned. Bill looked at the lad nonchalantly. 'Look at the state of him. He's pissed as a fart,' he said, shaking his head, tutting. There was a bit of twittering and comment from the punters, but they were keen to focus on us pitching, as if they were used to such goings-on. 'Sorry about that,' said Bill to the punters, straightening his tie and stepping back into the joint, resuming normal business after the interruption.

He looked around for the next item to bring up to sell. 'Where were we? Mick, pass me those china breakfast cups up. Let's see if we can treat the ladies and gentlemen who have come to see us today.'

The lad lay sprawled under Rushy's joint, and he was out sparkers. His friends grabbed him, tugging him up his feet. They bundled him into the middle of them, bolstering him up, and slowly sauntered away deflated. There was very little reaction from the punters; they were more bothered about watching us, eagerly eyeballing the next items for sale, hoping for a bargain.

Bill was mostly even tempered, but occasionally he'd lose his rag or 'cop the needle' as he called it. One day we were working in the market when a tourist, a German chap, came up and started chatting. As always, Bill was charming and friendly, and was more than able to put the Second World War behind him. They talked about the locality and somehow got talking about Sheffield.

The German chap said to Bill, 'Ah Sheffield famous for steel, but we have Solingen for steel. Sheffield steel eez no good.' The German rocked on his heels, tipping his chin upwards, smiling to himself.

Bill shook his head, shuffled and had to disagree with him saying, 'You're wrong, Sheffield steel's good stuff.'

The German chap stamped and blurted, 'Nein, eez no good, German steel much better. Eeez zuper-ioorrr; bestimmt.'

Bill was happy to forget the war, but this bloke's arrogance had got his back up.

The Deutscher continued, eyeing Bill with smug satisfaction, 'Sheffield steel...very, er, er, how you say, eez weak,' continued the visitor, doing an arm action that indicated a collapsing structure, scrunching up his face in an expression of dismissive contempt.

Bill was starting to get annoyed. He coughed and cleared his throat, leaning in to the chap, whispering quietly in his ear, 'Listen, old pal, it wasn't so fuckin' bad when we were dropping it on your nuts!'

The German jolted, pulled back and scuttled away.

I looked on in amusement, saying, 'They should get thee a job workin' for t' Council or t' government, international affairs or summat.'

Bill shrugged his shoulders and shook his head. Then he puffed, 'Well types like him make me badly[161]. Sorry I lost it... but he was giving me the right royal needle! The square–headed German berk!'

Sometimes the proceedings in the market ebbed and flowed, leaving us a little time to chat to the other stallholders. The atmosphere was friendly and cheery, even when we were struggling to take money. There was a sense of camaraderie and community spirit, and we had a lively interest in one another's lives, backgrounds and histories.

Bill and I liked to have a nobble with the other stallholders and proprietors. We liked to chat to Irene Granelli. She was a well-dressed, blonde–haired lady. She was a cut above the usual market traders; she lived in Calver, Derbyshire. She liked to let us know what it was like to live out in Derbyshire; something we could only dream of. We knew she was very proper and a bit particular, and so we could not resist winding her up if an occasion presented itself to us. We had been talking for some time about Bib's daughter's wedding. Anthea was marrying her Swiss boyfriend, Eugen, which was rather exotic in itself. The reception was to take place at the Maynard Arms, Grindleford, a salubrious and rather grand hotel with superb catering and delightful gardens. It was to be a summer wedding and all the family had been invited. We were looking forward to it. The Tuesday after the wed-

---

161   badly (adj)-ill, poorly, nauseous, bilious (colloquial)

ding, we arrived in the market and Irene came bustling out of her café to find out how things had gone.

She always referred to me by my full name, Michael, as if to mark herself out as more refined. She never called me Mick, as most people did.

She came over and sidled up to me, fishing for a good opening line.

'Where was the reception, Michael?' she asked.

'Maynard Arms, Grindleford. It was very nice, posh place that.'

'Mmn, I've been there, lovely place. Did it go well?' she asked tentatively.

Here was my chance to wind her up.

'Was it a nice occasion?' she persisted, trying to get more information from me.

I shook my head and sighed. 'Oh, Irene, it was a bit embarrassing really.'

She moved in closer eager to hear my news. She looked at me, trying to read my face for any clues as to what may have happened. She could not contain herself. 'What happened, Michael?'

'Aunt Violet disgraced herself,' I said fidgeting.

Irene started. She had seen Aunt Violet on her occasional visits to the market accompanied by her husband, Walter. She was a tall and broad imposing figure, with the demeanour and bearing of royalty. She was very proper and seemed to be a from a bygone age, always wearing her dark tailored suits, dresses and overcoats in Victorian style, wearing corsages on her lapel, carrying an umbrella, sporting matching shoes, handbags and gloves, bearing down on people imposingly from under her towering hats. The very thought of her doing anything improper was incalculable.

'What did she do, Michael?'

'She had a few too many sherries. Got a bit Mozart[162].'

Irene looked up with surprise. She knew of Aunt Violet and she was trying to reconcile the image she had of her as a Grand old Dame with this new picture I was painting of her recent misdemeanours.

'Oh my goodness...'

'Yes, she started doing cartwheels on the lawn,' I said.

Irene furrowed her brow and looked astonished.

162 Mozart (and Lizst)-pissed (rhyming slang)

'But, you know,' I added, 'that wasn't the worst of it... She'd got no knickers on, and every time she turned she was flashing her Harris! You know she's a bit bonny. Well, then she landed down hard with her high heels and got stuck fast in the lawn. Her stilettos went about four-inch deep.' At this, I couldn't help bursting out laughing. Irene realised I was having her on and thumped me.

'Oh, Michael, you devil. I thought you meant it.'

One day Irene and I were chatting to a friend of mine, Ken Thomson. Ken was another stallholder and was very sociable. Irene noted his smart mac and hat, and was clearly enjoying the attention of a nice professional gentleman as we chatted. She couldn't resist letting Ken know that she was a refined sort, even though she worked in the market. I can't blame her. People do tend to judge you.

'It took me a long time to get here today, Michael,' she said, clearly addressing both of us, trying to tempt our interest.

'Oh aye,' I said.

'Lately it has been so very cold out in Derbyshire.' She lingered over the last word, looking at Ken, to check if he was paying attention to her story. 'Yes. Do you know it has been so cold in Calver,' she continued theatrically, 'that the rabbits came down into my garden and ate all the vegetation, and then a fox came down from the woods into my garden, and he ate all the rabbits.'

Ken, unimpressed with Derbyshire life, piped up, 'Ugh, tha should ha' gi'n it a Fox's Glacier Mint!'

My mother taught us all how to talk ourselves out of trouble, but if push came to shove we could hold our own physically. We really didn't like fighting, but sometimes we had to stand up for ourselves and it was necessary to front up.

Bill went to live and work in South Shields for a while, working many markets in the North East. He worked at the Quayside, in Newcastle. He said some of the market people were rough there. He'd seen a man chained up in a sack and thrown into the Tyne by some ruffians for a bet, just to see how long it would take him to escape.

This was sport with serious consequences, and people there seemed to work and play with an intensity and danger unknown to us.

Bill hated getting up in the morning, and if you want to work markets you need to be an early riser to secure your pitch in a good spot. Bill had sussed how to manage this. At Newcastle he paid someone a knicker[163] to hold his pitch for him, meaning he could roll up to work later when he had had a good sleep. The chap who was Bill's pitch-nailing schlepper was called Stainless Steven. I don't know if this was his nickname or if Bill christened him thus. One morning Stainless Steven went to mark out Bill's pitch. Bill turned up at the market an hour later to find a chap encroaching, taking up half of his pitch. Bill challenged him in a polite yet firm manner, and asked him to move up as he'd paid for the frontage and he was being short changed.

'Just move up a bit, will you, so I can get set up?'

'I'm not moving,' he barked, setting up his fruit barrow, turning and ignoring Bill.

'Turn it up. Shift up.'

'Nah. Yow shift up.'

'Don't be a Tom Hunt. Budge up, will you? I've paid for eight foot; th'art on my pitch.' Bill was starting to get wound up, sensing that this geezer was just a wind-up-merchant and didn't really care that much about his few feet of pitch. A needless power struggle was going on here between an unknown newcomer and an established trader. Bill was getting riled; they weren't even selling the same goods so there was no competition. What was the problem?

'Shift up; be reasonable. I want to get to work, it will be spark on soon.'

'How many more times? I'm not moving.'

'I'm telling thee, th'art moving, otherwise thee and t' barrow are going in t' parney,' growled Bill, through gritted teeth.

At that moment another bloke rolled up.

'What's gan an?' he said. He was a very big bloke, and apparently he was the brother of the kid with the fruit barrow.

'I'm trying to set up and thy brother's on my chuffin' pitch. I've asked him to move up, but he's stubborn,' said Bill, now losing his temper. 'I'm going to stick him one on. I don't want to have to do the lot of you.'

---

163 knicker, nicker (n)-£1, one pound

'If you do me, you'll have to do him an' all,' said the fruiterer, gesturing towards his bigger brother.

'Aye no problem. I'll come back and do you one at once,' said Bill. 'Let's go across the road,' he added, leading them away from the other stallholders along the quayside.

The big bloke bounded up to Bill, and before he could place a punch near him, Bill had done one of his army moves on him, jabbing his fingers towards his throat. He went down immediately, and it looked to the others as if Bill had hardly laid a finger on him. Bill span round and started walking towards the crowd watching, seeking out the fruiterer and his barrow.

'Now then, are you shifting thy barrow or am I shifting it?' Bill yanked the barrow and started trundling it towards the edge of the quayside, tipping it persuasively towards the edge.

'Don't. I'll make room,' said the chap, and the hassle was over.

Bill worked the quayside regularly and the stallholders became quite welcoming. The fruiterer in particular couldn't be friendly enough. As Bill strolled up each time each week, he'd pipe up, 'Hello, Billy. Now then, make room, make room, Billy's here.'

There was only one time which Bill told me of, when he was fronting up and he came unstuck, as we term it, and had to back down, but even this he did in a masterly fashion. This move is called 'ringing it' in our family. Bill had rung it. An argument between him and another market trader had started in the market. The chap Bill was arguing with was seated on his stool behind a stall. The altercation went on for a few minutes and as was usual, Bill invited him out front, so he could stick one on him. The man stood up slowly. Bill swallowed hard and gulped to see his opponent was six and a half feet tall. Now he was stretched to his full height, Bill could also see he was muscled and well built, a big sterricker.

Bill was a quick thinker and he wagged his finger at him saying, 'Now turn it up, it's tha lucky day. I'm going to let thee off. I was going to give thee a tanning.'

With that Bill walked away, leaving the chap staring after him dumbfounded.

I chuckled as he told me the story, impressed at his front.

'Thi bottle twitched, ' I surmised.

'Aye, not 'alf,' said Bill. 'He was a big bleeder and I knew I was going to come a cropper, so I twirled it. He was built like a brick shit house.'

Bill was courageous and big-hearted. He'd been quite hot-headed in his youth, but as he settled into married life, he took on an altogether more peaceful personality. As he got older he didn't let anything excite him and he took everything in his stride. He liked quiet pastimes, including driving, going out for a run in the car, especially out into the countryside, or to visit Lincoln Cathedral.

Bill's wife was called Madge. I believe he met her at a dance, and she came from Darnall. Madge was buxom and good-looking, with a luxurious head of back-combed hair and good taste in clothes. Her make-up was always immaculate, with her expertly applied lipstick, eye shadow and eyeliner making her look like a starlet off the flicks. Madge often worked with Bill down at the market. She deferred to Bill in all her conversations with great reverence. Many of her sentences were tagged with 'Isn't it, Bill?' or, 'Didn't he, Bill?' — her voice always rising in tone, towards the end of the sentence, inviting Bill's confirmation and supportive acquiescence.

Bill and Madge were like a double act; she was the straight woman to his funny man. She had no idea that she could be comical, saying things with complete seriousness and gravity, completely unaware that she was amusing.

To anyone watching them, it was hilarious; Bill had a kindly but deadpan way of putting her straight.

She said to him once, recounting their day, 'That man down t' market had a lovely spotty dog, didn't he, Bill? A Daimler, weren't it?'

Bill replied, 'A Dalmatian, Madge, he had a Dalmatian. Daimler's a car.'

Another time she was telling us the story of how they'd seen a punk rocker, with a shock of bright dyed hair in a jagged Mohican hairstyle of multi-coloured spikes.

'Half his head were red, half were blue, and half were green!' she declared in astonishment.

'Madge, according to thee, he had one and a half heads,' piped up Bill, despairing of her grasp of fractions.

When he was laughing, Bill's whole body shook, and he struggled to stay upright and not keel over. He said he was always in danger of fainting if he got too excited. He'd pull out his handkerchief to wipe his eyes, stating how tickled he was, snorting with laughter.

I remember Bill told me a story about when they'd just got married. Madge was not very used to cooking and housekeeping, as her mother had looked after her at home; therefore the housewifely routine was fairly new to her. Bill had brought a nice piece of steak home for his tea and was puzzled at the time it was taking to get a meal on the table. He ventured into the kitchen to see how Madge was faring cooking the tea, looking forward to his sirloin.

'What's happening, Madge, how are you getting on with that bit of Sidrata[164] ?'

Madge tossed the frying pan to one side in frustration saying, 'This steak's no bleedin' good!'

'What's up with it?' asked Bill, examining it.

'T' pan's not big enough, steak won't go in. I can't cook it, I'll have to gid you something else for your tea,' she said, heading towards the cupboard to rummage around for tinned goods.

Bill took a knife from the drawer and handed it to her.

'Madge, just cut it in half,' he said.

'Oh yeah,' she nodded meekly.

As self-employed people, we did our own taxes. We didn't care for paperwork, which was not our forte, and occasionally we got behind with the books. Following a late tax submission, Bill once had a visit from the taxman in the early 1950s. Bill had inherited our father's insouciant defiance of officialdom, and he was cool and untroubled in his approach. The taxman sat down across the table from Bill, imperiously taking out his papers, pad and pen. He fired questions at Bill,

---

164 sidrata (n)-Bill's slang term for steak, possibly relating to meat produced by nomadic herding tribesmen.

who enjoyed playing it a bit daft. Bill minded father's advice to greet such officials in a particular manner: Don't give 'em a cup of tea, seat them in the kitchen, and don't invite them into the front room in any circumstances. Also, if possible open the back door and seat them in a draught too.

The taxman took up his forms and poised himself ready to write down notes from questioning Bill.

'Have you been abroad on any foreign holidays in the past few years?'

'Yes.'

'Where to?'

'Egypt.'

'Mmmnn, you'll need some good earnings to go there....very exotic. Did you stay in any nice hotels?' he asked, trying to gauge Bill's predilection for extravagant spending.

'Not really.'

'You must have stayed somewhere,' bristled the official, glaring at Bill, trying to drill down into his spending habits.

'I was camping.'

'Camping!' said the official incredulously. 'Well, you must have had to pay quite a bit, even for camping facilities.'

'It was a cheap break,' said Bill, 'I had a bivouac.'

'What, you took it with you? All that way?'

'The army provided it.'

'Eh?'

'I was in the army.'

'Oh,' the taxman wrinkled his forehead struggling to understand, '...in the army, you say?'

'I was a soldier.... It was a few years ago, in nineteen forty-six.'

'Oh,' he said crumpling up the paper form with irritation, tossing it into his briefcase.

The taxman left soon after, having nothing to report.

Bill closed the door after the visitor, watching him amble down the garden path. Bill muttered to Madge as he watched him go off, 'What a Pilkington. What an educated idiot. The pillock knows nothing about history.'

Bill loved to drive. As soon as he was old enough to drive he got a car and always had one. He wasn't a fast driver, but he loved to get around. I remember driving with him once and we were going up Snig Hill, stuck in a bit of traffic. Bill was holding the car on the clutch, and we were both watching a curvaceous woman walk by on the pavement.

'Cop a load of her. She's got a tasty bottle,' I said.

Both Bill and I had turned our heads to watch her and were mesmerised as she swayed by. There was a sudden crunch. Bill realised the car had been slowly edging forwards and had bumped the car in front of us. The man in front put his handbrake on and jumped out of the car, darting round to us, sticking his head through our side window.

'You've just bumped me,' he accused Bill, glaring at him.

Bill jumped out to check to see if there was any damage. There was none.

'Nah, pal, it was your fault; you were rolling back. You must have been looking at that tasty bird who's just walked up.'

The suited and booted gent was not inclined to argue. 'Sorry,' he offered, colouring up, and then he jumped back in his car and drove on.

In the late 1960s Bill bought an old Bentley. It was a beautiful, old-fashioned shape with wide running boards and big headlamps at the front and was painted a muted mid-china blue. He brought it to show me and I had to have one too. I loved the leather armrests that you could pull out, the walnut veneers and leather interiors. Bill told me they had another at the garage where he'd bought his, and I went to see it. I came away the proud owner of a deep blue-black Bentley.

My kids used to love to sit in the back, pulling down the little tables nestling in the back of the seat in front, for their pop and crisps. Whenever we passed a crowd at a bus stop gawping at us, I'd urge them to do the royal wave, which they did. We drove the Bentley on a great touring holiday to Scotland, visiting the Trossachs. The kids got me to sing *Chitty Chitty Bang Bang* which we'd just seen at the cinema, and I pretended that we were flying. Our grand vehicles did not reign long; they only did a few miles to the gallon so we downed them, but we'd had a brief taste of how the other half live.

When Bill retired, he loved to drive with Madge to Lincoln on a Sunday afternoon. It was a route he travelled frequently, driving to Lincoln and back, stopping there for a cup of tea and a peaceful moment of contemplation in Lincoln Cathedral. Sometimes he might call in at my house for a chat on the way back. Such visits could last for hours.

At family gatherings when we visited one another's houses, we'd sit in the best room, drinking tea from great teapots and best china, eating cake and buns, chatting long into the late evenings. Finally after ten or eleven o'clock, the women would then bustle into the kitchen, to make plates of sandwiches and a last cup of tea before the valedictory rituals. We named this sitting around and oral story-telling, 'telling the fanny' or 'fannying'. All the narratives, many of them concerning what happened to various family members working in the market, were rooted in truth, but there were embellishments: dramatic additions; hyperbole and colourful descriptions; minimoking (pretending to be other people and doing humorous take-offs) and mimicry; irreverent impressions; different accents and voices; physical depictions and jumping up to do actions; gurning with weird facial expressions, and rude gestures.

I often mused on the strange language we used when talking to one another, and reflected on how some words came to have certain meanings. Father never called an advert by the proper word for example, always referring to it as a 'chant'. Some words seemed to have no rational link to their meaning at all. When you think about it, how on earth did the word 'banjo' come to mean sandwich? My father had a very strange mixed vocabulary; he used bits of market slang, Yiddish, German, rhyming slang, local dialect, colloquialisms, and invented words and idioms, which meant we all had to understand his vernacular too. Eventually we all used the same language as him too, adding to it with our own inventions.

Most market traders from old market families who have been working the markets for years will have knowledge of market slang, a private and mutually understood language that they can use when talking to one another. This accepted slang probably evolved to enable them to talk to one another without customers understanding. All members of my family, young and old, had a grasp of market patois, together with the time–fashioned quirks of our own family parlance.

We found these linguistic capabilities very useful, you could have private conversations, which the punters could not understand. For example, you could ask what the profit margin was on a piece of china without a customer having a clue about it, by asking, 'What's the bunce[165] on that?'

If you saw a punter approaching, who was likely to cause you any trouble, you could warn your workmates accordingly saying, 'Pipe[166] this old gimma[167], she's a royal[168] Noah's.' We could also talk about our wares without the public understanding fully. You might need to tell a worker to throw a damaged pot away and you'd say, 'Schmeiss[169] that; it's Jekyll[170].' If you needed to encourage your schlepper to respond quickly to you, you'd urge him to act by saying, 'Look lively. Jildy![171] Jildy!'

Some words were more descriptive, enabling you to describe punters without them realising. You might say, 'Pass this carrier bag to the geezer with the big Derby[172] and the Irish[173],' or, 'Give this change to the mush with the funny naggins[174].'

On a more positive note, it was also useful for our courting fantasies. We could gawp at women and tip one another off about any attractive ladies nearby saying, 'Cop[175] the palone[176] to your right at twelve o'clock with the tasty scotches[177].' By so doing we could alert our workmates to any bobby dazzler[178] passing.

Our stories, which we enjoyed telling and re-telling, were effectively morality tales, fables and parables, passed down through each generation; they captured our beliefs and the essence of us collectively. They always had us rolling around laughing, and gave us a great sense of identity and strength as a family.

---

165 bunce (n)-profit (market slang)
166 pipe (v)-to see, look at, watch
167 gimma, gimmer (n)-old woman, old lady
168 royal –used as a modifier, emphasising meaning further, in this sentence *right* or *real*
169 schmeiss (v)-to throw, from German *schmeissen*, to throw
170 Jekyll (adj)-Jekyll and Hyde=schneid (rhyming slang), faulty, broken, damaged
171 jildy (adj, adv)-quick, quickly, fast (Anglo-Indian military slang, possibly from Hindi)
172 Derby (n)-Derby Kelly=belly (rhyming slang)
173 Irish (n)-wig= Irish jig-wig (rhyming slang)
174 naggins (n)-eyes (market slang)
175 cop (v)-to look at (market slang)
176 palone (n)-woman, this word is possibly of Romany origin
177 scotches (n)-scotch eggs= legs (rhyming slang)
178 bobby dazzler (n)-good looking person, well dressed person, (Northern term)

Our Bill was a brilliant 'fanny merchant'. It's not as rude as it may sound. It means he had the gift of the gab, he was a storyteller, a raconteur, someone who likes a laugh through spinning stories, creating illusions. A fanny merchant is someone who can draw people in with whimsy and flights of fancy, and have people on (carrying on with a pretence, either by an act, convoluted story, or running joke). Bill loved a bit of moody[179], and a bit of make-believe devilment. Bill was indeed the supreme fanny teller. He had a gift for drama, and an extensive command of language and could hold our attention for hours, with his stories weaving, turning and melding into one another, linked by theme, situation or character. He did have to rest sometimes, because he was laughing so much, saying, 'Hold on while I wipe mi clock[180].' I came a close second to him with my cheeky sense of humour and talent for mimicry. My only failing was that I could never keep a straight face and always laughed at my own jokes, forever tickled to death, sputtering with mirth and struggling to get my words out before I ever got to the punch line or dénouement of my story.

We never gave this use of language a second thought, until the real world encroached and made us conscious of our peculiar ways. Bill's son, Robert, was an only child, and like many of us in the Edwards family would often sit listening to family stories and market tales. In our family, children and teenagers have never viewed spending time in adult company as an endurance test, they relished ear-wigging these stories and begged to be allowed to remain present when relatives came to call. They did not want to be taken to bed, and so adopted strategies of sitting quietly at the edge of conversations, swathed in dressing gowns and nightwear, keeping quiet and laughing softly, in a bid to be allowed to stay up longer. Such evenings were always amusing, often shocking and were definitely an education.

It seems our use of private language rubbed off on Robert too and he had imbibed the lingo, incorporating it into his own language in use. He'd been set a writing topic at junior school, and the teacher invited the children to use all their powers of description depicting a busy, crowded scene.

Robert was called to the front of the class and he read out his story with gusto. The teacher strained to comprehend one particular

179 moody (n)-make believe, made up story, fantastical pretence (market slang)
180 clock (n)-face (slang)

191

section and had to ask him to repeat some words, but even then she could not decipher the meaning of the sentence. Robert had heard market language so often that he did not hesitate to include these terms in his work at school.

The English teacher telephoned his parents, expressing real concern, querying if Robert might have developmental problems, or delayed linguistic ability. It seems he'd written a story at school with a colourful account regarding a woman described as 'eating a banjo and wearing a pair of jazzy bins,[181]' which had caused great confusion and consternation in the staff room.

He was not reprimanded; his parents thought it was quite amusing. He was offered a little gentle advice not to use such words in his schoolwork, and to keep that language for home.

---

181 bins (n)–spectacles, glasses (market slang)

–11–
OUR ARTHUR

Arthur Edwards, age 50

Ask anyone who knew our Arthur and they'll all say the same about him; he was a lovely bloke, but crikey, what a temper he had. My mother used to joke about his temper, saying that he didn't need anyone else to wind him up, because he could wind himself up. Arthur had a kind nature, a great sense of justice, but if he got riled there was no calming him down and he'd be wanting to be having a pop at any comer. He would turn white with rage when he got revved up.

It is said that he once chinned a horse. He didn't mean to hurt the animal, it came up behind him at a fair somewhere, whinnied loudly and made him jump out of his skin. His instincts kicked in, and he lashed out and punched it on the nose-end, causing it to stumble.

He had a very poor track record with horses. At one time he decided that he was going to start riding. He bought all the gear, jodhpurs, riding hat, riding crop, and he went to the stables fully kitted out, looking forward to mastering the skills of a huntsman. He'd only been there a few minutes when he started coming out in a red rash and his skin started itching. It turned out he was allergic to them, so he never got his money's worth out of his riding kit.

When Arthur was faced with animals his courage often deserted him. In the 1960s Bill and I had a café at Waingate, in Castle Market. Bill was very good at getting things going, and he loved a new challenge. We'd put in a bid for the lease and we ran it for a few years before selling it on, to a Sheffield United ex-footballer.

Arthur came to visit our enterprise one day, and he sat down for a cup of tea and a bun. The Castle Market was overrun with mice, though we rarely saw them. There wasn't much any of us could do about it. It didn't matter how hygienic your premises were, they had the run of the place at night. Unfortunately a mouse chose to run down the market that day in daylight hours, and Arthur spied it. He started to jig and dance with fear.

'A mouse, a mouse aaah!' he cried, dancing up onto a chair.

'Nitto, keep stumm, th'art schreiing[182] like a bird. You're alerting the bleedin' billies. They'll clock it,' said Bill.

There was something very appealing about Arthur's personality; the combination of his manly strength and his softer sentimental side. It could engender a need to nurture and protect him. It was hard to get annoyed with him, even when he was being mischievous. Maggie Bailey used to work for the family and she loved and favoured Arthur, always referring to him affectionately as 'our Buck'. She had done the catering for my parents' wedding reception. Maggie had a slight speech impediment and she couldn't say her Rs. Arthur teased her gently about it and would ask her to say words with R in them.

'Say *tray*, Maggie.'

She'd try to pronounce it, saying, 'tway'.

'Say *tray*.'

Eventually she'd give in, losing her rag, saying to him, 'Oh fuck off, Buck.' Her annoyance was always short-lived; she couldn't be irritated with him for long and he could always win her round.

Before he got married, Arthur had a girlfriend who came from the Isle of Wight. Arthur was stationed there with the RAF and that's how they met. He used to have an ex-police Morris Minor, which he

---

182 schreiing (v)-to scream, cry, from German schreien, to scream, cry, wail

drove around. If you had a car, it was a pull for the ladies. She used to come and stay sometimes. From the age of sixteen he had also been dating a girl called Joyce. I'm unsure of events, perhaps he had started to see Joyce at some time, perhaps before this girl came on the scene. They were always falling out, and got back together frequently.

Joyce had a sixth sense when he was home on leave and would come to call knocking loudly on the door, even when his girlfriend from afar was visiting. She'd hover on the doorstep saying, 'I've heard Arthur's home.' Joyce would come in to join the company. As a kid I can remember the awkward silences, as Arthur tried to entertain his two lady friends. I sat watching the stilted conversation from my vantage point, behind a pile of ham and potted meat sandwiches on the table. I think he was innocent in all of this and had done nothing to lead them on, and was rather stunned at his sudden popularity, and unsure of how he should handle the situation.

It seems Joyce was determined to have him, and they eventually got married when she was twenty-four and Arthur was twenty-one. It could also be the case that Arthur was determined to have her. If Joyce fell out with him and withdrew from him, Arthur always chased her until he got her back. They were as bad as one another in this respect.

Joyce felt it was meant to be. She had been told by one of her friends when Arthur was just sixteen, 'Arthur Edwards says he is going to marry you.' Joyce had met Arthur at the City Hall and was three years older than him. She also knew him as she lived in the same yard at Brightside as Betty, who had married my brother Joe. So Joyce and Arthur were married and they clearly adored one another.

Arthur had really been too young to get into the forces, but he'd lied about his age and had been accepted. Mam used to say, 'He roared[183] to get in and he roared to get out.' He was in the air sea rescue. He had two jobs and was a gunner-cook. His hero was Winston Churchill, so he felt he had to do his bit.

His RAF days had instilled high standards of presentation in him. His trousers were always neatly pressed with sharp creases. He liked to look smart, wearing hand-made stag skin boots which were a yellowy tan colour. He had had them for years, buying lots of pairs of them, renewing them at intervals.

---

183 roar (v)-to cry, weep, (Yorkshire slang)

He used to clean them with a tan powder, brushing it into the suede-like finish to bring them up. He liked to line them up in the hallway in rows. One of his daughter's friends came to call, and saw the boots all lined up and commented saying, 'What's your dad, Anne? A centipede?'

He always had a good head of hair, and didn't go bald like the rest of the men in our family; he swore blind that he attributed it to the daily use of *Vaseline Hair Tonic*, which he'd used since his teens. He had a thick beard too, which was always well trimmed, which set off his handsome face with piercing grey-green eyes.

Arthur was generous and a soft touch. He was always moved by anybody's plight, and he loved kids. He'd give you the change in his pocket, if it made you feel better. When I came home from the army on leave whilst doing my National Service, I got straight off the train and called in at the market. I couldn't wait to see them all, and be amongst familiar faces and on my old turf. I went straight to see my Dad, Bill and Arthur, staying to chat with them for a while. Arthur took me aside and quietly asked me how long I'd be home for.

'Two weeks,' I said.

'Here thy art,' he said, peeling off some notes from his wad of cash. 'Thy'll need that,' he said, generously thrusting fifteen quid into my hands. It was enough money to live well on for more than two weeks.

When he was in the RAF he used to cry at having to leave my Mam when he was off on a tour again. They'd both be there hugging and cleaving to one another, tears running down both their faces. He had a safe job in a factory that our Joe had sorted him out, so it wasn't as if he was going to see active service, but he loved home and hated having to leave. He was also extremely fond of my sister Bib, and she was equally fond of him. He thought the world of her.

Arthur was 'as soft as a brush,' Mam always said. He'd go up to the orphanage at Easter, with bags of chocolate Easter eggs, and take baskets of fresh fruit and toys up there for the kids at Christmas.

Naturally he spoiled his own children at Christmas. Joyce and the kids were the most important thing to him. One year he came back to the market after the Christmas break, talking about a lovely gift he'd bought for his three children; it was a lovely miniature Austin pedal car, with a bonnet you could life up with a shiny, metal, replica engine underneath it. Arthur told us how he'd found the kids arguing on Christmas morning.

'Were they arguing about taking it in turns?' I asked.

'Oh no, they were fighting over the chuffin' empty box,' he said.

Joe Bennett and Arthur Edwards at a fair, date unknown

Arthur worked in the market too; he sometimes worked with us, but he also had his own stall and worked independently. The audiences in the edge were mostly benign, but he used to get particularly revved up when the perverts came calling. The market was an ideal place for them to conceal their priapic activity. The thickly-wedged crowd enabled them to sidle up to some woman surreptitiously, rubbing up against her, without people necessarily noticing.

Arthur could easily spot them, and he would often act to embarrass them publicly, shouting to the unfortunate woman to alert her, 'Are you uncomfortable, love? Kick back! Feel free, kick back, if you're uncomfortable. Give him a good thwack in the three-piece. Shall I come down there and give you a hand? Just shout, love.'

He'd then eye the perpetrator with a thunderous face, and the chap would soon shimmy off, moving on to pick his victims where the stallholders were less interfering.

Arthur couldn't bear these crafty operators and would alert other stallholders to their presence, ' Watch out, there's a Harris merchant[184] on the prowl; he's a big bloke, dressed smart with a hat.'

184 Harris merchant (n)-pervert who pinches/ likes women's bottoms (market slang)

One day when he had spotted a devious pervert in the crowd, Arthur made himself known to him and had a quiet, but threatening word in his ear.

Imagine Arthur's surprise when he came across the same chap the next day, at his appointment at the income tax office. The posh gent before him, directing proceedings, was no other than the pervert from the previous day. Arthur bit his lip and pretended he didn't know him.

Arthur was also intolerant of 'weeders' at the market. During one period he noticed that pottery biscuit barrels seemed to be disappearing from his display on his joint. He'd reckoned up and couldn't remember selling any, so he had to conclude that someone was stealing them. Week by week he put a couple of biscuit barrels towards the back of the joint, and with regularity they disappeared. Arthur got all the schleppers watching, to see if they could identify anyone suspicious. They noticed that one particular chap came week by week, and after he'd been around, another biscuit barrel had always gone. It was a difficult situation, and Arthur didn't want to put off any bona fide punters by making a public scene. A couple of weeks later, he placed another biscuit barrel strategically at the back of the joint again, in readiness for him coming. It was the last barrel he was going to get. Arthur put a note in it:

Come back next week and you can have the biscuits!

Arthur used to work many fairs all over the country, as we all did in our trading heyday. He worked Coventry, Tenby, Neath, and Brixham in Devon. I remember one year at Brixham he had the best year he'd ever had, and he didn't even go to work. He was setting up his stall by the harbour side when a trader driving his lorry drove past, caught one of the steel rods, which were part of the stall, levering the whole joint into the sea. It was an accident, but the stall and all his gear went into the briny and he had no gear to go to work with. Arthur salvaged a few pots, but they were ruined. He'd taken his best gear, tea services and dinner services. He managed to retrieve a few sets from the water, but many had lost a cup or two, rendering them useless. He couldn't sell them as best gear without twelve perfect place settings. He claimed on the bloke's insurance and got quite a lot of money back. Generally we weren't that lucky, and we usually had to graft hard for a living.

Arthur was less showy than Joe, but he also bought a lovely family home. It was a big old place at Crabtree Lane. In those days it had a massive garden and some woodland and it was relatively unspoilt and wild, though in a fairly busy suburb. It was the sort of house that attracted teenagers at night. Such a large garden was a big temptation, and Arthur and Joyce often heard people outside messing about.

One evening they were in the sitting room, and the curtains were open. It was dark outside. Arthur's daughter, Anne stood behind her dad's chair chatting to him. She looked up and screamed; she'd seen a man's face peering in through the window at them. Arthur jumped up and raced to fetch his twelve bore. Joyce flapped behind him, telling him not to do anything rash, but he'd already flung the front door open and was racing through the garden. He let rip and fired a warning shot in the direction of the thrashing and crash-ing figure plunging through the undergrowth. Their Doberman shot out, racing after the intruder too. All of a sudden they heard a yell, and the smash and tinkle of glass, and realised that the intrud-er had jumped the fence into next door's garden. In the darkness he had stumbled into the neighbour's greenhouse too, causing considerable damage.

Arthur liked his gun, so much so that Joyce eventually took it off him. The last straw was when he used it to shoot at the local wildlife. The house at Crabtree Lane had an old fashioned conservatory. Some old houses were being knocked down nearby, and the rats that had been living in the drains beneath them moved en masse, and settled under the conservatory. The scratching and sounds of these creatures drove Arthur wild. One night he lost his cool, fetched his twelve bore and got the whole family safely upstairs. He then hung out of one of the upstairs windows shooting at them, watching them scrabble and scuttle, excited at the growing tally of dead 'long-tailed uns'.

Joyce and Arthur liked their home comforts, even when working away from home. Arthur loved his food and had a sweet tooth, loving chocolate, sweets and ice cream, and he always carried a stock with him in his pockets. You could always cadge a few spice off Arthur. When he was working away, invariably Joyce went with him, and Arthur got her cooking proper dinners. He didn't make do with sandwiches, but tucked into roast beef, Yorkshire pudding, roasted potatoes and vegetables; proper meals, all cooked using the temperamental calor gas cooker in the caravan. He didn't like his standards to slip.

Joyce and Arthur adored one another, and she coddled him; he'd call her in to ask her what the time was, even when the clock was right in front of him. She did his bidding gladly. If Joyce went away, perhaps for a little holiday with the girls, he missed her terribly and his way of compensating was to always buy her something. One time he bought a big American-style refrigerator, which was so massive it blocked the gangway of the kitchen. Another time he put in a firm bid on a house they'd been to view. Joyce got to the stage that she didn't like to go away and leave him on his own; she missed him of course, but she was also conscious that he was likely to make extravagant purchases, to surprise her on her return.

I think Arthur encouraged me to buy a caravan. I bought one on his advice, and we took it on many trips away for work to shows and fairs. Locally I even took it to Hope Show in Derbyshire, so we could have cups of tea on tap all day. Grafting is thirsty work.

I had had some success working Hope Agricultural Show in Derbyshire and I persuaded Arthur to book it too. I worded him up about how things worked there; you needed to get there really early. We found it best to take the van and caravan the night before to position it in a good place, so we had somewhere near to the stall to prepare cups of tea and meals. I usually took all the family, and we had quite a nice day out as well as earning a living.

Arthur indicated that he was up for it and I got him a set of forms to book a pitch. On the day of the show he arrived on site with his caravan in tow and he set up near us. His wife, Joyce, was with him too. They set up the stall and he got to work. All day long visitors flowed; friends called in to see us and for the womenfolk it was a constant round of making sandwiches and teas. Joyce had got Arthur well organised and he had even set up a separate toilet tent, a small cubicle with their own chemical toilet outside, a few yards away from the caravan.

Halfway through the afternoon, Joyce glanced up from buttering scones to gaze out of the caravan window. She was astonished to see a long queue zig-zagging round through the vans, with people waiting patiently, outside their private toilet tent. She ran out of the caravan to find Arthur. She made him go and tell them it was private, turning them away. He put up a sign indicating that it was not for public use. We laughed about it and Arthur and I wondered whether we were in the wrong game[185]; it wouldn't have been a bad thing to set up a row of extra toilets and charge people for spending a penny. There were always long queues outside the official toilets provided.

Arthur's natural belligerence was not borne of fighting for fighting's sake; it was borne of the same pride and self-confidence which we all possessed. He could not bear liberty takers, and he hated anyone infringing his rights. His temper came from nowhere; one minute he could be laughing and joking and the next minute we'd be trying to restrain him. We once were out drinking in a pub where there was a little dance floor. We'd left our table, leaving our drinks, jackets, and the ladies handbags, signalling that we'd bagged the table to go up to the dance floor for a dance. We came back to the table after having had a dance to find a little moustached chap, who had seated himself and his wife exactly where we'd been sitting. He nursed his half of bitter and chatted to his wife.

'Excuse me, we were sitting here,' said Arthur, thinking that would be enough to get the chap to relinquish the seats.

'I'm not shifting,' said the little chap, screwing his backside more firmly into the seat.

'Aren't tha?' said Arthur reaching over, lifting the chap and the chair up into the air, and moving it out from behind the table. The chap looked horror-struck as he looked down from his throne, rocking in the air. After giving him this scare, Arthur set him back down and he and his wife stood up, gathered their things and moved quickly away, handing the table and chairs back to our group without further ado.

When the new Sheaf Market opened on the closure of the old Rag and Tag, Arthur had a stall outside, which he worked in all weathers. He started having health problems and trouble with his heart, so Joyce usually worked it for him. He worked some days though; like the rest of us he couldn't stay away from the gaff. One day he was working at the Sheaf Market and he suddenly felt ill. He sent a schlepper round to Bill's stall, to ask if someone could take him to the hospital, as he was

---

185 game (n)-business (market slang)

having chest pains. Bill's son, Robert, (who had been working with his Dad from the age of sixteen when he left school), volunteered, and he bundled Arthur into the car and they drove off.

Robert was worried as he drove, and he kept looking askance at Arthur. He was wearing a sheepskin coat and he was sweating so much that the coat lining was sopping wet. Arthur clutched his chest, beads of sweat dripping from his forehead. Just as Robert started to drive along West Bar, the car lost power, clunked and stalled and Robert realised they'd run out of petrol. The car jumped again as he started the engine once more to try to get it going, but it trundled to a halt. Robert pulled into the causeway edge.

'Chuffin' 'ell, not today of all days,' he sighed.

An irritated motorist behind them hooted loudly on his horn, annoyed at the stopping of the flow in traffic. Arthur was ashen by this time, but his illness did not stop him from jumping out of the car, threatening to chin the chap who had hooted at them.

Robert grabbed him, before he could start anything and said, 'Nitto, turn it up. Thy's badly; too ill for a scrap. Tha dunt wanna be starting a feight today.'

Eventually they did get to the infirmary and Arthur received treatment.

Arthur had heart attacks in succession at intervals. Following one serious heart attack, Arthur was not allowed to drive, though eventually he had his licence restored to him. Gradually he got used to driving again. One of Joyce's friends called to her on the stall in the market, to tell her she'd just seen Arthur driving the car.

'Where was he?' asked Joyce.

'Driving along West Street.'

'West Street? Mmn. I'm not sure it was him then, not sure if he'd be up there. Are you sure? Where exactly was he?'

'Well he was just hauling a bus driver from his cab...looked as if he was going to chin him.'

'Yes, that would be Arthur,' laughed Joyce, despairing at her incorrigible husband, who was unlikely to change his habits, even in the face of serious health problems.

Arthur had some good friends. Following one of his heart attacks, he was invited to work with his good friend, Joey Coupland, who lived in the West Country. Joey had a castle and grounds, which he involved Arthur in managing. Arthur took on a quiet job working for him, taking money and managing the entrance. In that way he could work peacefully and keep any stress under control after his heart attack. Arthur liked to get the kids at it, on tours of the castle. Many of the rooms were very dark, shrouded with heavy drapes, tapestries and hangings. Arthur encouraged the children to tickle people's faces from behind a curtain when the public went on tours around some of the dark rooms. They came out screaming and spooked, but it certainly helped Joey's publicity campaign to promote his haunted castle.

Arthur endured quite a few heart attacks, and he died at the age of fifty-two in the early 1970s. He was away from home the night he died, working at Coventry fair. He and Joyce had parked up the caravan and were with friends, Ted and Ivy Payton, dining out in town at the Leofric Hotel. It was a Sunday and the stall had been set up ready for the week's trading. Arthur and his schleppers had set up a right flash of gear, with a fantastic range of quality glass and china. Vases and figurines glistened under the lights and everyone agreed it was the best display on the fair and the consensus was definitely: 'Arthur's topped the gaff.'

They were all sitting in the bar, having a quiet drink before they went into the restaurant for a meal. Joyce noticed that Arthur was quieter than usual. Arthur unbuttoned his shirt and loosened his tie.

Joyce glanced over at him, knowing that this was a sign of discomfort when he was not feeling particularly well.

'Are you alright, Arthur?' she asked, getting up to go to her husband's side.

He whispered to her, not wanting to make any fuss. 'It's too late this time, Joyce.'

He died that night. Joyce was comforted by their friends, and she insisted on going back to the familiar surroundings of their caravan that night, although she could have stayed at the hotel.

The family were informed of the news. The next day Arthur's sons, Michael and Max, went to fetch the stall and to load the gear back onto the lorry, to drive it all home to Sheffield. They had loaded up and were just about to leave the fair, when they saw a stallholder putting up his joint, extending his pitch onto the area that should have been their father's pitch. They felt incensed at the lack of respect. Michael threatened to drive the lorry through the joint and his gear unless he moved it. They went to talk to the fair manager too, determined that his pitch would remain empty as a mark of respect. It was left empty in the end, in honour of Arthur, who should have been working there that week.

He was greatly missed. The doctors said he must have had a good heart to endure so many heart attacks, and indicated that he must have had excellent nutrition during the war; otherwise he wouldn't have lasted as long as he did. We toasted Mam, thanking her for giving him good scran throughout his earlier years.

Everyone liked Arthur. He had no enemies, and his friends would always remember him in the same way: 'What a lovely bloke, but what a bleedin' temper. He always wanted to be chinning somebody.'

-12-
OUR JOE

Bib and Joe, 1920s

Joe was the eldest lad in our family, and was a self-confessed big-head. My mother had a famous saying which she used in educating all of us, but which she often applied to him: 'Self recommendation is no recommendation.' I can still hear her saying it now.

Before the era of publicists and public relations, Joe was in a league of his own. He thought he was gorgeous, could pull any woman and he often did, frequently during working hours at some market. As a single young man he was famed for 'floating,' drifting off from his tasks to spend time with his latest honey.

Joe had lovely handwriting, which he had taught himself, using a little book on copperplate script. He had a lovely cursive flow to his lettering and had learned proper italic and copperplate script at school, Barton Academy. When he had time and was in the mood he perfected angular downstrokes in italic fashion, or added lovely copperplate flourishes to his letters. I watched him intently and tried to copy his style. He had proper quills and pens with little nibs, which he stored in a metal nib box. When he dipped his pen in the ink and glided it across the paper, he created this beautiful swirling writing. His interest in handwriting was not just an artistic interest; he liked to practise writing his unique signature ready for his autograph for when he became famous.

It seems he had exhibited this self-confidence from an early age. I don't know whether he was actively encouraged as a child to have such a good opinion of himself, but it was a trait that was with him throughout all of his life. He loved attention, and he had often sought it from being young.

My mother told me a story about his early life. At the time they lived in an ordinary terraced house and they had a pianola, which was a rather grand object. It was basically an automated piano. They played tunes on it by turning perforated paper rolls in the mechanism, powered by a foot pedal. You could easily give the impression that you were an expert player to anyone not familiar with this musical instrument. Joe liked playing with this as a kid. He had no real musical talent, but he liked to sit on the stool and play up and down the keys as if he were a top-class musician. It seems at the time he had also been boasting at school to his friends about his musical ability. Not surprisingly they wanted to check it out, and were angling for an invitation to come to play with him round at his house.

'Can we come round to your house to see you play t' piano?' they clamoured.

'Well, I can tell you this,' retorted Joe, who was always quick witted, 'you'll not be allowed in our house with mucky feet. You'll have to look through the window while I play.'

The kids agreed to his conditions and an arrangement was made for Joe's public piano recital at the Edwards's residence later that day at 4 o'clock. My mother tells me how she came into the lounge to see the amusing sight of a row of grubby faces outside in the front garden, noses pressed up to the glass, peering in through the window, and Joe flourishing wildly at the pianola, his feet pedalling, running his fingers feverishly up and down the keys like a concert pianist. The kids looked on dumbstruck, believing completely in his incontrovertible talent. As he finished he gave his assembled audience a grand wave, swept up from his stool with great showmanship and bent in a deep bow to accept his applause. It became a regular occurrence, and knowing our Joe, he probably charged them. My mother always said he was so professional at the piano that he could even make himself sweat.

When he was older, a man once approached him from the Council, asking him if he would consider playing the piano in public, at the City Hall. Joe was a bit stumped by the request, assuming that someone from his childhood who had witnessed his early promise must have recommended him as a potential recitalist. The official stood before him awaiting his response. Joe pondered for a while then shook his head, solemnly refusing the offer, stating, 'Sorry, I haven't really got time, and anyway it would interfere with my sex life.'

The official blinked back at him, flummoxed, yet unaware that he was joking. Joe didn't put him straight either.

Joe had always exhibited an early interest in money; he liked earning it, spending it, but was less keen on saving it. One year

Joe Edwards at the market, date unknown

he began to appreciate the value of saving; he was planning to go on holiday and had therefore started to save up. He did not trust banks and building societies so instead he used a square of linoleum on the floor as his makeshift safe, carefully moving around from one corner clockwise, positioning his half crowns under the lino rug, around the edge at intervals of every six inches, a couple of inches in from the side. As he moved along each week, making his deposits, he took great pleasure in mentally totting up how much money he had saved and reflected on what treats it would buy him.

Unfortunately this early style of banking is not to be recommended in a large family. Our Bill shared a bedroom with him and had watched him through a crack in the door, realising what he was up to and had twigged that he could start picking the coins up and could pocket them, following Joe from where he had originally started placing the coins down. Bill worked his way round each week, supplementing his income with a little extra spending money nicked from Joe. Joe was unaware. When holiday time finally came around, Joe flipped the lino back to reveal his amassed treasure and he got a shock to learn that he only had about ten bob extra to spend. Bill gave himself away by chuckling at Joe's discomfort.

Joe growled, 'Tha's swiped mi gelt! Thy cheeky bleeder!' He was half angry and half amused at Bill's entrepreneurial spirit, even though Bill had showed himself to be a bit schlant[186]. He couldn't help laughing as he looked at Bill who was stifling laughter, enjoying seeing Joe wound up.

'It's exactly what I'd have done. Th'art learning, old pal,' added Joe.

Joe and our Arthur had an opportunity to work together when they were in the RAF. When Joe landed a job in a factory, he also helped Arthur to get a role there too. Arthur was fairly passive in this; Joe made the entire running, manoeuvring to bring it about, possibly with some pressure from Mam.

Joe could not wait to get into the forces. He was interested in being a hero of course, but his main reason for wanting to be in the RAF was, in his own words: 'Birds love pilots.' He'd seen the films and heard the gossip about how women would give themselves to a pilot who might not return from a sally across the channel.

He went for his assessment and he was rejected in the medical because of his perforated eardrum, so a pilot's role was not to be. Joe impressed them with his confidence in the interview however. He cut a sharp figure, flashed up in a good suit and he was punching above

---

186 schlant (adj)-bent, dishonest, exhibiting behaviour which bends the rules (market slang)

his weight, making a favourable impression in the interview. The interviewer rustled his papers, eyeing Joe up and down.

'Where were you educated?' asked the chap.

'Barton Academy,' said Joe, watching the man place a tick in a box with his fountain pen. Joe always announced that he went to Barton Academy with some grandeur.

'Where are you from?'

'Sheffield, the steel city,' retorted Joe proudly.

'And what did you do?'

Bib dressed as Britannia and Joe seated on the floor on the right.

'I was a director of a company.'

The man bridled, suddenly more interested in him. The man assumed Joe had worked at a steel company. The interview continued, and Joe's nerve and directness impressed. Thus when he offered Joe the post of running a steel firm in Birmingham he wasn't going to put him right. The factory was called Green's.

My mother was pleased with that outcome. Joe was working under the RAF's auspices and was still doing his bit, but would be protected from the worst dangers. She knew him well, knowing his penchant for showing off and risk-taking, and voiced her private concerns to the rest of us. 'He's such a big-headed sod, if he gets behind the wheel of a plane, he'll only last a week! He'll be doing the loop-the-loop o'er the Picture Palace down Attercliffe!'

The small private day school, Barton Academy was therefore partially responsible for Joe's success in getting into management. Mam was keen on education for us, though our successes were patchy. She would have said that just because you work on the market doesn't mean you're a Yorkshire pudding. She was hopeful that we'd have education and common sense in equal measure, and she warned against too much bookish education, as she feared any of us might become 'an educated idiot' or a lump of wood.

In successive generations, for those of our offspring who excelled academically, parents have often rung out a warning not to become 'an educated idiot'. As part of the Edwards clan, it's always a great recommendation if you can also sell a box of gear, and work the gaffs[187].

Joe was in his element, at the thought of bossing other folk around; running around with a clipboard in his hands, swanning around the Birmingham factory. He worked there for the rest of the war and ensured Arthur's employment continued there too. They had never had a taste of such proper jobs, but ultimately they weren't for them, they were too restrictive and confining. The only thing they did envy people who stayed on there for, was their pension at the end of their working lives. We all expected to struggle in old age. Joe must have done quite well. He always liked to boast that he'd run round with a clipboard under his arm during the war.

He found it hard to accept that he had not become a pilot, and he often boasted about his fighter pilot exploits, especially to the ladies, making up stories of his exploits to impress. He could not refrain from showing off and always loved an audience. If he took a woman out he liked to queen[188] her, perhaps the date was even better for her, if she believed herself to be out with a hero.

Joe even bought some second-hand medals and wore them for a while, especially if he was going out dancing. Father made him take

---

187 gaffs (n)-markets (market slang)
188 queen (v)-treat woman like royalty on a date

them off and told him off, 'You'll get some porridge[189] if anybody sees thi wi' them on. Tek 'em off.'

Father was also more sensitive to the fact that some poor devil had been awarded them in honour, fairly and squarely, whereas our Joe was obtaining glory by proxy.

It would be fair to say that Joe always fancied himself. He liked attention, he liked to be noticed and he couldn't resist swanking. My Mam always went further and said he was in love with himself, which she found a little worrying, but also amusing. He had a number of schleppers, who got used to him floating, and they took over selling when he went off. One schlepper who worked for him for years was Walt Williams.

You couldn't help but be impressed by Joe's self-confidence and unswerving self-belief. He became something of a local character and started to get noticed beyond Sheffield, Rotherham and Barnsley.

Joe experienced a little celebrity in 1964, when the TV companies started taking an interest in him. The Rediffusion company made a documentary about the lives and language of market traders. He starred in a television programme about him, and other market men, called *The Grafters*. It was shown on ITV.

He also appeared on the *Dave Allen Show,* and in the local newspapers. Predictably it went to his head. He had just bought a big new wagon, a massive lorry with fresh cream paintwork. He always had a penchant for self-promotion so he also decided to have this new, special lorry sign written, vaingloriously capitalising on his new status as a TV personality. In great red and blue letters down both sides of the lorry it read:

Joe Edwards, Glass and China Salesman
France, Germany, Holland, London, England
Sheffield, Rotherham and Barnsley
As seen on the Dave Allen Show, ITV and the BBC

---

189 porridge (n)-prison (slang)

Joe Edwards in his 40s

Joe always needed an audience and so of course he could not resist driving the lorry down to Sheaf Market to give us a flash. He called in to see us and sauntered down to the stall where we were setting up. Bill nudged me at the sight of Joe as he rolled up in front of us.

'Come and look what I've done,' said Joe mischievously like a kid, beckoning to us to follow him. Bill and I trailed after him out to the street where he had parked outside the market. The great covered lorry with painted sides was parked up centre stage for all to see. People were already halting to look at it, stopping and pointing.

Bill and I had a similar sense of humour, and we twigged that it would pay to be nonchalant and that it would wind Joe up a treat. We tried to be blasé. We stood with our hands in our pockets silently, looking up at the lorry, holding our hands before our eyes to shield us from the glinting sun bouncing off its sheer, glossy surface.

'What do you reckon?' Joe asked expectantly, pushing for a response, nodding towards the great pantechnicon, hardly able to contain himself, bursting with pride.

'Yes, it's a flash, that,' I said nodding. 'Looks cushti.'

'Mmn, nice paint job,' said Bill.

'Did I tell thi, we've had our lorry sign written as well?' I said, lingering slowly over my announcement.

Joe's face dropped a bit; he was wary that our sign-writing might be competition for his grand efforts.

'No, I didn't know that... What's tha put on it?' he enquired.

I paused for effect, then continued, 'Have you seen our Joe on the telly?'

We all creased up laughing, Joe too, secure in the knowledge of his unassailable high status in the family. We have an old photo of his earliest lorry, where he is hanging out of the door, when he must have been in his twenties or thirties, cocksure and confident. How I wish we had a photo of this lorry from the 1960s, I can still see it now. It is only as time goes by, we realise what an achievement it was to stay in business successfully for all those years.

Joe was a self-confessed big-head, and therefore we always had some sport in taking him down a peg or two. He always was a cock bird and had no problems admitting it to anybody. Our jesting was always playful. He was as amused at his own conceit as we were, but he couldn't change and didn't want to change.

He worked the markets into his late sixties and early seventies. No matter how old, he was always immaculately dressed, always wearing a smart blazer, with polished brass buttons and polished shoes. I once went over to Barnsley Market and heading down the market I saw him, but I walked straight past him. I had seen him, but was pretending to ignore him.

He shouted after me, trying to get my attention, 'Mick! Mick! Now then, Mick!'

I turned on my heels, spotting him. He was standing chatting to another trader, flashed up in a superb new blazer, hand-stitched with lovely polished buttons and even with small brass buttons that you could undo at the cuffs. He looked very elegant, far too well dressed to be working on a market.

I smiled, acknowledging him. 'Oh hello, I'm sorry, Joe, I didn't see you there.' He looked at me affronted. He wasn't used to anyone failing to notice him. 'Well, I did see thi out of the corner of my eye actually,' I added. 'But sorry, I thought you were a bus conductor!'

He clenched his jaw, smiling and laughing through gritted teeth, as was always his way, which gave him the curious air of seeming at the same time to be both highly amused and irritated, like a wheezing dog that can't decide whether it wants to lick you or bite you. We both started laughing when he realised that I was having him on. There was of course no way that Joe's hand-stitched blazer could be mistaken for a corporation bus conductor's uniform.

Joe's interest in women was legendary, and as a young man he did not pass up any opportunity to flirt and get the attention of women. Bill told me this story about our Joe. Bill and Joe had gone to Cambridge Fair on Midsummer Common, an annual treat in the calendar for most grafters and showmen. It was known as the Holiday Fair; it wasn't particularly lucrative or known to be good for taking money, but falling mid-season it was a fair for catching up with people you knew on the circuit, for basking in the good weather, for sharing news, gossiping and chatting, for working half-heartedly, and for enjoying yourself. It was as much about socialising as it was about earning money. Joe fell easily into the spirit of having a good time and was already showing more interest in the local birds than he was in selling any china. Bill kept trying to pull him up and get him interested in taking some money, but it appeared to be a lost cause. They had secured a letty[190] on Mill Road. At the end of the day when Bill felt as if he had done most of the work, they went off to the pub. Joe had already set up an assignation with a couple of young women he had been flirting with, and they arrived excitedly. Joe flashed his cash, buying them drinks in the pub. Bill hovered and tried to make conversation, but after a while he decided to leave, realising he was in the way. Joe was engrossed, smooching and canoodling with both of them, sitting in a booth, with an arm around each of the girls, greedily hogging their attention.

Joe didn't come home that night, and Bill slept alone in the rented room. Bill got up early the next day and was at the fair setting up, when Joe rolled up, looking a little dishevelled and unkempt, still wearing his clothes from the night before, but looking rather pleased with himself.

'What's tha been up to? Tha's got eyes like lag holes in the snow. Get any kip?' asked Bill.

'I'm just nipping back to the letty to get changed!' Joe shouted across to Bill, not needing to answer his questions.

---

190 letty (n)-guest house, boarding house, small hotel (market slang)

Bill nodded and smiled to himself. He knew Joe would be gone for ages and would make sure he stopped off on his return to enjoy a hearty breakfast. He might see him before eleven o'clock, if he was lucky.

A little later Bill was dusting off china ready for sales, and clearing away the assorted rammel[191], when the young women from the pub the night before turned up, swinging on one another's arms, laughing and giggling.

'Have you seen our Joe?' asked Bill, guessing full well what had gone on the night before. 'He didn't come home last night. I'm worried about him.'

One of the girls looked sheepish and cast a knowing glance to the other before replying, 'Well...I've seen him this morning,' she said shyly.

'Yes we bumped into him this morning,' said the other girl, with mock innocence.

Bill couldn't resist making use of the opportunity to Noah's[192] it for Joe. 'He's having treatment you know,' he said, tossing his statement into the conversation with the ease of a kid dropping a stink bomb on the pavement. The girls paused and looked him straight in the eye, their faces suddenly more concerned than carefree. Bill could not resist building their fears. They stopped swaying and looked at him more seriously. 'Oh yes, he's in treatment and shouldn't tire himself out,' Bill said, polishing a cut glass bowl nonchalantly, turning away from them.

They moseyed up to the counter, suddenly more interested now in talking to Bill.

'What's he having treatment for?' asked the taller girl.

Bill was amused. She was obviously wondering if Joe had V.D. He continued polishing, and blew a cloud of dust off a fluted vase before rubbing at it frenziedly with a duster. He enjoyed making them wait. He turned his head towards them and threw them a charming smile.

'Athlete's foot!' he announced.

---

191 rammel (n)-rubbish, mess (local dialect)
192 Noah's ark it (v)-to nark it, to spoil, meddle in someone's business

Joe and Betty Edwards on their Wedding Day, ca. 1941 Mick Edwards, age 5.

Joe's single days were eventually curtailed when he was snared by his wife-to-be, Betty. She was quick witted and fiery, and a match for a man of his magnitude. By the time their wedding came round, Joe had been drafted into the RAF and was working as a factory manager in Birmingham. He had a miniature RAF suit made to fit me, and I took pride of place in my little outfit as page at their wedding. My mother had suggested we had the suit made for me. Bill had also ordered a suit for himself from the same tailor. Mine was ready and we went to pick it up on the Wednesday before the wedding. The tailor told Bill his suit wasn't quite ready as there was still some hand-stitching to do. A day later we heard the tailor's shop had been bombed. Bill's suit had been lost in the blast, so he never did get that new suit for their wedding. He wore his existing best suit. I still have the tiny replica RAF suit that I wore for the wedding, which fitted me when I was five years old.

We all loved Joe, but my mother, who thought the world of him, would have been the first to criticise him for believing his own fanny[193]. He was not exactly a fantasist, but he was proud, driven, focused and always thought he was special. Joe has a massive ego and liked himself, and did not entertain any self-doubt. He was a born show-off. He was not malicious in any way, but his over-indulgent

---

193 fanny (n)-story, tale, (sometimes make believe or tale of fact) (market slang)

self-belief and confidence drove him to over-reach on occasion. He liked the trappings of success, big houses, a Rolls Royce, best Cuban cigars, grand pursuits, riding, hunting, commissioning oil paintings and buying antiques. Coupled with this, he had an easy-going nature, characterised by a willingness to please all comers, which in actual fact meant he pleased very few people in reality. Mam used to say of him, 'He was any way for a little apple.' He tried to please out of a sense of romance and crazy idealism. We could always forgive him his conceit and scrapes; he was just our Joe.

Joe was friends with lots of people from different walks of life. He was comfortable with anyone, probably because he was so sure of himself. I once worked Cambridge Fair on Midsummer Common. I arrived and set up my stall then went for a walk around. I spotted Joe in the distance and walked up to him. It wasn't unusual for us to meet up at fairs around the country; sometimes we went for ages without seeing one another and we'd meet up by accident grafting away from home.

'Aye, aye, my old china[194]', I said

'Oy, oy my old mucker,' smiled Joe. We greeted one another warmly and walked around checking the grafting competition, seeing old friends and chatting to people we knew.

We went past a showman's caravan and the showman stuck his head out of the door and hailed Joe. 'Joe, how are tha, cock? Come in for a drink.'

Joe waved, but hesitated. He was aware of showmen's customs, and it wasn't the done thing to bring a stranger in for tea unless there had been a proper personal introduction and endorsement. He didn't want to appear to be rude.

'I've got my brother with me,' said Joe.

'Bring him in too,' said the showman and we were ushered into his vardy[195].

The caravan had the most beautiful interior, with cupboard doors of solid wood planed from the same piece of wood, with the grain

194 china (n)-mate (china plate = mate, rhyming slang)
195 vardy (n)-caravan, possibly Romany.

forming matching patterns. The wood shone and was highly polished. There were also wooden shelves with lace edging. On the shelves were the most beautiful pieces of Crown Derby bone china, of deep blue with burnished gold edging.

The man's wife served us tea from bone china cups and saucers and we chatted. Eventually after half an hour, we thanked them and left. I noticed outside the caravan nearby was their pale pink Rolls Royce. I was impressed.

When we were out of earshot, I said to Joe, 'He's loaded, what does he do for a living, then?'

'I don't know,' said Joe, 'but I don't think he sells pots in the market.'

I don't know whether Joe was inspired by his connections with such wealthy people, but he did end up with a Rolls Royce of his own. One afternoon in the 1970s I was relaxing in my front room when I was surprised to look out of the window to see a silver-grey and black Rolls Royce glide up to park outside. My kids shot to the window to catch a glimpse of the celebrity.

'It's Uncle Joe!' they yelled, dashing into the kitchen to greet him. The Rolls was part of the trappings of success; he just had to have one, even though the damn thing guzzled petrol.

At that time I was selling car polish, and I had the bottles filled at an industrial unit at Middlewood Hospital, the old asylum. On one trip there I had discovered that they also ran a car washing service, and I recommended it to Joe. He loved to give people a flash and he said he'd call next time I was there. I told him how they used old-fashioned methods, buckets of soapy water and soft cloths.

'Tha'll not get thi Roller scratched there,' I assured him.

The next time I was due to go to Middlewood I arranged for Joe to call too. His arrival caused the usual furore; people looking at the car, peering through the windows at him, the cheekier ones asking to sit at the wheel to pretend to have a drive. If anyone had a camera you could guarantee they would want their photo taking, preferably with him.

The patients crowded round him and the gaffer[196] set them to washing it, bringing buckets of hot water, sponges and foam cleaner. Joe preened himself proudly, watching the team get to work, taking time to smoke his cigarette.

'I've set three of 'em on. It's a big car,' he said, gesturing towards where the band were busy sloshing water onto the sides of the car. 'I'll give 'em a bung-on[197]. I've promised 'em a best cigarette each if they do a good job.'

He had made quite a show of promising each one of them a best cigarette, by this he meant *Players*, which were considered better quality. They might only be used to *Woodbines*, but Joe was going to give them a treat today.

The service manager offered us a coffee and Joe and I went into the office with him. We sat chatting for some time and eventually came back out to see what quality of job they had done. The Rolls was gleaming. A group of patients, who had been assigned to the industrial unit, were hanging round doing nothing, while one or two of the keener workers amongst them continued leathering it down, drying the last drops of water from the shining bodywork. Joe smiled, appreciating their efforts and walked round to inspect the job.

One big chap rhythmically wiped leather round in little circles, uttering quietly, 'Looks better nah.'

Joe skirted round to the boot end and nodded approvingly. Deeming the job to be satisfactory, he started handing out a couple of his ciggies. The workers fell upon him, nearly knocking him over in the frantic rush to get their prizes. As Joe moved around to the front of the car he was aware of a sudden torrent of water, splashing over his shiny, leather shoes.

'What the bleedin' hell??!' he said, dashing round to the front to check what was happening. There he spied a big chap with the bonnet of the car propped up. He looked more closely to see that he was showering the engine with a hosepipe. Water splashed around hitting the plugs, the electrics, and the battery. 'Turn it off. You'll knacker it!' shouted Joe, but the chap continued to shower the inside of the bonnet with water, only turning round to see what Joe was

196 gaffer (n)-manager, boss, person in charge
197 bung-on (n)-tip, additional money in recognition of good work (market slang)

wailing about. The manager frantically turned the tap off a few feet away, and he wondered what had stopped the flow of water.

The big chap ambled up to Joe with his hands out saying, 'Can I have my ciggie now, Mister?'

'Never mind your ciggie. You'd better get me a bloody tow truck!'

'You told us to do a good job, Mr. Edwards,' he said.

'Good job?' huffed Joe, thrusting a whole packet of fags into his hands, which were also dripping wet by now, as he hopped into the car to try to start the engine. There was a whirring and screeching sound. It wouldn't start. Joe hit the dashboard in frustration with his fist. 'These chumps 'ave knackered the bleedin' electrics,' he said to the manager, any sense of political correctness deserting him. The manager stood dumbfounded, then he shot into the office to phone for help.

I stood watching the scene.

'They've done a good job there, Joe, reight good job. That engine's clean as a whistle. Ey, it was the promise of those fags that got them at it.'

'Piss off, clever chuff!' said Joe, scowling at me.

'Serves thi reight for being a big hitter.'

Joe had a charmed life and did very well. He had a succession of love-ly old houses: one at Birkdale and later a farm at Grenoside with an orchard. He enjoyed hunting with the hounds, strutting around in his hunting pinks, and had stables with horses. He was a member of the Grove and Rufford hunts, and Master of the Wentworth Trail Hunt for a while. He liked to live the life of a country gent, with roses round the porch, and a little Jack Russell snapping at his heels. Joe hated being a skint member, but good times come and go. Joe did more than anyone in our family to create the myth of the Edwards' millions. I always said of him, 'He's not really a millionaire, he just lives like one.' I assure you the idea of the Edwards' millions was always just a fantasy, though Joe would have been the last one to dispel such a myth.

As he became infirm, he lived in a nursing home at Dodworth, and even then he still had an eye for the ladies, flirting mercilessly with the nursing staff. Though he was older and a bit unsteady on his feet, he was still a character.

As I left him, after visiting one day, he shuffled off, helped by a nurse, heading back to his room, holding onto her outstretched arm for support. Slowly he turned round and looked at me, giving me a cheeky wink and a little wave. He shrugged his shoulders, stating without a shred of self-pity, 'How the mighty have fallen.'

–13–
THE DECLINE OF THE RAG AND TAG

Many Sheffield people have fond memories of the characters from the old Rag and Tag. We'll never see such characters again; though real characters, they are the stuff of myth and folklore.

There were characters you wouldn't see these days. I remember being mesmerised by watching Leo Huntridge, a medical herbalist. He would hold up a giant glass jar, allegedly with a massive coiled tapeworm inside. He claimed as part of his spiel[198] that a sufferer had ejected this parasitic tapeworm, by taking his potions.

Leo was always dressed in a classy British officer's overcoat, woven from wool worsted cloth, top of the range, with leather buttons. He always looked smart, wearing a clean shirt every day, with a tiny Windsor knot at his throat. He looked like an officer and a gentleman, and traded on the fact that he had army connections, endowing him with instant authority and credibility. He was a man who revved himself up when pitching, his fanny becoming more exaggerated. He used to sell tablets, tincture and medicines. His stall was lined with jars and bottles, full of pills and potions, Epsom salts, syrup of figs, senna pods and other assorted opening medicines. He had a wooden hut where he kept his stock. His mother used to sit in the hut when she wasn't working on the joint.

He had a big picture of himself outside his laboratory, propped up for customers to see where his medicines were manufactured, a great long building with many windows. He stood proudly in his army captain's uniform outside the factory, the photo hazy, sepia-

---

198 spiel (n)-patter, learned talk, presentation, set patter delivered to the public

tinted and dog-eared with use behind him. I watched him point out to the crowds that this was a picture of his manufacturing set-up in Derbyshire. They nodded and nudged one another, impressed. He pointed at it, waving his arm.

'I'm Captain Leo Huntridge of the Royal Medical Corps. I shall be with you all the day, purveying my finest medicines. Note my laboratory, ladies and gentlemen. Yes, here is where we manufacture the tablets that we bring to you, using only the purest ingredients from nature's harvest,' he bellowed.

At that moment, a little kid, who was obviously working for him, rolled up to the front of the crowd. Unconcerned that Leo was in the middle of pitching, holding the crowd in thrall, he asked of him, 'How many tablets shall I put in these little packets, Leo? How many did you say, thirty?'

Leo grimaced and ushered him quickly behind the joint, whispering in his ear, 'Shift, out o' t' road, you little prat.'

By the entrance to Pet's Alley at the top of the market by the old brass weighing scales stood Rix Amoid. You could buy anything at Pet's Alley: cats, dogs, hens, ducks, rabbits, budgies, fowl, and ferrets. This was at the top of market under the arches. Rix Amoid used to graft his Magic Elixir; a blend of herbs, roots and spices, which could free anyone of their great pain and suffering. He also used to graft 'Miracle Tablets'. I was watching one day as he demonstrated them. It amused me how he'd dramatically place one on his tongue and let it melt, his eyes rolling a bit for dramatic effect. I watched him for many hours, as he was constantly doping himself as part of his demonstration. He must have consumed dozens of tablets a day, demonstrating his medicinal wonders. After he'd placed them ceremoniously in his mouth, he'd lick his fingers. When he died, I questioned my sister why this tragedy had befallen a man whose livelihood was health care. Surely taking all those tables should have kept him well.

'Bless his soul. God rest him,' she said, 'he was a lovely man. It's a pity he's tailed 'em[199]. Mind you, he ate enough tablets to kill a bleedin' elephant.'

Some of the items for sale on the stalls in those days were a bit hooky[200]. You could buy a little block of buck fat, with added men-

199 to tail them (v)-to die (slang)
200 hooky (adj)-dodgy

thol, purportedly for use as an insecticide, which you burned to get rid of flies. I have no idea whether it worked, but in the absence of more effective products, the salesmen made a lot of money from such wares and the punters were regular buyers.

In both my father's, and grandfather's time, there were idiosyncratic characters getting a living on the markets. My father used to talk about his childhood and seeing a massive bloke dressed like a German warrior at the bottom of Snig Hill. He used to pull a pitch by wearing a German Pickelgruber helmet, one of those metal helmets with a great spike on top. He'd then place a big wooden cartwheel on top of it and spin it. I think he was some sort of escapologist, and this shenanigans was his prelude to his main performance.

Whenever he told this story my father started laughing. He sputtered, not able to get his words out, continuing with his description, still chuckling, he told us how the cart wheel was so heavy it nearly bust the bloke's neck and his head used to bob and bounce up and down with the weight of the wheel spinning; his eyes bulging in his head with the extreme weight and exertion required to perform the feat.

I asked innocently, 'What did he do that for?'

'To pull a pitch!' he said, still chuckling. 'What a way to get a living!'

Many of Sheffield's market families were year-round workers, working in all weathers, eking a living from market trading all year round, in summer and winter, and in all conditions. Then there were the fair weather grafters, who only came out in spring as soon as the weather got better, which was the only time of year that they could get a living. We referred to them as 'crocus workers' because like the crocus, they were first to be spotted regularly each year in spring. Grafters had to work hard and save a proportion of their takings while they could, for when the kipper season[201] came, it was much harder to get a living.

When we found it hard to sell things in the market and when the punters weren't biting, we often referred to it as 'being in a cemetery with lights on'. Neither of us was good when business was slow, and time could drag. In the late sixties we had more and more days which

---

201 kipper season (n)-winter (market slang) so called because you had to eat cheaper food in winter, such as kippers

were like this. Rising rents and the high cost of employing people meant that my brother Bill and I found it increasingly hard to generate enough income for two families. Things were quite desperate.

On one slow afternoon I ambled off for a break, to Granelli's café. Inside I found a trader, with a camera and a little fruit monkey wearing a little hat. It was about twelve inches high and was dressed in a jaunty scotch plaid suit with royal blue trousers. The punters in the café loved it and he was getting attention. I thought to myself narkily, *I wish the bleeding punters got as excited over me and Our Bill.* I was rather envious, but on my way back to our stall it gave me an idea. I nodded at Bill as I approached and eyed him chatting to a customer. I greeted her and started with my fanny[202].

'There's a monkey missing in the market,' I announced. The woman stopped mid sentence and looked at me inquisitively. 'Yes, there's a chap up in the café who's lost a monkey,' I continued. 'It's one of those little ones. He puts it on people's shoulders. You know; one of those little fruit monkeys. The photographer has him, and it sits on your shoulder while he takes your photo. Anyway he was having a cuppa in Granelli's café and the bleedin' thing's escaped.' Bill raised his eyebrows and I mouthed to him, 'It's moody[203].'

Bill smiled at the woman and added, 'Yes, it could be anywhere.' Bill gazed around, looking up into the eaves.

The woman gathered her handbag to her and looked up into the rafters of the market.

That day everyone who came within ten feet of the stall found themselves being dragged into conversation with us about the monkey. We even got the other grafters at it. Bill had spied Rushy, the fruiterer, with a few punters round the joint and had spotted the opportunity to get the story spreading through the market.

'Now then, Rushy,' said Bill, 'tha wants to get them apples covered up. There's a bleedin' monkey loose up in the rafters. If it comes down, it might crap on 'em!'

Rushy, who was not inhibited at all by the presence of any animal-loving punters, said, 'If it shits on my apples, I'll kick its bollocks up!'

His audience bristled with interest regarding the monkey, and the

---

202 fanny (n)-tale, anecdote, made up story
203 moody (adj.)-make believe, fabricated, not true

rumour spread quickly around that such exotica was on the loose in the Rag and Tag. Every conversation rippled with the unusual news that there was a monkey loose in the market.

When we met punters that day we talked about the monkey. 'Hello love, have you seen a monkey?' What a conversation starter it was. We pulled them in every time.

People came nearer, looked at our goods, chatted. We noticed the rumour spread like nettle rash, and before long the place was heaving. The only trouble was the punters were walking round with their heads turned heavenward.

Later that day a chap approached us with a camera and tripod.

'Hello, I'm from the Star and Telegraph. I've come about the monkey that's escaped. So you actually saw it?' he said pulling out his notepad and grappling with his camera.

'Yeah. It was up in the roof.'

'Where's it from?'

'It's the photographer's monkey. It got loose and got lost.'

'How big is it?'

'About a foot high,' said Bill holding his hand out flat in front of him to indicate the petite monkey's height.

'Wearing a little scotch plaid suit.'

'You've just missed it. About ten minutes ago it was swinging up on those bars up there', said Bill, pointing up into the roof.

'Look's like it's gone now,' I said nodding.

'Where's it gone?' asked the reporter.

' I don't know,' said Bill.

'Where do you think it is?' asked the reporter.

'I think it'll be up in one of those lights.'

'Or in some boxes somewhere keeping warm,' I added.

The photographer moved a few feet away, angling the camera atthe lights, itching to get a picture, fiddling with his lens, hoping preferably for a shot with a monkey swinging from the rafters.

We enjoyed the buzz that day, and sales picked up a little. The reporter came back later and stopped to chat to us. Harry, a nearby stallholder, came staggering forward to join the conversation. Harry was a grafter, but he didn't get much work done, as he spent most of his time in the peever,[204] so by three in the afternoon he was well and

---

204 peever (n)-pub

truly bevvied[205]. He mooched forward, keen to get in on the action.

The reporter glanced over at him, asking, 'Have you seen it?'

'Yes,' he slurred, continuing, 'it stood there, run up, jumped up on the stall, then run up that pole.' The reporter nodded with interest and took out his notebook. He didn't seem to notice that Harry was inebriated.

'It was wearing a scotch plaid suit, weren't it, Harry?' Bill added, feeding him his next line.

'Yes, scotch plaid,' slurred Harry. 'Looked like one of Barney Goodman's!' he confirmed.

'How big was it?' asked the reporter.

'It were that bleedin' big,' said Harry swaying and emphatically holding out his hand in front of him, at a level of about three feet high.

When the reporter had gone and the punters had drifted off, we killed ourselves laughing, re-telling the afternoon's events. Bill's eyes were watering as he mimicked Harry, the shickory dick[206] putting his hand out in front of him indicating the alleged height of Harry's purported monkey, staggering and swaying and pretending to slur his words.

'Oh dear God, that Harry. He'd seen it and course the bleedin' thing was three foot high. It had grown. It started out as a miniature monkey a foot high and we've ended up with a bleedin' gorilla. What a nobble! He's a right bevy merchant[207], that Harry.'

The next few days in the market were very busy. We had not seen such throngs of punters for ages. All stallholders benefited. Everyone who came in was looking for the monkey.

There was another occasion when we had dealings with a photographer and his monkey. It was when he'd just got it, and he wasn't very used to it. He couldn't control it. It had been pulling people's hair, nicking their glasses and causing mayhem. In desperation, he'd put it back in its cage, hoping it might calm down a little, and was consoling himself with a mug of tea from Granelli's.

'Have you got any ideas?' he asked me. 'I've got to get to work today; I've took nowt. The bleedin' thing's goin' mental, can't do owt

205 bevvied (adj)-drunk, inebriated, sozzled
206 shickory dick (n)-drunkard (market slang)
207 bevy (bevvy) merchant (n)-heavy drinker, drunkard, someone who enjoys alcohol (market slang)

wi' it. It's on springs. It wayn't stand for being photographed today.'

'What's up with it? Has it got the horn?' diagnosed Bill.

'I don't know, perhaps it's on heat. Could be, aye,' said the man, shaking his head.

'Tell you what. Go and get a Mogadon off that woman down there. She'll gi' thi one, takes 'em hersen,' offered some bright spark schlepper.

The photographer jumped up and went on the hunt for this tablet. We saw him later; the monkey sprawled across his shoulder drooping everywhere. It seems Mogadon was a strong sedative, and it had made the monkey too dopey. He shrugged his shoulders, adjusting the monkey to try and make it look livelier.

'Now it's too laid back. Had to flop[208] it to try and wake it up.'

A woman came up, prodding and stroking at the creature with concern.

'What's up with it? It looks ill.'

'It's just a bit tired, love, he's been grafting all day.' Then he said hopefully, 'Let me take this last photo of you, then I can get him home to kip.'

He trailed off keenly behind her, in the hope of achieving a sale.

Bill's son, Robert, left school at sixteen and had gone to work with his dad in the market. He'd been working with him on Saturdays for some years, so was used to the work and the punters. They worked together for a while in the newly built Sheaf Market, a great soulless concrete box, for all its mod cons at the time. Robert was a different temperament to his dad and did not suffer fools gladly. It sometimes irritated Robert that people would talk to him with little respect. He'd say to his dad, Bill, 'They think you're a lump of wood, because you work in the market; it annoys me.' So if anyone was cheeky to him, Robert could give as good as he got.

One day a woman was trying to get his attention, and cheekily she yelled across at him, 'Oy, nah then, thee. Are tha crackers?'

---

208 flop (v)-to tap, hit, slap (slang)

As quick as anything he fired back at her, 'Why, love, are you looking for a boyfriend?'

He was also amazed at the ridiculous requests he'd get from people, as if they thought the Potty Edwards were omnipotent. They rolled up every week with special orders and requests for replacements.

One day a woman addressed him. 'Hello, Mister, have you got a spare teapot lid for me? I've dropped mine and bust it this morning.'

'How big is it, love?'

'A little white pot.'

'Two cup, three cup, any idea?'

'Dunno.'

'Round, oval, square, ogee?'

'Who?'

What shape is it, love?'

'Round.'

Robert bit his lip. As if he'd have spare miscellaneous lids for any and every teapot in Sheffield? That would fill a ruddy warehouse.

'Tell you what, love, I've not got one in today, but I'll have a look for you. Anyway the Teapot Lid Factory lorry will be delivering next week, come back again when you're passing and I'll see what we can do.'

She ambled off and he knew she was unlikely to return; such odd requests usually demanded instant gratification.

We Potty Edwards also liked to think that we were at the vanguard of emerging table fashions, and were able to spot developments in culinary presentation, appreciating trends in tableware and pottery. We regularly took the trade magazine, *Pottery Gazette,* and liked to read through it to see what the latest fashions in pottery were. Whatever the public wanted we'd try to get it, even if it meant a special order or trying to buy special items and trialling sales of new wares. Often this left us exposed to the vagaries of fashion, and there were piles of lines in the warehouse that hadn't taken off amongst the trendsetting public. Oval steak plates, novelty-shaped salt and pepper pots, platters to hold bread for fondue evenings, whatever the punters wanted we tried to get hold of it. One day Robert was at the stall during a quiet period. A woman approached, puffing on a fag. She nodded to him, as she got close up.

'Alright, love, what can I do for you?' he asked.

'I'm after a dish.'

'Oh aye, what type?'

'I want one of them new dishes.'

'Oh aye, what sort, love?'

'A Keith and Lorraine dish.'

'A what, love?' he strained to hear what the woman was requesting above the hubbub.

'Have you gor any Keith and Lorraine dishes?' she asked more loudly.

'I beg your pardon.' He wasn't sure he'd heard right.

The woman glared at him and rolled her eyes, barking, 'A Keith and Lorraine dish!' as if he were an idiot.

'No sorry love, never heard of 'em.'

'Y'ave,' she tutted. 'Ya know, put pastry in t' bottom then fill it wi' egg and chayse.'

Robert paused as the penny dropped. 'Oh, a quiche lorraine dish.'

'Yes, that's wor I said!'

'Come back next week, love, and I'll get one for you.'

People always enjoyed coming up for a chat in the market. It always amused me how people liked to claim to be related to us. I wondered why this should be. People often liked to lay claim to us: third cousins removed; distant relations by marriage; old relatives found through distant third parties. They all wanted to belong to the family, but we were nothing special and we had nothing worth laying claim to. We always emphasised we were skint and we couldn't pass on any of the Edwards' millions. One day I was passing time chatting to one of Joe's sons, Lance. Joe had two sons, David and Lance. Lance was the younger son; he grew up to make a living as a comedian and I witnessed his early promise that day, when he had just started to make a living working in the clubs. As we were chatting about the strange way in which people liked to think they were distant relatives, with incredible comic timing, a stranger rolled up and started chatting to

Lance about the very same subject.

'I'm one of yourn, tha knows,' said the stranger.

'Oh aye,' said Lance, humouring him.

'Which side? Edwards or t' Lockwoods?' he asked.

'Lockwood side.'

'Aye, I could tell. I can see t' family resemblance. All t' Lockwoods have got reight big blackheads in their noses like thee!' chirped Lance.

Lance was fearless. The man went off feeling he'd been recognised as a family member, and was too thick-skinned to be offended by Lance's quirky humour.

We had some good times; we had a nobble and a laugh. With our daft antics we squeezed a few more sales out of people, and they had a bit of excitement too, but inevitably we could not stop the rot. We went our separate ways as business partners in the late 1960s. Bill went into the new Sheaf Market, (now demolished) in 1973.

The Council had built a great new modern box of a building at the bottom of the Parkway roundabout, which promised to modernise our whole approach to working in the market, taking our business indoors under cover. The day came around for us to go and view the new site. Our new allotted pitch was in a corner, the site we'd had in the Rag and Tag Market had been on an island site, where we'd got the crowd all round, meaning you could have a chance to draw in the people from all sides. I knew it would have been better if we could have had the same layout, but we couldn't. There was no atmosphere in there: harsh electric light and pale grey concrete all around, with just a limited number of fixed market stalls outside. I fancied it would go pear-shaped. I had a chat to Bill and he said he thought it would be all right there. I was uneasy and I didn't fancy our chances in this new building. Eventually I suggested to him that he would be better off if he went on his own. Bill and I had tried valiantly to get a living for both our families, but it was becoming too hard: two lots of wages out of one business in the rag market had been difficult enough. My father's words rang in my ears: 'The worst person to fanny to, is your sen.' It was time to face reality. We discussed our options. I was the youngest, and we decided Bill should keep the pitch and continue on his own. So Bill moved into the new Sheaf Market on his own and his son, Robert, joined him with help from their schlepper, Alan Chambers. Bill worked it for a few more years. Arthur and Joyce took a stall outside. After Arthur's death, Joyce worked it on her own.

I enjoyed every minute I had working with Bill, as we always got on well. I was sorry to leave the pot job, but times were changing so I had to have a go at something different. The split was amicable, but it was not without some sadness that we went our separate ways. We were proud of the family business and would have liked it to continue as successfully as in the earlier days.

The rents went up relentlessly in the new market building, and as traders left, unable to keep up with spiralling costs of running a business, the Council seemed to put the rents up even more to make up for lost income; that's how traders saw it. Eventually Bill retired. He bemoaned the fact that the markets seemed to be run by Council bigwigs, who'd never done a day's proper work in their lives in his view; as usual he liked to depict them seeming busy doing nothing, envisaging them all running about with clipboards.

Robert worked in the market for a while and then gave up the business too. We could not blame him at all. We celebrated his success at getting 'a proper job' with benefits and a pension.

Do you know how to make a million on the market? Borrow two million. Nowadays it's a mug's game. It's enough to drive you potty...

As for me, I still had to make a living somehow. Selling things was all I knew. I thought about it though and decided I would try to find a line to sell requiring less investment. Pots required great expenditure — big vans, big warehouse, big rents. I decided I wanted to try something I could run without all the extra expenses. My idea was to demonstrate. I took a look all round to see what they were demming[209] on the markets at that time, to investigate who looked as if they were getting a good living. The carpet cleaner mop was one product. I saw they blacked the carpet up with shoe polish and then they cleaned it up, so I concluded you'd always have dirty fingernails. That put me off; I discarded that idea.

I had to keep my family and I briefly got a job at Gross cash registers, demonstrating them to shop keepers and selling them. It was a job that I did well in, and I was often top salesman, but ultimately it wasn't for me. I didn't like keeping records, and going to the meetings about sales figures, where the bosses tried to gee us up.

One day whilst still working for Gross, I had gone to Rotherham Market to see if I could sell any cash registers to any traders. I was even drawn back to what I knew in the sales job. I found myself on my rounds trying to find the dems[210] on the markets. Not many stall-holders had any use for electric tills so I just had a look around. I saw a chap demonstrating paint pads, a mohair flat pad for emulsion and gloss. I thought they looked alright so I had a chat to the chap and bought twenty-five sets off him to have a go with them. I went to Hoyland Market on the Saturday. The first time I had a go with them, on my first time out, I sold twenty-four sets and I kept one set back to demonstrate with. Within three weeks I was demonstrating this product on most weekdays at different markets round about. I rated this product, as the pads were made of good quality mohair. I started to have to buy lots of gear to keep up. I finished up working at shows and exhibitions all over England.

I once turned up to get a pitch at Bakewell Market on August Bank Holiday. I was too late to get on the ground proper, but a chap saw me as I was hanging around on a patch of ground by the river and came up to chat. I had been hoping to get a pitch to be able to get to work to dem the paint pad.

'You're Joe Edwards' brother, aren't you?' he asked.

'Yes, I am. I'm Mick.'

'Well, you can work here,' he said outlining a good bit of ground abutting the car park, which was just a rough field by the water in those days.

'How much rent do you want?' I asked him.

---

209 demming (v)-demonstrating (market slang)
210 dems (n)-demonstrations (market slang)

'Nowt. You can have it.'

I worked it for years and it was the best pitch on the gaff. One year I lost a gold ring whilst working there. I was swilling out a bucket of water and the ring must have fallen off my finger. I emptied the water onto the ground. It could be anywhere.

It had my initials on it: M.D.E. If you find it, give me a call…

I used to tell the punters this true story at Bakewell, and they'd walk off after the demonstration, eyes on the ground, looking for treasure.

I always enjoyed having a nobble with the punters. Demonstrating the paint pad was a good experience. Invariably I usually got someone in the edge who had bought one the week before, and they would pipe up when I was demonstrating, 'It's good. I painted my front room last weekend.' If anyone recommends your goods, the punters are always a bit nervous, thinking you might have a friendly endorser planted in the audience. I liked to play up to their fears.

One day a wizened little old man piped up that he had used it and found it an excellent tool. I laughed and smiled at the punters, waving my hand. 'Take no notice of him. He's my eldest lad.'

The punters turned to look at the old boy in the audience, obviously a good twenty years older than me and then looked back to me, tittering. The old chap laughed. He knew my micky taking was not meant to be malicious.

I also ventured over to Germany to sell them. I sold them in Germany for five pounds a set, at that time about twenty Deutsch Mark. I stayed there four years. I worked in Hamburg, and worked all the markets thereabouts. On arriving, I had a lucky break and struck up a chance conversation with a German grafter called Günther, who set me on the right track to deal with Germanic officialdom and who tipped me off about which markets to work. I was well known in Sheffield, I was Potty Edwards, but in Germany they called me, Herr Malermeister[211].

I came back from Germany following a long summer working away. My son came running towards me to give me a hug. I was surprised to see that he was in long trousers. When I'd left, he'd been in shorts, as little kids used to be in the sixties and seventies. This was significant; I realised I was missing his childhood, and resolved to start

---

211 Herr Malermeister- Mr Painting Expert

working in England again.

I continued working on the markets, selling paint pads, car polish, a vegetable peeler and various items. Often after a break, finding new lines, I'd return to selling paint pads. I knew the demonstration off by heart.

My work experience in Germany was educational and I learned a lot from it. I had seen how the traders in Germany sold goods; they knew you sell the sizzle not the sausage, and their standards of presentation and gift-wrapping were amazing. I came upon the idea of selling toffee. I wanted to tap into the idea of toffee being an old-fashioned sweet and I thought I'd try selling it from an old costermonger's handcart. I asked around if anyone had such a cart, but such items were long gone. By this time, my son, David, was making steel joints for markets and I set him on designing a handcart. He spent some time crashing and banging in the shed, and a few weeks later out he came with a gorgeous full-sized handcart with wooden wheels. It looked so old fashioned and Victorian. He had gloss-painted it and finished it

Joe Bennett and Mick Edwards, mid-1990s

with polished brass rails. I had it sign-written and I re-christened myself Old Lockey, after the Lockwood side of the family. Well, it was a change from Potty Edwards, and signalled the reinvention of myself.

My daughter wrote a story about toffee in her nice handwriting for the wrapping paper, and I had a few reams printed up. My idea was to put the toffee in a cup, roll it around into a cone, as the old sweet shops used to do, and finish it off with a nice bow. Sure this would cost a bit more, but hopefully people would come away feeling they had made a special purchase. I had a long Victorian-looking overcoat made and bought a bowler hat, and I looked the part. I was ready to launch this new venture.

One of the first gaffs I worked with my new toffee venture was at a Dickensian Fayre at Rochester, Kent. I was excited to be going there. I had a good feeling about this, and fancied we were going to have it spark off and sell out of gear. I invited my brother-in-law, Joe Bennett, to come along. Joe was old enough to have retired, but he liked to come along to such events, enjoying the chit-chat with people we knew and the excitement of going somewhere new and strange.

It used to tickle me how Joe would look up into the air in new places, gazing around, and point out stunning architecture or local sights to me. He'd look up from his work in a dream sometimes, completely losing track of unpacking boxes or setting up the joint. Notwithstanding his age, I used to cheekily remind him that we were working. 'Now then, Joe, we're not on holiday; we're here to graft, tha knows.'

'Oh, aye,' he'd say and he'd shake himself and come back to the present.

I was sorted with my coachman's outfit, but I had to ensure that Joe was dressed appropriately too. The terms and conditions clearly stated that all traders had to comply, and be dressed in Victorian fashion to attend.

I explained to Joe that he needed to find a suitable outfit and that we would not be allowed on the gaff unless we were dressed up. 'Joe, you need to dress in keeping, a bit oldie-worldy. Has tha got owt?'

'Nah, I don't think so.'

'Wait a minute. What about your riding gear?'

'Aye, I never thought of that. I could wear my hunting pinks and jodhpurs.'

He hadn't been riding for some time and he wasn't sure that the clothes would fit him. Joe didn't have a big appetite and hadn't got any fatter as he got older. I thought they'd probably fit. I had driven to the gaff in my outfit and had also added a jaunty neckerchief to my costume. Joe went in search of the toilets when we arrived and went off to get changed.

I spotted Joe from afar as he came strolling back down the market, in his red hunting jacket and jodhpurs. Over his outfit he wore a white cotton apron. He clutched his riding hat. He had a classic look, and looked vaguely Dickensian.

'Tha's got a good get-up there; tha looks cushti in that,' I said.

A few minutes later we got to work, unpacking the boxes and setting up the handcart. Joe bent over to pick up a box of toffee and I heard an almighty rip. As he'd bent over, his trousers had split.

'Bleedin' 'ell! What a Noah's! I've split my keks,' said Joe.

'Watch your sen, Joe. Your Harris is hanging out the back. You'll have to smother that, or you'll get the punters at it,' I replied.

His trousers had split right around the centre seam from his flies and under the undercarriage, leaving his two trouser legs dangling down, separate, hanging off his thin frame.

'These rowmies[212] have had it,' said Joe, examining the seams. It looked as if the trousers were so old, the cotton stitching had perished in places. 'I'll have to go back to the letty and get changed.'

'Tha can't do that. It's snided and will be spark on soon.'

'Perhaps I can punt for a new pair on the gaff.'

'Tha'll not get a pair of new rowmies here,' I said. Then I thought of a solution, and grabbed hold of Joe and twizzled the white apron round to create a flap at the back covering his backside.

'There, problem solved. Thy 'rt decent now.'

Later on that day I swathed Joe in another white cotton apron that we usually wore over our outfits. He then had an apron front and back, effectively cocooning him to cover his embarrassment. So we went to work. He got a few funny looks, but as soon as we started taking money, we didn't bother much about whether or not we looked Victorian. Our old-fashioned outfits were spattered with toffee by the end of the fair. The Dickensian Fayre at Rochester became a fair we worked for many years.

Joe and I also regularly worked Lincoln Christmas Market in our Victorian get-up. One year we stayed at a letty on Carline Road. We'd left our big van on site ready for the first day of trading. On the first morning of the market, my daughter, Michele, was coming to pick us up in her battered old Vauxhall Estate, which was also laden with boxes of toffee. We were expecting a sell-out fair so we needed two vehicles to transport all our gear. She called for us at the letty, and we traipsed down to the roadside with our overnight bags, cramming them into any spare nook and cranny. It was a cold December morning and we didn't fancy a walk into town. Now we had a dilemma,

---

212 rowmies (n)-trousers, from round the houses=trousers (rhyming slang)

there were three people to transport to the market. My daughter was driving, that left Joe and me to seat too. I figured Joe was thinner than me and he had more chance of fitting in the back.

'Thee hop into t' back, Joe,' I said, raising the van's door at the back, pointing to a little space.

Joe sighed, 'Jesus, I can't get in the back. I'll cripple mi sen.'

I was keen to emphasise why Joe should get in the back. 'No, thee get in t' back, Joe, thy are not carrying any extra weight like us.'

My daughter started laughing.

'What are you laughing at?' I asked.

'I might have to report you to Age Concern, asking an old gentleman to ride in the back like that,' she jibed. Joe was twenty-four years older than me; she had a point. Joe acquiesced and could not help smiling at my arrogance. He made his way to the car and wriggled into the back, feet first. I gave him a gentle push to shove him further down the centre of the van. Boxes of toffee were piled up all around him. He slid into a space about eighteen inches high and a foot square; he had to narrow his shoulders as he squeezed himself into the small space.

We arrived at the market and we pulled up and undid the van's back door.

'We're here, Joe,' I called, and I could just see the crown of his head poking out of the hole.

'I'm stuck; get me out. I'm dying for the khazi,' said Joe.

I leapt forward and grabbed hold of his shoulders and tugged at him, pulled him out of his coffin-like space. It was hard to get him out; he was firmly wedged in. Finally I pulled him free and helped him stand up. He was out of breath and red-faced at the exertion of freeing himself. He eyed me, half annoyed, half amused at my lack of chivalry.

'Your lot are a right bleedin' team! Knackerin' t' workers before we've even got to bleedin' graft!' said Joe rollocking us.

It might seem as if we are always fighting. We didn't go looking for trouble, but it seemed to find us. Joe Bennett was my unlucky companion when we got into a spot of bother down south. Now you might think only young men get into trouble, but I'm pleased to report that testosterone-fuelled violence got us into bother when we were in our dotage, already hurtling into semi-retirement. I was sixty and Joe Bennett and his brother, Mark, were much older. Joe must have been in his mid-eighties at the time.

I had invited them both to come and help me work a Dickensian Market in Rochester, Kent. We'd loaded up my van in the daytime and set off from Sheffield late one afternoon, planning to get us to Rochester in the early morning. This was partly planned to help us avoid paying for a night for three at a letty. It always helped to save on exes[213]. We set off and had got well down the M1, when the van started to make grinding noises and the cab was filled with an acrid burning smell. We pulled off the M1 at Luton and called in at a garage, dumping the van on the forecourt for repair, leaving a note with our details, not daring to risk driving it any further, resolving to pick it up on our way back. We managed to find some car hire place nearby and hired another means of transport, choosing a van. We drove back to our abandoned vehicle, transferred our cargo and after stopping off for some food and a drink, we set off again, heartened by having a roadworthy vehicle under us once more. We went a few miles, but I noticed the empty fuel tank light was glimmering. By this time it was getting dark. I suggested we pull off the M1 fancying our chances of filling up more easily in a town. Joe and Mark agreed and we pulled off at an exit off the motorway. We drove slowly, trying to preserve every drop of fuel as the light blinked at us on the dashboard.

'This bleedin' petrol tank's nearly empty. We need to find somewhere soon,' I warned. Joe and Mark looked around us; we were desperately lost and had no idea which direction to drive in for our best chance of petrol.

Suddenly it seemed things were looking up. We saw a young lad, about twenty years old, walking arm-in-arm with his girlfriend. We drew to a halt in the van alongside, winding the window down to enquire if he could help.

I leaned across Joe to have a word with the kid. 'Excuse me, sorry to trouble you, we're not from round here. Could you tell me where there is a petrol station please, pal?'

The kid looked up at us. 'Fuck off!' he cried fiercely and walked

---

213 exes (n)-expenses (market slang)

on.

We were a bit stunned, and were used to better manners than this.

'Christ there's nobody round Joe. Who else do we ask? If we keep driving, it's going to conk on us. Let's pull up again near on and ask him again.'

Perhaps we were being a bit naive, but we were used to northern hospitality and helpfulness.

The kid was striding on ahead, so we drove on a bit further and pulled up alongside him again. He looked at the van, scowling at us.

'We'll try again Joe, although this kid has obviously had too much pongo[214], but we might appeal to his better side,' I suggested hopefully. 'If we ask him again, he might have come to his senses and will be a bit more helpful this time.'

Joe nodded, huddled up in the front, looking tiny, old, and totally knackered; he looked apprehensive. Joe was at the kid's side of the road and I urged him to wind the window down so I could chat to him. Joe did my bidding, wound the window down and in the most friendly, polite voice he could muster said, 'Excuse me, son, sorry to trouble you again, but be a pal, give us a hand, we really could do with knowing where a petrol station is. We're nearly out of gas and are just trying to get to London. Could you please just give us a clue, which direction? Is there one open anywhere?'

The kid bobbed and lunged forward jutting his neck out and thrusting his chest forward in an aggressive bouncing gesture, flailing his arms.

'I've told you once, leave me alone and fuck off! If you ask me again, I'm going to come and grab hold of that old fucker and stick one on him!' he jeered at Joe.

Joe shrank back in shock and sank down in his seat, raising his eyebrows, as he threw a glance towards me beside him.

I leaned forward to address the lad through the window. 'Now then, now then, there's no need for that sort of language, we're just asking a civil question.'

'Fuck off, you old bastard!' spat the youth.

I was getting riled now.

---

214 pongo (n)-booze

'There's no need to be so rude in front of this elderly gentleman,' I said.

'I don't give a fuck. I'll fuckin' twat him in a minute!' threatened the youth, pitching his head forward towards Joe in a threatening head-butting gesture, giving us a taste of what we had coming.

'For your information,' I yelled, 'he's been in two world wars and fought for thee, you schmock[215]!'

The lad lunged forward menacingly gravitating towards the van.

I said to the young lad whilst pointing at Joe, 'He's over eighty odd years old! I'm only sixty, pal. If you fancy a having a pop, tha'd best have a pop at me. I'm a bit fitter and younger than him. If you want to be on, come on then, let's be having ya!'

I yanked the handbrake on and started to get out of the van, chucking my coat to Joe, tensing my muscles as I climbed down.

'Steady on, Mick, I'm going on holiday to Spain next week,' twitched Joe. 'I don't want my bleedin' passport taken off me by the nick, or customs stopping me from going through, on the bloody Wanted List for GBH!'

I wasn't to be halted; he'd really wound me up.

'It's reight Joe, don't thee worry, I'll sort it. Stay there. I'm not standing for it,' I said, jumping out of the van, slamming the door, urging Joe to stay in there.

I walked round to the front of the vehicle, where laddo was already fancying himself as a bit of a Cassius Clay. He was peeling off his leather jacket, mouthing obscenities at me, bobbing about, dancing and shuffling towards me with his fists up.

'Are we feighting or dancing, you prick?' I said. Then I fronted up, standing two feet away from him, pulled back my arm ready to land him a punch on his chin. I was getting ready to hit him. Bosh! Down he'd go. I imagined I'd stroke him with my first punch, sticking him one on the chin. He'd go down and I'd peer at him, flat out lying on the deck, out sparkers. I looked him over; he was tall. I suddenly thought he might be a match for me and decided to change tactics. I kicked up my leg karate-style, uttering what I hoped was a scary Oriental war cry at him, designed to spook my competition. I was thinking that I'd have a better chance if I kicked him in his tender parts.

---

215 schmock, schmuck (n)-idiot, (Yiddish)

I hovered for a moment with my leg in the air and looked up at Joe, seeking his approval. He looked back at me wide-eyed.

He shook his head and held his head in his hands in despair, hissing at me to get back in the van so we could scarper. 'No, Mick, no, leave it. Think of my holiday. Let's schmeiss!'

I thought better of it too and lowered my leg, turned away and jumped back into the van.

Joe was scared and he wanted to be off, but he couldn't help commenting, 'We must be the oldest bleedin' thugs in Southern England!'

The lad's girlfriend, who was half Mozart[216] herself, was fretting around her boyfriend, tending to the hero, who hadn't even a scratch on him.

I said, 'Joe, he had it comin' and I was up for it. You get what you stand for and I wasn't standin' for him! Never mind, th'art reight. Let's get off.'

The lad's girlfriend looked on. I was sorry for her that it had had to come to this, her boyfriend having to resort to fisticuffs with us, but she can't have been very bright, dating a Pilkington[217] like him.

As I released the handbrake, ready to drive off, I called to the lass out of the window, 'You must be proud of him, love. What a pillock!' I said as we took our leave. 'You want to get your sen a man, not a boy.'

Since then, I've never been very keen on the South.

I don't have many regrets, but I do have one, how I wish I had saved more pots. Many pot banks smashed up their old designs when they closed or changed hands. I was so busy selling pots I never gave any thought to my old age. I often used to say to our Bill, 'I wish I'd had enough gelt to buy a lorry load of pots and bury them in the bleedin' garden, instead of ending up potless[218].' Not that the damp

---

216 Mozart (adj)-drunk, pissed from, Mozart and Liszt (rhyming slang)
217 Pilkington-pillock, idiot (Potty Edwards slang)
218 potless (adj)-skint (slang)

earth would have done them any good, but I'd be selling them now to collectors and antique dealers. If I see any china my instincts are still the same; turn it over to have a look at the back stamp to identify the maker; flick it, to hear if it's still sound.

In particular, I wish I had saved a few more pieces of Midwinter porcelain and *Carltonware*. I think they were my favourites. I have a few favoured pieces and I derive great pleasure from drinking a good cup of tea from a bone china cup and saucer, turning the cup in my hand to appreciate the shape and decoration.

Sometimes when I am looking around a car boot fair, I see items, which my brother Joe, used to sell. I once saw a big Arthur Woods' Paris basket. Our Joe used to sell loads of them. They were very popular. It had a big handle, and it was quite a heavy substantial piece. Joe used to sell it for a quid when people might have bought it for three or four quid in the shops in town. I said to the lady behind the stall, 'Save me that, love. I'll be back in a bit. I'll have that.' When I went back, it was gone. Nowadays I have learned to buy something beautiful when I see it.

I have now retired from demonstrating, but when I was still working around the markets hereabouts, the comment I most often heard was, 'I seem to know your face.'

The punters would look at me quizzically, trying to think about where they could know me from, from which context in life they might have met me.

I'd then reply, 'Did you ever buy pots in the market?'

They'd think for a moment, then their face would break out in recognition, like the sun creeping from behind a cloud. They'd smile at me knowingly and say, 'Oh yes, you're one of the Potty Edwards, aren't you?'

'I am, love, I am.'

Invariably they'd hover, itching to ask another question. After a pause they'd ask, 'So why are you working the market? I thought you were millionaires.'

'You work it out, love. Do you think I'd rather be in Barbados sunning myself, sipping a Pina Colada by the swimming pool with some tasty, little, young bird fanning me, or working here at Barnsley Market?'

'Hmm.'

'If we are millionaires, love, all I can say is some other bugger's got my share.'

ACKNOWLEDGEMENTS

Grateful thanks to the following for stories, anecdotes, photographs and press cuttings: Robert Edwards and Anne Edwards for anecdotes, David Edwards for photographs and Gaynor Edwards for the loan of photographs, information on the family tree and research into family history, also Tony and Irene Hall for press cuttings, and John Lockett for information on pottery kilns.

Thanks also to Steve Ostler, Andrew Hall, Julia Binns, Dene Lindley, Joti Bryant and Pamela Marin-Kingsley.

ABOUT THE AUTHOR

MICHELE LOCKWOOD-EDWARDS

Michele with her father, Mick Edwards

Michele Lockwood-Edwards is part of the 'Potty Edwards' family. This book is the result of years of work — talking with her father Michael 'Mick' Edwards and family members — collecting their anecdotes and bringing them together in this biographical story of the family.

She has been writing since she was a child, inspired by her Uncle Bill, who wrote verse, and encouraged by her parents, who bought her first Oxford English Dictionary when she was 9 years old, because she had announced she was going to be a poet! She is now a business coach and teacher, but her main passion is writing.

Lightning Source UK Ltd.
Milton Keynes UK
21 June 2010

155894UK00002B/1/P